BUSINESS STRUCTURES

IN A NUTSHELL

By

JOSEPH SHADE

Professor of Law
Texas Wesleyan University School of Law
Fort Worth, Texas

DAVID G. EPSTEIN

Professor of Law
Southern Methodist University
Dedman School of Law
Dallas, Texas

Charles E. Tweedy, Jr. Chair in Law
The University of Alabama School of Law
Tuscaloosa, Alabama
(1998–2003)

THOMSON
—————*————— ™
WEST

Mat #40082511

Nutshell Series, In a Nutshell, the Nutshell Logo and West Group are registered trademarks used herein under license.

COPYRIGHT © 2003 By WEST GROUP
                610 Opperman Drive
                P.O. Box 64526
                St. Paul, MN 55164–0526
                1–800–328–9352

ISBN 0–314–14356–4

TEXT IS PRINTED ON 10% POST CONSUMER RECYCLED PAPER

May 13, 2003 1:16 PM Shade 015227 TPC

DEDICATION

LOUIS SHADE and ISAAC EPSTEIN: Immigrants from Eastern Europe, pillars of the community in Temple, Texas, two extraordinary men, close friends, our fathers.

We are proud of our fathers who provided us with a way of life and opportunities unimaginable in the villages of Lithuania and Poland in which they grew up. We dedicate this book to their memory.

Joseph Shade
David G. Epstein

PREFACE

This book was written for law students taking the first course offered in law school in business organizations. Different law schools have different names for the course—"business associations," "business enterprises," "business organizations," "business structures" or "corporations." We use these terms synonymously and also refer to the course as the "basic business course."

The differences in the business background and motivation of the students who take the course are even more diverse than the names given to the course. For some, who aspire to become "corporate lawyers," it is an introductory course which lays the foundation for advanced courses in securities regulation, corporate finance, mergers and acquisitions, etc. For others, who aspire merely to fulfill their law school's required curriculum and pass the bar, it is the first and last business course they will take.

Regardless of your reason, we are glad that you are taking the course and reading our book. Our goal is the goal expressed on the cover of each West Nutshell, namely to provide:

> A succinct exposition of the law to which a student or lawyer can turn for reliable guidance.

We have worked hard to make our book "succinct," and we have tried to emphasize "explanation."

More specifically, we have focused on (1) explaining the basic concepts that you cover in class, (2) providing a business and practice context for those concepts and (3) showing how the concepts are consistent (and inconsistent) with each other.

Our objective is to have all students, finance majors and fine arts majors alike, say, "Now I understand that."

We thank Alan Herda and Kimberly Latham, students at the Texas Wesleyan School of Law, and Anna Teller, research librarian at Texas Wesleyan, for their valuable help in proofreading the manuscript, checking citations, researching legal points, etc. Last, but not least, we thank Patty Lovelady Nelson of The University of Alabama School of Law for turning our manuscript into a book.

JS
DGE

Dallas, Texas
Washington, D.C.
April 2003

OUTLINE

TABLE OF CASES

References are to Pages

BUSINESS STRUCTURES

IN A NUTSHELL

CHAPTER I

WHAT DOES THE BASIC BUSINESS COURSE IN LAW SCHOOL (AND THIS BOOK) COVER?

Enron. *What do you think about when you see or hear the word "Enron"?*

Most people think of Enron as a single "evil empire." In reality, Enron was a large number of different business structures: (i) corporations, (ii) partnerships, (iii) limited partnerships and (iv) limited liability companies. At its peak there were over 3,000 business structures in the Enron family of companies.

Different schools use different names for the first course in business structures. The course is also called business associations, business organizations, businesses enterprises or corporations. In this book we treat all of these as synonymous terms and refer to the course as "the basic business course." Many students have different names— very different names—for the course.

Whatever your law school or you call the course, you are going to be called on to learn about different business structures. More specifically, you are going to learn about what is common to all forms of business structures and what distinguishes one form of business structure from another.

A. WHAT IS COMMON TO ALL BUSINESS STRUCTURES?

1. BUSINESS STRUCTURES AND A SEPARATE "LEGAL" PERSON

A "business structure" is not a real person, not a flesh and blood human being. Microsoft's Bill Gates is not a "business structure." The Simpsons' Monty Burns is not a "business structure."

A "business structure" is a device through which real people like Bill Gates and Monty Burns conduct business. And while a business structure is not a flesh and blood human being, legislatures and courts treat business structures as a person or "entity" for some purposes.

2. BUSINESS STRUCTURES AND STATE STATUTES

Most business structures are "creatures" of statutes. State statutes. Each state has statutes governing each of the types of business structures covered in this book: corporations, partnerships, limited partnerships, limited liability partnerships and limited liability companies.

There are also federal statutes that affect business structures. Federal securities laws and federal tax laws are the two most obvious and most significant examples.

The federal tax laws, among other things, significantly impact both the choice of the appropriate form of business structure for a particular business, as discussed in Chapter II, *infra* and how much of the money made by the business, the real people who own the business get to keep as discussed in Chapter IX, *infra*.

The main impact of the federal securities laws is in the areas of capital raising (see Chapter V), governance of certain larger businesses (see Chapter VI), and potential federal remedies for wrongs in the nature of fraud (see Chapter VIII).

There are, however, no federal statutes that govern the creation or regulate the internal operation of business structures. The creation and regulation of business structures has been left to the states. While similar, the governing statutes vary from state to state.

In the main, these state business structures statutes deal with (i) the relationships among the real people who are a part of the business structure and (ii) the relationship between these real people and the business structure itself. For example, you would look to the relevant state business structures statutes to resolve a dispute among Microsoft stockholders as to who should be on the Microsoft Corporation's board of directors or a dispute over whether Microsoft should pay a dividend to its shareholders.

For these Microsoft disputes, you would look to the State of Washington's corporate code. Bill Gates, and the other "real people" who formed the Microsoft business structure, chose the corporate form of business structure and chose to form the corporation in Washington.

The real people that create a business structure have a choice not only as to the form of business structure but also as to the state in which they form the business structure. And, the business structure laws of that state then controls the disputes among the real people involved in the business structure and disputes between those people and the business structure. Your professor may refer to this concept as the "internal affairs doctrine."

Almost all large businesses are structured as corporations. A majority of them are Delaware corporations. Thus many of the cases that you study in your basic business course involve Delaware corporations.

Under the internal affairs doctrine, lawyers or law students working on a dispute among the real people involved in a business structured as a Delaware corporation or a dispute between those people and the corporation will look to Delaware corporate law even though the business and all of the real people are in states other than Delaware. Accordingly, this book will explain provisions in the Delaware corporate code.

While no other state has a corporate code exactly like Delaware's, a number of states have borrowed heavily from Delaware. Even more states have adopted statutes modeled on the Model Business Corporations Act ("MBCA") Accordingly, this book will also explain certain provisions of the MBCA.

We don't know what form of business structure Monty Burns used for the Springfield Nuclear Power Plant or even in what state he formed it. And, unless your professor is a bit weird you do not need to know that.

What you do need to know is that if the Springfield Nuclear Power Plant is a partnership, then the relevant state partnership statute will be based on either the Uniform Partnership Act ("UPA"), a 1914 statute, or the Revised Uniform Partnership Act ("RUPA"). Since almost half the states still have UPA-based statutes, this book covers both. Similarly, there is both a Uniform Limited Partnership Act ("ULPA") and a Revised Uniform Limited Partnership Act ("RULPA"), and a significant number of state statutes based on each.

The limited liability company and the limited liability partnership are comparatively new forms of business structures. All states have statutes governing limited liability companies and almost all states have statutes governing limited liability partnerships but these statutes vary widely.

3. BUSINESS STRUCTURES AND OTHER LAWS

Obviously, the law of business structures must also involve case law. Why else would your professor require you to buy a "casebook" and assign cases. And, if you buy the casebook and read the assigned cases, you will find not only cases that interpret the applicable state corporate, partnership or LLC statute but also cases that establish concepts and rules independent of any statute—cases such as *Meinhard v. Salmon* which imposes the duty "the punctilio of an the honor the most sensitive" on a manager/owner of a business structure to the other owners of that business.

Less obvious, but at least as important, the law of business structures also involves contract law. In significant part, state business structures statutes establish "default rules"—rules that govern only if there is no contrary provision in any relevant business structure agreement. (For partnerships, that agreement is called the "partnership agreement"; for corporations, look to the "articles of incorporation" and "bylaws"; and limited liability companies will typically have both "articles of organization" and an "operating agreement.")

4. BUSINESS STRUCTURES AND MONEY

People start a business to make money. And, flesh and blood people form a business structure to be able to get, make and keep money.

Many of the issues that you will see in your basic business associations course will be about money. Issues about how to get money into a business structure so that it can operate and grow:

– Should an "interest in" or "share of" the business be sold to investor(s)?
– Should the business borrow?
– Should the business retain and use its earnings?

And you will see issues about how to get money into the hands of the real people who own the business structure:

– Should the business pay salaries to its owners who work for the business? To owners who do not work for the business?

– Should the business distribute the money it is has to earned to its owners?

– Should the owners of the business be able to sell all or part of their ownership interest?

And, of course, you will see assigned cases and you may encounter exam questions with issues about who gets to decide these issues about money.

5. BUSINESS STRUCTURES AND FINANCIAL INFORMATION

Because many business structures issues involve money, you need to know (i) what money a business structure has and (ii) whether it is making money. This means that you need to know "something" about accounting and financial statements.

We knew that even before Enron. Now, however, after the accounting fiascos in Enron, WorldCom, Tyco, HealthSouth and . . . your professor is even more likely to expect you to know something about accounting and financial statements.

Accounting is the process of recording, classifying, and communicating financial information. Just as lawyers have cases and statutes (and nutshells) to look to, accountants have GAAP—Generally Accepted Accounting Principles. Financial statements are prepared according to GAAP. And, under GAAP, just as under business structures law, a business structure is treated as an entity.

If your professor talks about financial statements in class, she will probably talk about the (a) balance sheet and (b) income statement. The purpose of a balance sheet is to provide information about what a corporation owns and what it owes as of a particular date. Kind of like a photograph. In contrast, an income statement is more like a video. Its purpose is to provide information about business' revenues and expenses over a particular period of time.

a. Balance Sheet

A balance sheet is a called a balance sheet because it is typically one sheet of paper that has a column of numbers on the left hand side of the page and another column of numbers on the right hand side of the page and the total of the numbers on the left hand side and the total of the numbers on the right hand side are the same. They "balance."

The numbers on the left hand side are the values of the stuff that the business owns, its "assets." You don't have to be an accountant for Enron to see opportunities to be "creative" in determining what assets belong to a particular business structure and even more opportunities to be creative in determining what values to assign to such assets.

The top numbers on the right hand side are the amounts that the business owes, its liabilities. Less "wiggle room" in determining the appropriate numbers for liabilities.

There is no reason for the total number assigned as the value of the company's assets to turn out to be the same as the total number for liabilities. And, usually it isn't. Usually, it is necessary to plug in another number for the left and right hand sides of the "balance sheet" to balance.

That "plug number," the difference between the assets and liabilities, is the owner's "equity." That needs to make sense to you.

Let's try again. The assets are the value of what the business owns and the liabilities are the creditors' claims on that value. If the asset value exceeds the liabilities, then the excess is what the owners have a claim on and we need to add that number on the right hand side of the balance sheet for the owners' equity.

What is less obvious is that even if the amount of the liabilities is greater than the value assigned the assets, we need to add that number on the right hand side of the balance sheet for the owner's equity. It is just that it is a negative number.

The balance sheet reflects the basic accounting formula: **Assets = Liabilities + Equity**.

You do not have to be a "finance maven" to understand the basic accounting formula or enough about accounting to survive nicely in the basic business course. Once you learn the basic terms it is mostly boils down to common sense.

Two of the three main sections of the balance sheet, assets and liabilities, are basically the same regardless of the form of business structure. However, the equity section varies depending on the type of business structure.

In a partnership separate equity accounts, which are discussed later, are maintained for each partner.[1]

Corporations do not maintain a separate equity account for each investor. However the equity section of a corporation's balance sheet usually consists of three separate accounts, which unfortunately go by different names that mean the same thing: (1) capital stock, common stock or stated capital, (2) paid-in capital or capital surplus and (3) retained earnings or earned surplus.[2]

b. Income Statement

Like a balance sheet, an income statement can be reduced to a formula: **revenue – expenses = income (or loss)**. Unlike a balance sheet, an income statement covers a period of time, not a specific moment in time.

---

1. Equity may appear as a single line on the balance sheet, but, at least internally, separate equity (or capital) accounts are maintained for each partner.

2. (1) and (2) reflect the amount the corporation receives when it sells its stock to investors. The allocation of the proceeds from the sale of stock between these two accounts involves a concept called "par value" (which is discussed later). (3) reflects the cumulative earnings of the corporation from the sale of its products or services, less the amount paid as "dividends" (also discussed later).

There is discretion in terms of the time period covered by an income statement: income over the past month, past quarter, past year. More important, there is discretion in terms of what revenues and, especially, what expenses to assign to a particular accounting period. A business that wants to show potential investors or potential lenders a strong income statement might be creative in attributing revenues to that accounting period or in not attributing expenses to that time period.

6. BUSINESS STRUCTURES AND THE REAL PEOPLE WHO ARE ITS AGENTS

Even though a business structure is a legal person, a business structure needs flesh and blood people. A business structure needs real people to provide the capital and own the business: investors and owners a/k/a shareholders of a corporation, partners in a partnership, members in a limited liability company.

And a business structure needs real people to make decisions for it. It wasn't a cute little girl with pigtails named Wendy who made the (unfortunate) decision that Wendy's International. Inc. should buy Baja Fresh or a clown named Ronald that decided that McDonald's Corporation should invest in Chipolte Mexican Grill.

A substantial part of your law school course (and so a substantial part of this book) will deal with which real people make which decisions in various forms of business structures. For now, we simply need to understand the legal basis for imposing liability on one legal person, a business structure, for the acts of other legal persons, the flesh and blood persons involved with the business structure. We need to do some agency law.

When courts (and law professors) discuss agency law, they typically look to the *Restatement*, more specifically the *Restatement (Second) of Agency*. Section 1 of the *Restatement* provides:

> (1) Agency is a **fiduciary** relation which results from the manifestation of **consent** by one person to another that the other shall act on his **behalf** and subject to his **control**, and consent by the other to so act.
>
> (2) The one for whom action is to be taken is the **principal**.
>
> (3) The one who is to act is the **agent**.

In sum, the business structure is the "principal" and the flesh and blood person or persons acting on its behalf are the "agents."

Hundreds of other *Restatement* sections follow that first section of the *Restatement (Second) of Agency*. In your business associations course, you will deal primarily (if not solely) with the sections dealing with the principal's contract liability.

And, under agency principles, a business structure is liable under a contract made by some flesh and blood person only if the real person had "authority." **That authority can be either express or apparent.**

The existence of "express authority" (called simply "authority" by *Restatement (Second) of Agency* § 26) depends on statements from the principal to the agent. A common example of such a statement is a provision in the partnership agreement that "The Managing Partner shall have the authority to enter into contracts binding the partnership to pay up to $5,000, without obtaining the approval of the other partners."

Under *Restatement (Second) of Agency* § 27, the existence of apparent authority depends on manifestations from the principal to third parties. Assume, for example, that the partnership has regularly paid *T* under contracts for more than $10,000 even though the managing partner did not obtain the approval of the other partners. *T* enters into a new $10,000 contract with the managing partner to supply products to the partnership. The partnership has contract liability. Even though the managing partner did not have actual authority, she had apparent authority and so the partnership would be liable on the contract.

Again, in the previous paragraph, note the focus on the principal. Apparent authority depends on the manifestations of the principal to the third party, not the manifestations of the "agent." We can not create apparent authority to contract for Microsoft Corporation by claiming that we have that authority.

B. HOW DO THE DIFFERENT BUSINESS STRUCTURES DIFFER?

The real people who form business structures have choices as to the form of business structure to use. And there are business and legal differences among business structures.

The five main legal differences among the various business structures are (1) tax treatment, (2) owners' liability exposure, (3) management (or governance) of the business, (4) opportunities to raise funds for the business and (5) exit strategies—opportunities for investors/owners to sell their ownership.

Your basic business course will likely cover these differences. So will the next nine chapters of this book.

Further, in your basic business course (and in the next nine chapters of this book), you will see legal differences not only among the various forms of business structures but within the business structures which depend on whether the business is "closely held" or "publicly held."

As discussed in Chapter II, a closely held business may be any of the business structures covered in this book—*i.e.,* general partnership, limited partnership, limited liability partnership, corporation (either an S corporation or a C corporation) or limited liability company. Almost all publicly held businesses are C corporations.

What distinguishes a "closely held" from a "publicly held" businesses?

A **closely held business** usually has the following characteristics: (1) Few owners, most of whom are usually (2) active in the business and often depend on the business for their livelihood (through salaries and to a lesser extent, dividends). They are more than capital providers. They are the managers of the business. The owners typically (3) operate the business informally. They tend to cut corners in the formal requirements of governance imposed by the statutes. Shareholders and directors meetings are typically held infrequently, if at all, and notice and quorum requirements are often ignored. The most significant distinction between closely held and publicly held businesses is that there is (4) **no market for ownership interests** (*e.g.,* shares) of a closely held business. If an owner of a closely held business becomes disenchanted with the way the business is being run or its future prospects, she rarely has the option of selling her interest.

The characteristics of a **publicly held business** are just the opposite. There are many shareholders; managers of publicly held businesses typically pay attention to corporate formalities. Most are required to do so under the SEC's proxy rules. If a shareholder doesn't like the way things are run she takes the "Wall Street option" and sells her shares. By law, other than electing directors, shareholders have no power to take an active role in managing the company. As a practical matter, the only important decision a shareholder of a publicly held company has to make is whether to sell her shares.

We will explore the similarities and differences of the various business structures as well as a number of the legal issues that commonly arise in the life cycle of a business in the chapters of this book that follow.

CHAPTER II

HOW DO YOU SELECT THE BEST BUSINESS STRUCTURE FOR A PARTICULAR BUSINESS?

Historically the selection of a business structure mainly revolved around consideration of relatively clear cut issues related to providing **limited liability** for the owners of the business and **avoiding double taxation.** As late as the early 1990s, only three types of business structures were widely used by businesses with more than one owner—the general partnership, the limited partnership and the corporation. The tax rules as well as the rules pertaining to the owners' personal liability for obligations of the business pertaining to all three were relatively well-defined. Today, limited liability is readily available not only to the owners of corporations but also to the owners of many unincorporated business structures such as LLCs and LLPs. In addition, under the "check the box" regulations adopted by the Internal Revenue Service in 1997, the selection of a tax regime for closely held business structures is now a matter of elective choice. Thus, the process of choosing an appropriate business structure for a particular business is now more complex.

What choices are available today?

- The Partnership
  - General Partnership (GP)
  - Limited Partnership (LP)
  - Limited Liability Partnership (LLP)
- The Corporation
  - a C Corporation

■ an S Corporation
■ The Limited Liability Company (LLC)

What factors will govern the choice?

Today, whether a law student is trying to solve a choice of entity question on an exam or an attorney is hired to create a business structure for a particular business, the **process** of selecting the most appropriate business structure for a given business involves analyzing (1) a variety of factual considerations, (2) a number of legal questions and (3) the basic attributes of the various types of business structures.

A. FACTUAL CONSIDERATIONS

Obviously, the decision as to what business structure to use for a particular business will be driven by the facts surrounding the particular deal. Facts can be infinite, they appear in various combinations and all won't be present or relevant in any given situation. Some of the facts which may influence the choice of a business structure are as follows:

Nature of business. What is the nature of the proposed business? Is it a business that is capital intensive, labor intensive, etc.? What will be the name of the business? Does the name have any special importance to the proposed business?

Participants. Is there **unanimity of interest** among the participants as in the case of a "family" corporation? Or are their **interests diverse** as in the case of a money/talent type deal? What will be the respective functions of the various participants? Who will contribute what to the deal—*i.e.,* money, service, property, patent rights, etc.? Do any of the participants have substantial outside income or a substantial net worth?

Management. Who will manage the business? Who will actively participate? Will some owners be mere passive investors? What salaries are to be paid to any of the participants? What person or group will manage the business?

Funding. How much money will be needed to get the business started? What are the sources of funding? How much money will the business make during its first years of operation? How long will it take for the business to reach a break even point, begin showing a profit, etc.?

Dividing the attributes of ownership. How will the profits be divided among the participants? If the business fails, how will the assets of the business be divided among the participants in the event of liquidation?

Exit strategy. How do the participants expect to make money from the business—through salaries, distributions, sale of all or part of their interest in the business?

Much of the above and similar data is often incorporated into a business plan prepared by the client. Often counsel of an experienced attorney is sought by clients in working-up the business plan and/or working-out the business bargain. The above is a partial checklist of the factual data on which to focus when faced with a choice of entity situation.

B. LEGAL CONSIDERATIONS

Main legal considerations. The three central legal questions usually considered in selecting a business structure for any business enterprise are:

1. Will the participants be personally liable to third parties for the debts of the business?

2. How much will the government take in the form of taxes?

3. How will the business be governed?

Additional legal considerations. Two additional legal questions are often factored into the selection process, and sometimes may control the decision:

1. How will the attributes of ownership—*i.e.,* profits and assets—be divided among the owners?

2. What are the owners' expectations relative to getting money out of the business?

The above questions translate into what, today, are generally considered the five principle legal considerations that govern the choice of a business structure. These need to be understood by all students because they, and the many legal issues that flow from them, are the foundation upon which much of what the basic business course is about rests.

- Limited Liability
- Tax Considerations
- Management
- Capitalization and Financing
- Exit Rules

1. **Limited Liability** means that the owners of the business structure are not personally liable for the debts or obligations of the business structure. The business structure, as a legal person, is liable for its debts. The real people who own the business structure may lose their entire investment in the business structure, but if the assets of the business structure are not sufficient to satisfy the business structure's obligations, creditors of the business structure cannot reach the personal assets of the owners—*i.e.,* their homes, cars, personal bank accounts, etc.

2. **Tax Considerations** revolve around the question, how much will the government take from the business in the form of taxes. They involve contrasting so-called "**double taxation**" with so-called "**pass-through taxation**." **Double taxation** means that the business structure itself pays taxes on the income it earns and the owners of the business pay taxes on the income they receive as dividends. This tax regime is imposed on most corporations under Subchapter C of the Internal Revenue Code ("IRC"). Under **pass-through taxation** no tax is payable at business structure level, but only at the personal level on the individual owners' share of income. This tax regime is

available to closely held businesses organized as partnerships, LLCs or S corporations, under Subchapters K and S of the IRC.

3. Management basically involves consideration of who decides what as to how the business operates. This is often called "governance" in corporate lingo. It involves contrasting centralized management or management by representatives with direct management where each owner participates in management. The basic concept can best be understood by contrasting the management structure of a corporation with that of a general partnership. In a corporation the owners (called shareholders) elect a board of directors. The board sets policy, appoints officers to manage the day-to-day affairs of the business and oversees the officers. Except for electing directors, the shareholders have no authority to manage the business. In a general partnership all of the owners have the right to participate directly in the management of the business, unless by agreement they delegate the management function to one or more of the partners.

4. Capitalization and Financing relate to the process of (1) establishing a financial framework (called a capital structure) and (2) raising money (called "financing") for the business. Capital structure relates to the manner in which the attributes of ownership can be divided among the owners and managers of the business. Usually corporations provide greater flexibility of the capital structure. In a corporation the different aspects of ownership can be divided up and packaged in various ways; while in partnerships or LLCs, the owners are more limited in the way they can divide up these attributes of ownership. In corporations the capital structure can be designed to meet the preferences of the marketplace and the desires of the various constituencies.

Whether or not capital structure becomes a consideration usually depends on the capital needs of the business, how the business is financed and what the exit strategy of the owners might be. In general the corporate form of business structure provides distinct advantages over the other business structures in the area of capitalization and finance.

5. Exit Rules generally relate to the means by which the owners expect to get their money out of the business—*i.e.*, the duration of and means of terminating the business structure and the owners' expectations for harvesting the value of their investment.

All of these matters will be dealt with in much greater depth later in the book.

C. TYPES OF BUSINESS STRUCTURES

The main types of business structures available today and the only business structures covered in this book are:

1. **General Partnership**
2. **Limited Partnership**
3. **Limited Liability Partnership**
4. **Corporation**
5. **Limited Liability Company**

The main attributes of each of these business structures are summarized below. All of these attributes will be dealt with in greater depth later, but the sooner you get your arms around the basic attributes discussed below, the better you will likely do in the course.

1. General Partnership

A General Partnership ("GP") is defined as an association of two or more persons to carry on as co-owners a business for profit.

Each partner has unlimited joint and several personal liability for the debts and obligations of the business—*i.e.,* **unlimited liability**. Legal claimants can pursue all assets of partners, not merely assets used in the business. The partnership files a tax return but it is only an information return. No tax is payable at the partnership level. Taxes are paid only at the personal level on the individual partners' share of income—*i.e.,* **pass-through taxation**. In the absence of an agreement to the contrary in the partnership agreement, all of the partners have the right to participate in the management of the business. The partners may agree among themselves to delegate management authority to one or more managing partners. Such delegation, however, is not binding on third parties who are unaware of the delegation. In essence, as between the partners, the partnership agreement is the "law," but as to third parties, agency rules as to actual and apparent authority generally govern. Also, all partners have broad-based fiduciary duties to one another.

While today GPs are governed by statute, they were originally creatures of common law. At common law, "partnership" was a label for the relationship between the participants when two or more individuals agreed to operate a business for profit as co-owners. By definition, they legally became partners, whether they realized it or not, and certain legal consequences followed. When one realizes that the common law courts conceived of partnerships simply as a group of individuals, the rules that govern the relationship, including the important principles of unlimited personal liability, mutual right of management and pass-through taxation, logically follow. This is sometimes referred to in the legal literature and cases as the **aggregate theory**, to conceptually distinguished the theory governing GPs from the **entity theory**, which is a concept central to the corporation, discussed in § II.B.4, *infra.* Today, general partnerships are considered aggregates for some purposes such as tax and unlimited liability, but entities for other purposes such as owning property and bringing legal actions in the name of the partnership.

While partnership law does not require that there be a written partnership agreement, partnership agreements are very important. A partnership agreement is a contract and it is enforceable like any other contract. Basically the partnership statutes provide "default rules." The partnership agreement can change many of the default rules in the law such as the rules as to how profits and losses are divided, how the partnership is managed, etc.; however, the partnership agreement cannot change certain basic attributes of a partnership such as unlimited liability and fiduciary duties.

2. Limited Partnership

Limited Partnerships ("LP") are creatures of statute, which were unknown at common law. An LP is a partnership in which there are one or more general partners who manage the business and one or more limited partners who have virtually no management authority. A limited partnership is a hybrid business structure. It is like a general partnership for tax purposes—*i.e.*, it provides pass-through taxation for both general and limited partners. It provides limited liability for the limited partners similar to the limited liability that a corporation provides its shareholders. The general partner has management responsibility and unlimited liability for the debts and obligations of the business. Limited partners have no voice in management and no liability over and above their capital contribution. Today, the "no participation in management" rule has been slightly relaxed. Most modern limited partnership statutes have safe harbor rules that enable limited partners to participate in management to a limited extent without losing the shield of limited liability.

The conceptual foundation of the limited partnership is found in history. During the industrial revolution of the 19th century, business units became larger and required more capital than the active participants in the business could provide. Passive investors were reluctant to risk unlimited liability by investing as general partners in a business run by someone else. Borrowing a concept from Europe, state legislatures in the United States adopted statutes which came to be known as Limited Partnership Statutes. The central concept in all these statutes is that

passive investors, who have no control over the debts or operations of the business, **should have no liability over and above their original investment**. These statutes reflect a trade-off to facilitate raising capital from passive investors for the more capital intensive businesses started during the industrial revolution. For example, Andrew Carnegie's original steel company, which ultimately became U.S. Steel, began as a limited partnership.

Today, limited partnerships are primarily used in three specialized areas: (1) tax shelter investments, such as oil and gas and real estate, where pass-through taxation is critical and centralized management is desired; (2) venture capital and leveraged buy out firms; and (3) estate planning tools called family limited partnerships. The need for pass-through taxation and desire for strong central management in the operator of the business is common to each of these situations. In most modern limited partnerships the general partner is a thinly capitalized corporation, wholly owned by the promoters of the deal. Thus, in effect, today's LP can be structured to provide limited liability for all participants. General partners have fiduciary duties to their fellow general partners and to limited partners similar to the fiduciary duties in a general partnership.

3. Limited Liability Partnership

A limited liability partnership (LLP) is a type of general partnership in which, by simply filing a certificate with the appropriate state official, stating that the firm is an LLP, adopting a name that includes LLP or similar words in the firm name, and otherwise complying with the requirements of the statute, partners can protect their personal assets from vicarious personal liability for partnership obligations that exceed the assets of the partnership. In modifying the rule of unlimited joint and several personal liability of partners, the LLP statutes fundamentally changed a rule of Anglo-American partnership law that had existed for centuries. The provisions authorizing LLPs are typically part of a state's general partnership statute rather than a separate statute. **LLPs are simply a subset of general partnerships, which permit general partners to limit their personal liability**. Despite the similarity of names limited liability partnerships have less in common with limited partnerships than they do with general partnerships.

The LLP statutes of the various states differ significantly in the degree of protection from personal liability they afford partners. The main distinction is between what are now called "**partial shield**" statutes and "**full shield**" statutes.

The original LLP statutes were partial shield statutes, which grew out of the failure of many banks and savings and loan associations in the late 1980s. Many large law firms had to pay large settlements resulting from malpractice suits arising from work done by the firms for defunct banks and savings and loans. In some instances, due to the joint and several liability of partners in a general partnership, partners in the law firms who did no work for the defunct banks and savings and loans, but who had deep pockets were required to pay substantial sums of money to satisfy judgements or settlements arising from acts of their partners. A **Partial Shield LLP statute** permits a general partner to limit his liability for the malpractice of his partners, who he does not supervise. In other words a partner in a Partial Shield LLP is not vicariously liable for the negligence of other partners or employees, who are not under his supervision, but he has unlimited personal liability for his own negligence, for the negligence of those he supervises and for all other partnership obligations, including partnership contracts.

Many states subsequently expanded the scope of protection by providing a broader shield against personal liability of partners than that provided in the original partial shield statutes. These second generation statutes extended the shield of limited liability to provide protection against contract claims as well as malpractice claims against nonnegligent partners or persons not under their supervision. These are called **Full Shield LLP Statutes,** even though none of the LLP statutes shield partners from personal liability for their own acts of malpractice.

There are numerous other variations in the LLP statutes of the several states. Under most state LLP statutes the LLP is a business structure which is available to any type of business. However, to date the LLP has predominantly been used by professional partnerships, particularly large law and accounting firms.

4. Corporation

The fundamental bedrock attributes of a corporation are (1) separate legal entity status, (2) limited liability of shareholders, (3) double taxation and (4) centralized management. To solve choice of business structure problems and other problems involving the application of these basic concepts, students must clearly understand what they mean.

Separate entity status means that the corporation is a separate person in the eyes of the law. The corporation has a life of its own, separate from that of its owners who can come and go by transferring their ownership interests. The corporation is created by filing a document, called articles of incorporation with the state. In concept, when the state accepts the articles for filing, it grants the corporation life by issuing a concession or franchise usually called a "charter" or "certificate of incorporation." As a creature of statute, the corporation has an existence separate and independent from its owners (shareholders) and those who manage it (directors and officers). This artificial entity may conduct business in its own name in much the same way that a real person can. It has the power to own property, to make contracts, to sue and be sued, to acquire assets and to incur liability in its own name, separate and distinct from its owners.

Limited liability on the part of shareholders flows naturally from the concept of separate entity status of the corporation. It might be thought of as the opposite side of the same coin. The owners are not personally liable for the debts or obligations of the corporation, subject to certain some exceptions discussed in § IV.B, *infra*.

Double taxation means that the corporation itself pays taxes on the income it earns and the owners pay taxes on the income they receive as dividends. A change in the tax laws recently proposed by President Bush, if adopted, would significantly modify the principle of double taxation. Also, under "Subchapter S" of the IRC close corporations, which meet certain requirements can elect to eliminate double taxation. See § IX.B.3.b, *infra*.

Centralized management. The way corporations are managed is totally different from the way any of the unincorporated business structures, such as the various types of partnerships and LLCs, are managed. The owners of the corporation (called shareholders) annually elect a board of directors to set policy for the corporation. The board appoints officers to carry out the day-to-day management of the corporation. Except for electing directors, the shareholders have no authority to manage the business. They do have a veto power over certain fundamental acts of the corporations—such as dissolving the corporation, changing the capital structure or making a major acquisition. Conceptually, management of a corporation is vested in three tiers of the corporate hierarchy—shareholders, the board of directors, and officers. Corporate management requires observation of certain formalities, such as shareholder and director meetings, notices, quorums, etc. In close corporations often all three tiers of the corporate hierarchy consist of the same people.

Separate existence, limited liability, double taxation and centralized management are the bedrock attributes of a corporation. Each are more fully discussed in later parts of the book. Two other attributes of a corporation, mentioned earlier and discussed in detail later, while not rising to the level of the above, may come into play in selecting the best form of business structure for a

particular business. They are **capitalization and financing**
and **exit strategy**.

5. Limited Liability Company (LLC)

The LLC is a hybrid business structure which combines
the tax treatment of a partnership with the limited liability
of a corporation and allows more flexibility of management
than either a corporation or partnership. The LLC came
into wide use in the 1990s, the decade in which most of the
LLC statutes were passed. Today all 50 states have LLC
statutes. However, there is much more variation in the
LLC statutes of the various states than in the states'
corporation or partnership statutes.

The LLC statutes are enabling statutes. In the main,
the LLC statutes merely establish default rules that govern
if there is no contrary provision in the LLC's operating
agreement. Thus, the law of LLCs is primarily contract
law. The statutory default rules for LLCs are in part
drawn from corporate law and in part from partnership
law. A filing with the state is required to create an LLC.
The filing requirements vary from state to state. The
document filed to create the LLC is similar to the articles
of incorporation filed to create a corporation. The owners
of LLCs are called "members," rather than shareholders or
partners, in the LLC statutes of all states.

Once the LLC is organized the members usually enter
into an agreement which is called an **operating agreement**
in most states. The operating agreement is a cross between
corporate by-laws and a partnership agreement.   It
provides the members maximum flexibility in creating a

business structure tailored to the members' particular needs and desires. As previously stated the LLC statutes mostly provide only the default rules. The operating agreement, which is a contract, largely governs the organization, structure and management of the LLC. It also allows great management flexibility. For example, in most states members are allowed to directly manage the business. This is called a "member managed" LLC. Or the members can elect one or more mangers to manage the business. This is called a "manager managed" LLC. The scope of the fiduciary duties owed by the managers of an LLC is not clear at this time.

In summary an LLC can be described as an unincorporated business structure which provides its members with limited liability (similar to that traditionally provided by corporations), pass through taxation (similar to that traditionally provided by partnerships) and management flexibility (which exceeds the management flexibility provided by either corporations or partnerships).

A business structure which combines all of the above features would predictably have wide appeal and the LLC has become the business structure of choice of thousands of closely held businesses in recent years. While publicly held businesses can legally be LLCs, few have chosen this alternative because, if the LLC is publicly traded, the tax rules change. Publicly traded LLCs are taxed as corporations.

D. APPLICATION

Two hypotheticals, both involving business structures created for businesses composed of two basic constituencies, the "money" and the " talent," will illustrate the process involved in selecting a business structure for a particular business.

1. The Taco Stand

FACTS: David, who manages a Taco Bell restaurant, and Joe, an accountant, who believes in David's business abilities and loves tacos, decide to open a taco stand. Joe prepares a business plan in which he estimates it will take a $100,000 investment to get the restaurant started. David will work full-time managing the restaurant, for which he will receive an annual salary of $35,000. He will also invest $10,000 in the business and receive a 20% ownership interest in the business. Joe will serve as a part-time bookkeeper and will handle tax, administrative and financial matters. He will receive no salary, but after the first year, he may bill the business as a consultant if he spends more than 10 hours a month on the restaurant's business. He will invest $10,000 in the business and receive a 20% ownership interest in the business.

David's sister, Lee, has expressed a willingness to invest $80,000 in the business. She hopes for an annual return of 10%-20% on her investment, but she realizes that there are no guarantees. Lee, a highly successful business woman, is president of a large corporation earning an annual salary in excess of $250,000. She has neither the time nor desire to be involved in day-to-day operations of the taco stand but wants a say in fundamental policy decisions of the business and the power to veto such decisions. She absolutely wants no exposure to personal liability, over and above her $80,000 investment. In return for her investment she will initially receive a 60% ownership interest in the business. David and Joe will have an option to buy an additional 20% (10% each) of the business from Lee during the first three years of operation for $40,000.

What would be the best choice of business structure for the Taco Stand?

Applying the various factors and considerations outlined above, this is a closely held small business, initially financed through a typical money/talent deal between three individuals, who have a preexisting relationship. The talent intends to operate for the foreseeable future and increase their equity ownership if the business is successful (sometimes called "sweat equity"). The desired combination of legal attributes which will clearly control the choice of business structure for this business will be: (1) limited liability, (2) pass through taxation and (3) an internal governance structure more flexible than that provided by the typical corporation.

Lee, the money, obviously wants limited liability, and the talent, David and Joe, would also prefer limited liability. This eliminates the general partnership. Lee also wants a veto power. This is likely more participation in management than the LP statute allows since "veto power" is not one of the safe harbors allowed under the limited partnership statutes. Since Lee does not want to risk the unlimited liability which would flow as a result of being deemed a general partner, this eliminates the LP as a viable choice of business structure.

Clearly, all the parties would want pass through taxation. This eliminates the C Corporation as a viable choice of business structure. However Subchapter S would clearly be available in this situation and would be an acceptable choice. Subchapter S probably would have been the choice prior to the mid-90s. However, flexibility of management probably makes the LLC a better choice. All things considered, **the LLC, which provides limited liability, pass through taxation and flexible management, would be the best business structure for the taco stand.**

2. The High-Tech Start-Up

FACTS: Epstein and Shade (the "founders"), two computer engineers, have designed a prototype of a new computer program, which their research indicates will enable computers to perform applications for which there is a large market. Their business plan indicates that it will take a minimum of $5 million to get their business up and running. They estimate it will take approximately two years of operation at a "burn rate" of approximately $500,000 per month before operating revenues are sufficient to meet operating expenses.

Value Venture Capital Co ("Value"), agrees to invest $6 million in the business, which they decide to call Wonder.com ("Wonder"). Value also agrees to use their best efforts to raise between $10 and $20 million more for Wonder in the next couple of years through private or public financings. In return, Value will receive   52%

ownership of Wonder. The founders, Epstein and Shade, will each retain 24% ownership interests in the company. Both Value and the founders agree that to develop the business, the company will need to attract several high level computer and marketing people. They recognize that to attract such people, they will need to give them an opportunity to acquire equity interests in the company through a stock option plan.

What would be the best choice of business structure for Wonder?

Here there are conflicting considerations. Obviously, this is a risky venture and all parties want limited liability. Since the business is projected to incur large losses in its early years, the participants investors would prefer pass through taxation, which would allow them to offset these losses against other income. This would be a factor for considering an LLC. However, in the case of Wonder, this would probably not be the controlling factor.

The identity of the investors and owners is an important factor that often governs the choice of business structure. So is access to capital. In this case the "money" in this marriage of money and talent one frequently sees in new business startups is a venture capital firm ("VC"). The VC will control the board of the start-up company and decide the form of business structure. VCs are usually partnerships and thus not eligible to be shareholders in S Corporations. VCs do not generally like to invest in LLCs. The VC's exit strategy is a public offering. They want to create a capital structure which will enable them to implement this exit strategy. This entails creating

securities that can be sold and used as currency to fund
options plans necessary to attract talented employees,
make acquisitions, etc. The VC also wants a capital
structure that would allow it to possibly exit with
something if the deal does not pan out. This would
probably involve creation of a class of convertible preferred
stock which would be issued to the VC. This gives the VC
a preference over the founders, who would likely be issued
common stock, if the start-up does not make it and has to
be liquidated.

**In short, this business will require substantial cash
investments over a relatively long period and the board is
controlled by a VC, whose exit strategy is to harvest the
value through a public offering if the business is
successful. If the business is not successful, it would like
to salvage something through its liquidation preference as
a preferred stockholder. A corporation will likely be the
business structure chosen in this situation.**

E. SUMMARY OF BUSINESS STRUCTURES AVAILABLE TODAY

While the business structures listed in subsection C,
above, are by no means the only business structures
available today, they are the main choices and the only
ones considered in this book. Today while many factors
must be weighed in determining the best form of business
structure for a particular business, the analysis must start
with the most fundamental of factors—the number of
owners of the business:

1. Single Owner Businesses. The default form of business structure for a business owned by a single owner is called a sole proprietorship. In the sole proprietorship there is no legal separation between the business and the person who owns and manages the business. Thus, a sole proprietorship does not fall within the definition of a business structure, as defined in this book. However, since there are more than twice as many sole proprietorships in the United States as all other types of business structures combined, we would be remiss if we failed to make the point that **there are far more sole proprietorships than there should be**. The owner of a sole proprietorship is subject to the law of agency and she has unlimited liability for obligations of the business. Today it is possible to significantly reduce one's exposure to personal liability by forming either a corporation (which would likely elect Subchapter S tax treatment) or a single member LLC. Today, most but not all state LLC statutes permit single member LLCs.

2. Closely Held Businesses. Business with more than one owner, but which do not have ownership interests which are publicly traded or readily saleable have a wide variety of choices. They can choose from any of the business structures listed above, namely: (1) GP; (2) LP; (3) LLP; (4) LLC; or (5) Corporation. As discussed in the above hypotheticals, tax considerations, limited liability and flexibility of management are likely to be the main factors weighed in making this choice.

3. Public Corporations. Business whose ownership interests (*i.e.*, shares) are publicly traded because of tax

considerations discussed above are virtually always C
corporations.

It is arguable that the current menu of business
structures available to closely held businesses is larger
than it needs to be.   This is confusing and there is
significant overlap among many of the currently available
business structures. *Why is this so?*

The only explanation we can offer is that business
structures are currently going through an evolutionary
period, which occurred mainly in the 1990s. This evolution
is part of the ongoing evolution in the law of business
structures briefly described in the following section.

F. THE EVOLUTION OF
BUSINESS STRUCTURES
(a little history and a short look at the future)

As described in the famous dissent of Justice Brandeis
in *Liggett v. Lee*, in the last half of the 19th century, in
response to the large amounts of capital needed by
businesses as a result of the industrial revolution, modern
corporate law evolved from the era of special charters and
tight state controls to the era of laws of general
incorporation. Prior to changes in corporate law during
this period, it took an act of the state legislature to get a
corporate charter.   Such charters were typically only
granted in connection with special types of projects such as
building a railroad or opening a large mine. However,
following the industrial revolution, large amounts of capital
were needed to finance businesses. The laws governing

corporations were changed, and we moved from the era of special charters and tight state controls to laws of general incorporation. Today, anyone can form a corporation for any lawful purpose. The same corporate statutes apply to all corporations, both close and public, but these statutes were clearly originally written in a way that contemplated large public corporations. Primarily because the corporation offered its owners limited liability, it became the dominant form of business structure for both public and closely held businesses. It remained the dominant form of business structure through the 1980s and is still the most frequently used form of business structure.

However, as more fully discussed later, the corporation may not always be the best suited business structure for a closely held business. Thus, just as the modern corporation was created in the second half of the 19th century in response to the economic needs of that day, several different business structures, the most notable being the LLC, were created in the 1990s for closely held businesses under the laws of all the states. These new business structures provide their owners limited liability like a corporation but have tax and management attributes that may make them more attractive to closely held businesses than a corporation.

The proliferation of business structures during the 1990s and beyond has been dramatic. For example, in 1990 only Wyoming and Florida had LLC statutes. By 1996 all states had enacted LLC statutes. Texas passed the first LLP statute in 1991 and by 1996, 45 states had statutes authorizing the use of LLPs.

The LLP significantly overlaps the LLC in many respects. In general, the proliferation of new business structures in recent years is confusing and has resulted in much overlap. The LLC may become the dominant form of business structure for closely held businesses in the future. Some scholars have suggested that one day there will be only two types of business structures in the U.S.—the publicly held C Corporation and the LLC. Such a degree of logic and tidiness is more likely to remain a scholar's dream rather than a practical reality. In fact, as this book is written, state legislatures, in their infinite wisdom, are continuing to invent new types of business structures. Whatever the "new, new thing" in business structures turns out to be, a body of jurisprudence must develop around that business structure. That body of jurisprudence will likely be developed by courts and legislatures through analogy to both corporate and partnership principles from the past.

CHAPTER III

HOW ARE THE VARIOUS BUSINESS STRUCTURES FORMED?

A. PARTNERSHIPS

The action necessary to form a partnership varies depending on the type of partnership being created.

1. GENERAL PARTNERSHIP (GP)—THE DEFAULT FORM OF BUSINESS STRUCTURE

While today general partnerships are governed by statute, they were originally creatures of common law. At common law, "partnership" was a label for the relationship between the owners when two or more individuals agreed to operate a business for profit as co-owners. The statutes of all states have incorporated this common law concept. Accordingly a GP is defined in both the UPA and RUPA **as an association of two or more persons to carry on as co-owners of a business for profit.** While most modern state partnership statutes contain refinements to the general definition, they do not change the basic concept. Thus, the owners of a business may create a general partnership without intending to do so or knowing they have done so. Absent the statute of frauds, no written agreement is required. Further, no filing of any kind with the state is required to create a GP. While no formal partnership agreement is legally necessary, such an agreement is highly desirable, as discussed later.

The general partnership is the "default form" of business structure in businesses owned by two or more persons. If two or more persons own a business and they do not take the necessary action to create a limited partnership, corporation, LLC, or other business structure they become partners in a general partnership. A GP is the only business structure covered in the basic business course that can be created without some type of filing with a governmental authority.

a. Inadvertent Formation

Because the general partnership is the default form of business structure, co-owners may create a partnership without knowing that they are doing so and certain consequences might follow, including joint and several personal liability for the debts and obligations of the partnership.

The 1927 New York case of *Martin v. Peyton* is the leading case in which the court enumerated the test for determining whether a partnership has been "inadvertently formed." The test for determining the existence of a partnership, enumerated in that case, is still used today.

> Partnership results from contract, express or implied. If denied, it may be proved by the production of some written instrument, by testimony as to some conversation, by circumstantial evidence. If nothing else appears, the receipt by the defendant of a share of the profits of the business is enough. . . . Mere words will not blind us to realities. Statements

that no partnership is intended are not conclusive. If as a whole a contract contemplates an association of two or more persons to carry on as co-owners of a business for profit, a partnership there is.

The issue of whether a partnership or some other legal relationship was created usually arises in the context of a failed venture, where creditors seek to hold a solvent individual liable as a partner for unpaid business obligations of the alleged partnership and the alleged partner argues that she was merely a creditor, landlord, employee or the like, whose compensation was, in part, based on profits of the business. These are usually fact-sensitive cases. Most modern statutes contain a number of helpful guidelines as to which facts are important. For example, most state statutes provide that the sharing of "gross returns" does not give rise to any presumption of partnership, but the sharing of "profits" is prima facie evidence of the existence of a partnership. However, even the sharing of profits does not give rise to a presumption of partnership when the share of such profits was received as payment for debts, wages, rent, and the like.

b. The Desirability and Effect of a Written Partnership Agreement

Although many thousands of so-called "handshake partnerships" (partnerships that have no written agreement) are created every year, written partnership agreements are highly desirable. For one thing, if the partnership is to last beyond a year, involves real estate or is otherwise within the statute of frauds, a written partnership agreement is required by reason of the statute of frauds.

More importantly, the UPA, RUPA and modern state partnership statutes mainly provide default rules—rules that govern only if the partners have not agreed otherwise. For example, absent a partnership agreement, the default rules under the governing statute may preclude payment of salaries to partners or may provide for an equal division of profits and losses among the partners, even though the respective partners contributed different amounts of capital to the partnership. Therefore, if the partners want to modify the statutory requirements, they need a partnership agreement. In other words, if the partners do not make a deal for themselves the state will make a deal for them. Most partners would prefer to make their own deal. To do so they need a partnership agreement.

Partnership agreements are enforceable in the same way as contracts generally. Thus, much of the law of partnerships is contract law. Whenever legal issues arise concerning internal relationships within a partnership the two most basic questions likely to be asked are: (1) Was there a partnership agreement; and (2) If so, what does the agreement say about the issue in question? Usually it is only in the absence of a partnership agreement that one must look to the default provisions contained in the partnership statutes.

The partnership agreement may set out the division of profits and losses among the partners, prescribe the standards by which the duty of good faith is to be measured, enumerate the rules governing dissolution and windup of the partnership, set the standards and procedures for the admission of new partners or expulsion of partners and govern the operations of the partnership. In short, as to questions involving the internal rights and obligations of the partnership and its partners, **the primary source of "partnership law"** is not the statutes or case law. **It is the partnership agreement.**

While a partnership agreement can govern almost every aspect of the partnership, there are a few mandatory rules in the UPA, RUPA and partnership statutes of the states that can not be trumped by the partnership agreement. These include: (1) varying the partners' rights to information regarding partnership affairs, (2) eliminating the duty of good faith and fair dealing, (3) eliminating the partners' fiduciary duties to one another, (4) varying the principle of joint and several personal liability of the partners and (5) varying a partner's power to dissociate from the partnership.

2. LIMITED PARTNERSHIP (LP)

Unlike general partnerships, limited partnerships are strictly creatures of statute. The LP was unknown at common law.

In all states, in order to form a limited partnership, the general partners must execute a Certificate of Limited Partnership and file it with the appropriate state official, usually the Secretary of State. In general, the certificate must set forth the name of the limited partnership, the address of the registered office and registered agent for service of process, the name and address of each general partner, and any other matters that the partners deem necessary to include. Once the certificate has been filed and fees paid, the limited partnership is deemed to have been legally formed, so long as there has been substantial compliance with the statute.

The partners typically enter into a limited partnership agreement, which is executed by all general and limited partners. As is the case with general partnership agreements, limited partnership agreements are governed by contract principles and are the main source of the "law of the limited partnerships."

The limited partnership agreement may contain provisions governing matters such as the admission of new general and limited partners, procedures for voting, procedures for withdrawal or removal of general and limited partners, remedies for breach of the partnership agreement and the manner and process for dissolution and wind up of the limited partnership. It may also enumerate the powers and liabilities of the general partner(s) and set forth the manner and amount of distributions. In addition, the agreement will set forth the amount and form of contributions. The limited partnership agreement will also set forth the manner in which the profits and losses of the limited partnership will be allocated among the partners and classes of partners. If the agreement is silent as to allocation, the profits and losses will be allocated on the basis of the value of the partners' contributions to the limited partnership.

Once created, the limited partnership has two classes of partners—**general partners** who have full management responsibility and unlimited personal liability for the debts and obligations of the partnership, and **limited partners** who have no voice in management and but whose liability is limited to their capital contribution. While the original concept of the LP was, and continues to be, a tradeoff under which the limited partners relinquished all management rights in exchange for the limited liability granted them under the limited partnership statutes, today that concept has been slightly relaxed. Most modern limited partnership statutes now contain safe harbor rules which enable limited partners to perform certain acts and engage in certain practices without being deemed to "participate in management or control" and thus lose their shield of limited liability.

3. LIMITED LIABILITY PARTNERSHIP (LLP)

An LLP is a type of general partnership, which for most purposes is governed by the same rules that govern general partnerships. Unlike limited partnerships, which are governed by separate limited partnership statutes, LLPs are typically authorized and governed by provisions found in a states' general partnership statutes such as § 15-1001 of the Delaware Revised Partnership Act.

The one difference between the LLP and the GP is, however, very significant. An LLP enables general partners to protect their personal assets from personal liability for partnership obligations that exceed the assets of the partnership. In modifying the rule of unlimited joint and several personal liability of partners, the LLP statutes fundamentally changed a rule of Anglo-American partnership law that had existed for centuries.

LLPs are creatures of statute. Thus a filing with the the appropriate state official, usually the Secretary of State, is required for formation. There is great variation in the LLP statutes of the various states. The statutes vary in the form of document they require, in the terminology they use and in the degree of protection they afford to the partners. In most states, however, the required filing is relatively simple and requires some or all of the following information: the name of the partnership, the address of the registered office and registered agent for service of process, the number of partners in the partnership, a statement that the partnership elects to be a limited liability partnership, and adoption of a name that includes a reference to the partnership being an LLP. While generally available for use by any type of business, LLPs, to date, have mainly been used by professional partnerships such as law and accounting firms.

Most states also have a minimum capital requirement and/or a requirement for minimum liability insurance coverage. In addition to other variations the LLP statutes of the various states differ in the degree of protection from personal liability which they afford partners. Some states have so- called "**full shield**" statutes and others so-called "**partial shield**" statutes. See § II.C.3, *supra*. **Bottom line: LLPs are simply general partnerships which permit general partners to limit their personal liability in varying degrees** (which differ from state to state) by filing a simple document with the Secretary of State, complying with relatively meager statutory requirements, appropriately revising their partnership agreement to provide for limited liability, and paying the prescribed fee.

B. CORPORATION

While the statutory requirements for forming a corporation differs slightly from state to state, the general pattern is similar in all states. The procedure for forming a corporation has become quite rote. The incorporation procedure is substantially the same for both close and public corporations. Approximately 17 states have special provisions in their corporate statutes, that allow corporations, which meet certain requirements (which vary from state to state) to elect special "close corporation" status. These special close corporation provisions will be discussed later. See § VI.B.3.a.(1), *infra*.

1. INCORPORATION AND ORGANIZATION

a. Formation

Formation of a corporation requires the filing of a document, called articles of incorporation, in most states with the appropriate state official, usually the Secretary of State. The articles must be signed by an "incorporator" and accompanied by the prescribed fee. Any person can serve as an incorporator, whose principal function is to sign the articles. Often the attorney for the corporation is the incorporator.

The articles of incorporation **must** include the following: the name of the corporation, which in most states must must include words such as "corporation," "company," "incorporated," or abbreviations thereof; the address of the corporation's registered office and registered agent for service of process and the nature of the business of the newly formed corporation. The nature of the business is set forth in the so called "purpose clause," which historically was detailed. Today, the standard practice is just to say that the purpose of the corporation is to engage in "any lawful act or activity for which corporations may be organized."

The articles **must** also set forth the aggregate number of shares the corporation is authorized to issue and a description of those shares, including par value. If more than one class of shares is authorized the articles must so state. "Authorized" is a word of art under the corporate statutes. It means the maximum number of shares the corporation can issue as set forth in the articles.

The articles of incorporation may also contain: provisions that create, define, limit or regulate the powers of the corporation, directors, and shareholders; provisions that regulate the voting rights of shareholders (such as straight voting or cumulative voting), provisions that give shareholders of the corporation preemptive rights, a provision that limits the duration of the corporation's existence (though most articles provide for perpetual existence) and a provision indemnifying directors from liability. In some states, it is still necessary to include in the articles a "minimum capital" requirement: that the corporation will not conduct business until a minimum amount (usually $1,000) has been received for the issuance of shares.

When the state accepts the articles of incorporation for filing it issues a form of receipt typically called a certificate of incorporation. At that point in time, the corporation's existence begins.   The date on the certificate of incorporation evidences the corporation's beginning of existence in the same way that a birth certificate evidences the birth date of a real person.

b. Organization

In addition to the steps necessary to form the corporation, additional steps are required to complete the organization of the corporation.   First, bylaws must be prepared and adopted. Bylaws regulate the internal affairs of the corporation and provide a structure for governance. Among other things the bylaws set forth the procedures for calling and conducting meetings of both the board of directors and shareholders, including notice and quorum requirements.   The bylaws also provide the basic rules for governance of the corporation and define the duties and authority of the various corporate officers.   Unlike the articles, the bylaws are not filed with any governmental authority.

Second, organizational meetings of shareholders and directors must be held (or in the alternative unanimous written consents in lieu of meetings must be adopted). Unless the first board of directors is named in the articles, the shareholders must elect directors to serve until the first annual meeting of shareholders. The directors must adopt bylaws, appoint officers and perform any other acts necessary to complete the organization of the corporation.

Additional steps, which should also be taken to complete the organization of the corporation, include: opening of a corporate bank account, obtaining a minute book and seal, obtaining share certificates and duly issuing the shares acquired by the initial shareholders, obtaining the necessary tax identification numbers, determining whether an S corporation tax election should be made and, if so, making that election. All of the "steps" recommended in this subsection are important to the operation of the corporation, but they are not conditions to the creation of the corporation.

c. Ultra Vires

You should be aware of "ultra vires," both the word and the legal doctrine called the "ultra vires" doctrine. While the doctrine is a relic of the past and essentially a dead letter in the law, the word is still frequently seen in judicial opinions. In the case of ultra vires, understanding the word and the doctrine will reflect the insignificance, rather than the significance, of the doctrine in modern times.

The word "ultra vires" literally means "**beyond the power**" and the word is seen in judicial opinions where it is usually used to characterize illegal acts performed by corporations such as improper bribes, political contributions, charitable donations, etc.

The term ultra vires also serves as an icon for a common law legal doctrine, which bears its name. That doctrine, which had its heyday in the 19th century in the era of "special charters," described in § II.F, *supra,* relates to the consequences of a corporation doing an act that exceeded the corporation's purpose, as stated in the "purpose clause" of its articles.

During the era of special charters the purpose clauses in corporate articles used to be specific and verbose. For example a corporation might have been organized to build a railroad and its specific purpose was so reflected its purpose clause. If that corporation also engaged in general construction work, it might be characterized as performing an ultra vires act—*i.e.*, an act beyond the purpose for which the corporation was organized.

The main use of the ultra vires doctrine was to disaffirm contracts. It was used for this purpose both by the party who contracted with the corporation and by the corporation itself to weasel out of contractual commitments on the grounds that the contract was ultra vires, beyond the purpose for which the corporation was created.

Ultra vires is no longer a viable legal doctrine for that purpose because: (1) today corporations have broad purpose clauses (*e.g.*, "to engage in any lawful activity . . .") and (2) modern corporate statutes have provisions, similar to § 3.04 of MBCA, that state "no contract or conveyance shall be invalid because it was beyond the scope of a corporation's power . . . ." These provision typically do give the state power to enjoin ultra vires acts, but such actions are rare.

The result is that the state can enjoin ultra vires acts; but private parties can no longer use ultra vires as a defense to performance of their contracts.

The ultra vires doctrine and its decline does reflect a historical policy concern, namely the fear that corporations might get too big and powerful. That fear still exists today, but the primary tools used to prevent this from happening are the antitrust laws, not the ultra vires doctrine. The recent Microsoft antitrust litigation is a good illustration.

2. Where to Incorporate—The Internal Affairs Doctrine

Creation of a corporation merely requires compliance with the applicable provisions of the corporate statute of any one of the fifty states. The incorporator(s) can choose any state. It does not have to be the state where the corporation will have its principal office and the corporation does not even have to do business in its state of incorporation. For example, a corporation, whose entire business is in California, can incorporate under the law of any of the fifty states.

This brings into play the concepts of "foreign" and "domestic" corporations. A corporation formed in any state in the United States is a domestic corporation in its state of incorporation and nowhere else. Thus, if a corporation is incorporated in Delaware but does all of its business in California that corporation would be considered a foreign corporation in California. That corporation would have to qualify to do business in California, as well as in every other state, other than Delaware, in which it does business.

Qualifying to do business is a simple statutory procedure, which generally entails: filing certified copies of the articles; filling out a simple form provided by the state, paying a filing fee and appointing a local agent for process. Qualifying in multiple states increases the filing fees and franchise taxes that corporations must pay. Thus, the choice of the state of incorporation usually boils down to incorporating locally or in Delaware. A corporation that does the bulk of its business in one or two states will almost invariably incorporate locally—simply because of considerations related to costs and convenience. On the other hand, a corporation which does business in multiple states may choose to incorporate in a particular state and qualify to do business in the other states. In these situations Delaware is by far the most popular choice. More than one-half of the companies on both the Fortune 500 list and the New York stock exchange are incorporated in Delaware.

The most important legal consequence of the choice of the state of incorporation is the "Internal Affairs Doctrine," a conflict of laws rule which provides that the law of the state of incorporation, called the corporate domicile, determines the rights and duties of shareholders, directors and officers. The Restatement of Conflict of Laws states that foreign courts should apply the law of the state of incorporation to issues relating to the internal affairs of a foreign corporation. Thus, when a matter related to the inner workings of a corporation is before a court in any state, the court will apply the laws of the state in which the corporation was incorporated to resolve the dispute. This does not mean that the law of the state of incorporation would govern all legal issues involving the corporation. Disputes involving transactions with third parties would likely be governed by local law.

3. Subchapter S Election

Recall that many closely held corporations may avoid double taxation by filing an election to be taxed as a

Subchapter S corporation. If the corporation meets the requirements for subchapter S taxation, it may file an election with the IRS at any time during the first quarter of the tax year in which the election is to take effect, or during the preceding year. Once the election is made and accepted by the IRS, it remains in effect until it is terminated by the corporation.

C. LIMITED LIABILITY COMPANY (LLC)

The LLC is a relatively new business structure which is neither a corporation nor a partnership. The LLC has attributes drawn from both of these older business structures. Today all states have enabling statutes which authorize the creation and use of LLCs. The variations in the LLC statutes of the several states are much greater than the variations in the states' corporate or partnership statutes. Despite these statutory variations, there is one important similarity which needs to be understood. **In all states the law of LLCs is primarily contract law**.

1. FORMATION

A filing is required to create an LLC in all states, but the states vary significantly as to specifics required in that filing. In some states, formation of an LLC requires the filing of a certificate of formation with the Secretary of State. The certificate of formation must include the name of the LLC, the address of its registered office and registered agent and any other matters the members deem necessary. If there has been substantial compliance with the statute, the LLC is formed when the certificate is filed.

In other states, articles of organization, which are similar to articles of incorporation, must be filed with the Secretary of State. The articles of organization must include the name of the LLC, the period of duration, the purpose for which the LLC is organized, the address of its registered office and organizers, and such other provisions as the members elect to set out in the articles. In some states, if the LLC is to have managers, the articles must include a statement to that effect and must name the managers.

2. THE OPERATING AGREEMENT

Regardless of whether the relevant state law uses the term "certificate of formation" or "articles of organization" to describe the document that must be filed to create an LLC, that document is not the most important document relative to the LLC. The state LLC statutes merely establish "default rules" that govern, if but only if there are no controlling provisions in the operating agreement. The operating agreement can best be described as essentially an amalgamation of corporate bylaws and a partnership agreement.

The operating agreement governs the internal operation of the LLC and defines the relationships among the members of the LLC as well as the relationship between the members and the LLC itself. More specifically, it may establish the process for the admission of new members, set forth any requirements for contribution, define classes of members or managers, govern voting rights, provide for the dissolution and windup of the LLC, provide for the allocation of profits and losses as well as distribution and set forth the remedies for breach of the agreement. It can govern all of the above and more, as the members choose. The LLC provides more management flexibility than any other business structure.

An artfully drafted operating agreement can be used to structure the LLC in accordance with the owners' desires. There are no statutory requirements for a corporate-like hierarchy of shareholders, directors and officers. The LLC statutes of most states give the members the option of electing to manage the business themselves—in which case the business structure is called a "member managed LLC" or to have one or more managers manage the business—in which case it is called a "manager managed LLC."

Most LLC statutes incorporate a policy of giving maximum effect to freedom of contract. For example, § 18-1101(b) of the Delaware LLC statute clearly enunciates this policy as follows:

It is the policy of this chapter to give maximum effect to the principle of freedom of contract and to the enforcement of limited liability company agreements.

Flexibility of management, coupled with pass-through taxation and limited liability of members, has contributed to the dramatic growth of the LLC as a business structure in recent years.

CHAPTER IV

WHAT ARE THE LIMITS OF LIMITED LIABILITY?

Limited liability is one of the main factors considered in selecting a business structure. It also plays a key role in operating, financing and managing a business. Today, limited liability is readily available, as a matter of elective choice, not only to owners of corporations, but also to the owners of certain forms of unincorporated business structures such as LLCs and LLPs. The shield of limited liability, though broad, is not absolute. This chapter explores the scope of the limited liability protection afforded by the various business structures.

A. THE CONCEPT OF LIMITED LIABILITY AND THE POLICY UNDERLYING THE CONCEPT

While relatively simple, the concept of limited liability is sometimes misunderstood. Limited liability in no way limits the liability of the entity which incurs the legal obligation. For example, a corporation, as a separate legal entity, is fully liable for its obligations to the extent of its assets.

Limited liability only limits the liability of the owners of the entity. Anyone who invests in a corporation risks losing all or part of their investment. However, to the extent that the concept of limited liability is recognized and enforced, creditors of the corporation may not reach the personal assets of the real people who own the corporation (*i.e.*, its shareholders) to satisfy corporate debts.

The policy behind the notion of limited liability is clear. If the courts routinely looked behind the separate entity status of the corporation (or other business structures offering protection from unlimited personal liability) and routinely held shareholders personally liable for obligations of the corporation, the free enterprise, capitalistic system as we know it would not exist. Business structures with limited liability are critical to capital raising, risk-taking, diversification and other aspects of our economic system. For example, how many people would buy stock in companies such as Microsoft, IBM or General Electric (or the start-ups, which might be the Microsofts of tomorrow), if they knew that they might face liability in excess of their investment (*i.e.*, if, not just their investment in a particular company, but their home, bank account, car, savings, and other investments were at risk). Thus, the concept of limited liability is critical to capital formation and encourages business risk taking, savings, investment and diversification.

On the other hand, there are situations in which the individual shareholders or in the case of subsidiary corporations, the parent corporation, have used the corporation as an instrument to defraud creditors. A consequence of limited liability is to leave creditors of a failed corporation unpaid. Sometimes basic fairness dictates that the shareholders of the failed business structure, rather than its creditors, should bear the loss. Thus the courts recognize limitations to the general rule that shareholders are not personally liable for corporate obligations.

B. CORPORATIONS

1. THE GENERAL RULE—NO PERSONAL LIABILITY

The most fundamental attribute of the corporation, which flows naturally from the separate entity status that the law affords corporations, is that the **owners of the corporation are not personally liable for the debts or other obligations of the corporation**.

2. EXCEPTION TO THE GENERAL RULE— DIRECT LIABILITY OF SHAREHOLDERS UNDER CONTRACT OR TORT LAW

There are situations in which shareholders are directly liable for corporate obligations under either contract or tort law. First, under contract law, shareholders often assume personal liability for corporate obligations. A lender may refuse to extend credit to a corporation with limited assets unless one or more of that corporation's shareholders agree to personally pay the debt if the corporation does not do so. In this situation, shareholders are personally liable for corporate debts under general contract principles.

Second, if a shareholder of a corporation commits a tort in the course of the corporation's business, he will be liable under general principles of tort and agency law. For example, if in a closely held incorporated furniture store, the majority shareholder of the corporation injures a pedestrian while making a delivery, he would be liable as a joint tortfeasor. Even if he wasn't driving the truck, a shareholder, who is also an officer, might be liable for negligent failure to supervise.

3. EXCEPTION TO THE GENERAL RULE— "PIERCING THE CORPORATE VEIL"

The principal limitation to the general rule of limited liability of corporate shareholders is the common law concept known by the colorful name of "piercing the corporate veil." If the corporate veil is "pierced" the court will hold one or more of the corporation's shareholders liable for a corporate debt. The classic fact pattern is a situation in which liability has been incurred in the name of a corporation, which has become insolvent. Creditors, trying to reach the assets of a solvent defendant, sue some or all of the corporation's shareholders and argue that they should be held liable for the corporation's obligations. This situation has arisen in hundreds of reported cases and the courts have not been consistent in either their decisions or reasoning.

The policy which underlies the law of piercing clearly indicates that the doctrine should be applied as a narrow exception to the general rule of limited personal liability. In 1985 (then) Professors Esterbrook and Fischel observed in an often quoted statement: "Piercing seems to happen freakishly. Like lightning, it is rare, severe and unprincipled."

Many years ago, in a case called *Berkey v. Third Avenue Railway* Justice Cardozo expressed the same notion as follows:

> The whole area [of piercing] is one that is still enveloped in the mists of metaphor. Metaphors in law are to be narrowly watched, for starting as devices to liberate thought, they often end by enslaving it. We say at times that the corporate entity will be ignored when a parent operates a business through a subsidiary characterized as an 'alias' or 'dummy'. All this is well enough if the picturesqueness of the epithets does not lead us to forget that the essential term to be defined is the act of operation. Domination may be so complete, interference so obstructive, that by general rules of agency the parent will be a principal and the subsidiary an agent. Where control is less than this we are remitted to tests of honesty and justice.

Cardozo was telling us the same thing in 1926 that Easterbrook and Fischel told us in 1985, namely: as a general rule the corporation is a separate entity from its shareholders and that limited liability should be recognized as the general rule. Cardozo went on to say that sometimes in unusual or compelling circumstances courts may disregard the corporate entity and hold the shareholders personally liable for corporate obligations when" honesty or justice" requires.

Piercing is an equitable remedy that courts sometimes impose to avoid injustice. This rule rest on the rationale that since doing business as a corporation is a privilege allowed by law, the law can limit that privilege in the interest of fairness, equity or public policy. While both the rule and underlying principle make sense, they are too broad to give much guidance as to what specific facts establish grounds for piercing. The judicial opinions are in conflict, both in their results and reasoning, and they tend to be long on metaphors, but short on meaningful analysis.

a. Factors Considered in a Leading Piercing Case

Piercing cases are very fact dependent. While no one case can serve as an icon for the many cases considered in this area, a good beginning point for analysis is a case that appears in most of the casebooks—*Dewitt Truck Brokers, Inc. v. W. Ray Fleming Fruit Co.*

Fleming Fruit Company (the "corporation"), a close corporation controlled and managed by a single individual, sold fruit for growers on commission. When the fruit was sold, the corporation would pay the growers the sales price less the corporation's commission and transportation costs. The corporation had contracted with Dewitt Truck (the "Plaintiff") to transport the fruit but defaulted on its obligation to pay Plaintiff $15,000 for transportation costs, despite the fact that the corporation had collected the money to pay these costs from the fruit growers.

Plaintiff brought suit to collect the money due from Ray Fleming ("Fleming"), the corporation's president and principal shareholder. Noting that Fleming had orally assured plaintiff that he would personally pay the transportation costs if the corporation did not,[1] the Court pierced the corporate veil and held Fleming personally liable for the debt of the corporation. In its opinion, the court listed a number of factors, that influenced its decision to pierce the corporate veil:

(1) Gross "undercapitalization" and "insolvency of the corporation,"

(2) Failure to observe corporate formalities or keep adequate corporate records,

(3) Nonpayment of dividends,

(4) Control or domination of the corporation by Fleming,

(5) Siphoning of corporate funds by Fleming, and

(6) Nonparticipation by officers, directors or shareholders, other than Fleming, in the affairs of the corporation.

While this case was probably decided correctly, the multiple factors cited in this case as the basis for decision confuse the issue and provide little analytical guidance for future cases. First, there are questions as to how many of the factors on the list must be present and in what combination. Second, one can question the relevance of some of the factors listed by the court. For example, how is the unpaid corporate creditor harmed by nonpayment of dividends to its shareholders. Many loan agreements limit dividend payments to protect the creditor. If the corporation was grossly undercapitalized and insolvent, why did the contract creditor fail to require an enforceable

---

1. The oral promise was not enforceable because of the statute of frauds.

personal guarantee from Fleming? Is the creditor really prejudiced by the fact that the corporation failed to keep adequate records or observe corporate formalities?

It is questionable whether the first three factors listed above were relevant to the decision. The remaining three factors are evidentiary facts that bear on the more basic questions of whether Mr. Fleming was in control of the corporation and whether he did a "fast shuffle" with the intent of defrauding the corporation's creditors. That was the real issue in the case.

b. Factors Considered in Piercing Cases

Numerous writers over the years have analyzed the reported cases and given us a number of factors, which in some combination, might persuade a court to pierce the corporate veil in a given case. One such study cited in most law school casebooks is Professor Robert Thompson's 1991 empirical study of the over 1600 reported piercing cases (the "Thompson Study"). These studies provide valuable insight into the various factors which may influence decisions in piercing cases.

Piercing only occurs in close corporations. The Thompson Study showed that piercing only occurs in close corporations or corporate groups. It does not occur in publicly held corporations. Professor Thompson's database showed that piercing did not occur in any case in which the corporation whose veil was pierced had more than nine shareholders.

Tort or contract creditors. Many writers have stated over the years that courts are more likely to pierce the corporate veil in favor of tort claimants than in favor of contract creditors. Their basic reasoning is that contract creditors, such as customers, suppliers and lenders, who voluntary deal with corporations and do not require personal guarantees, assume the risk of the consequences of limited liability. By contrast, involuntary creditors, such as tort victims, did not voluntarily choose to assume that risk and could not protect themselves contractually. While logic supports this reasoning, the case law does not. The Thompson Study found that courts pierced a greater percentage of the time in contract cases than in tort cases.

Professor Thompson's findings notwithstanding, the insights of the scholars that it is important to distinguish between contract and tort claims in evaluating piercing claims is correct. Professor Gevurtz explains in his outstanding *Hornbook on Corporation Law*, that the question is not whether a tort claimant is a more sympathetic or deserving plaintiff than a contract creditor in a piercing case, but rather what sort of conduct justifies piercing in contract cases as opposed to tort cases. Contract cases usually involve situations where the contract creditor was (1) induced to do business with the corporation through misrepresentation or fraud, or (2) the person in control of the corporation dealt improperly with the corporation's assets—*i.e.*, the control person took money out of the corporation's bank account to pay personal debts.

On the other hand, in tort cases, the question usually boils down to one of public policy. Is it reasonable for the owners of the corporation to transfer a risk of loss to a third party by conducting business through a marginally financed corporation? In this type of situation liability insurance or the lack thereof should be considered in deciding whether or not to pierce. For example, assume an airline created a separate corporation for each airplane in its fleet and that the airplane owning subsidiary corporations have inadequate equity capital or liability insurance to cover losses which are foreseeable in the event of an accident. The parent corporation would risk piercing liability in the event of an accident where the liability exceeded the assets and liability insurance of the subsidiary corporation, which owned the airplane involved in the accident.

Undercapitalization. In piercing cases, inadequate capitalization means a capitalization that is very small in relationship to the foreseeable needs of the business. Inadequate capitalization alone is not sufficient to cause a court to pierce the corporate veil. On the other hand inadequate capitalization plays a supporting role in many piercing cases and coupled with other factors such as wrongfully dealing with corporate assets or creditors might become a factor that has a powerful influence on a court. For example, if assets that could be used to purchase insurance or pay creditors are siphoned off by the controlling shareholder as salary, dividends or similar payments, this might be viewed as purposeful insolvency rather than mere undercapitalization—a practice which might influence a court to pierce.

Fraud or deception. Using the corporation as a device to defraud or deceive creditors can be a powerful factor in piercing cases. Sometimes the undercapitalization cases are more about fraud or deception than about inadequate capitalization.

Commingling. "Commingling," when done by a person who "dominates" the corporation, is another powerful factor which might influences a court to pierce. "Commingling" includes failure to keep separate bank accounts for the corporation and the controlling shareholder and writing checks to cover personal expenses out of the corporate account. It also includes situations in which the dominant shareholder treats the corporation's bank account as his private "piggy bank." In some cases the personal assets of the dominant shareholder and the assets of the corporation may be so commingled that the third party may think she is dealing with the shareholder rather than the corporation.

Self-dealing. Abusive self-dealing, like commingling, can take many forms and is often a powerful factor in piercing cases.

Control or domination. In piercing cases, courts often speak at length about the degree of control exercised by the defendant over the debtor corporation. They sometimes say that domination is so complete that the corporation has become the "alter ego" or "instrumentality" of the controlling shareholder. Some opinions even seem to suggest that excessive domination or control can itself be a grounds for piercing.

This is not "good law." People control all corporations. Since piercing is a close corporation problem, all of the corporations whose veils are pierced are likely to be under the control of one or a few decision makers. If control alone were grounds for piercing few, if any, close corporations could be counted on to provide limited liability. There must be some kind of misconduct—fraud, self-dealing, commingling, etc., which tells the court **when** to pierce. However, control does play a part. The control factor may tell the court **against whom** to pierce. Shareholders not in control of the corporation are unlikely to be held personally liable in piercing cases.

Failure to follow corporate formalities. Courts often cite failure to follow corporate formalities, such as holding shareholders' and directors' meetings, issuing stock, keeping corporate minutes, etc, as a factor they consider in piercing cases. This factor has been criticized by many scholars because failure to follow corporate formalities is not a factor that often prejudices the plaintiff seeking to recover a corporate debt from an individual shareholder. At best it may furnish some evidence that the shareholder treats the corporation as an "alter ego" and does not recognize its separate existence.

Language in many piercing cases notwithstanding, unless the complaining plaintiff can show they were harmed by such informal conduct, failure to follow formalities should not be a significant factor in the decision of whether or not to pierce. A few states have passed statutes which mandate that failure to follow corporate formalities will not be a ground for piercing.

The factors discussed above appear in an infinite variety of combinations. No one factor controls nor does any combination of factors. Many of the traditional piercing factors were present in the *Fleming* case. Piercing involves a weighing test. The cases reveal highly impressionistic results, many of which are irreconcilable. In the last analysis it is an equitable doctrine, which should be applied sparingly as an exception to the general rule of limited personal liability.

4. PIERCING CASES INVOLVING MULTIPLE CORPORATIONS

a. Parent-Subsidiary Cases

In many piercing cases the controlling shareholder is another corporation rather than an individual. This is called a parent/subsidiary relationship. In these cases, the plaintiff is seeking to hold the parent corporation liable for the subsidiary corporation's debts.

Some writers have suggested that courts are more willing to pierce when the shareholder seeking to be held personally liable is a corporation rather than an individual and only business assets rather than personal assets are sought in payment of the unpaid debt. However, the Thompson Study found that courts actually pierced more often when the defendant was an individual than when the defendant was a corporation. Further, courts cite prior cases against corporate and individual defendants interchangeably, without making a distinction.

This raises the question should the standard be different when the defendant is a corporation rather than an individual:

(1)   If there is abusive self-dealing by the parent, fraud
       on the subsidiary's creditors or the parent
       improperly deals with the subsidiaries' assets.

(2)   When the parent does not allow the subsidiary to
       have adequate capital or insurance to cover a
       foreseeable risk.

Logic would suggest that the answer to both (1) and (2)
should be no. The Thompson Study seems to confirm that
answer. So long as the reasonable expectations of creditors
or other third parties are not abused by
misrepresentations, fraud or improper dealings with
corporate assets or public policy is not violated, it should
not make a difference whether the owner of the corporation
whose veil is sought to be pierced is an individual or a
corporation.

Often, however, cases involving attempts to pierce the
corporate veil when the defendant is a parent corporation
have a somewhat different flavor than cases in which the
defendant is an individual shareholder. This is mainly due
to differences in fact patterns involving parent/subsidiary
relationships. For example, sometimes the relationship is
structured so that all profits of the subsidiary inure to the
benefit of the parent; or there is no clear delineation as to
which transactions are the parent's and which are the
subsidiary's; or the board of directors of the parent makes
decisions for the subsidiary. Thus, while the underlying
principles should be the same, the factual context in which
the problem arises may be sufficiently different to influence
a court in a given case. And of more immediate
importance, this type of an insight in answering an exam

question involving a parent/subsidiary relationship may have a positive influence on your professor.

b. Sister Corporations and the "Enterprise Theory"

Either an individual or a corporation may own controlling interests in a number of corporations which are engaged in related activities. These are called sister corporations. Many large corporations own subsidiaries, and usually there is a legitimate business purpose for conducting operations through subsidiary corporations. However, sometimes multiple corporations are used to artificially divide what is essentially one business enterprise into segments in order to unreasonably limit liability or to mislead creditors or customers.

Consider *Walkovsky v. Carlton*, a case in most law school casebooks. Carlton was the controlling and dominant shareholder in each of ten cab companies in New York City. Each of the ten corporations owned two cabs, which reflected a common practice in the New York City taxi cab business. Expensive licenses granted by the city entitled the owner of the licence to own and operate two cabs. None of the corporations had much equity capital, and each carried the minimum amount of liability insurance required by law—$10,000. The driver of a cab owned by one of the ten corporations ran over Mr. Walkovsky, who sued (1) the corporation which owned the cab that hit him, (2) the other nine sister corporations on an enterprise liability theory, and (3) Carlton, individually, on a theory that he was personally liable.

In an appeal from the trial court's order granting a motion to dismiss the case against Carlton, the court accepted enterprise theory liability on the part of the nine sister corporations, since what was held out to the public as a single enterprise was artificially separated into different corporations. But the court rejected the theory that Carlton's use of the minimally capitalized multiple corporations made him personally liable.

In cases involving enterprise liability courts often cite confusion as a reason for disregarding the separate corporations. Customers may be justifiably confused about which entity they are dealing with or creditors may be confused about whose credit is on the line. Mixing assets, failing to observe formalities, having officers who do not identify in what capacity they are acting and using the same trade names, stationery or common facilities are other factors often cited in imposing liability based on the enterprise theory. The motive and business purpose, if any, for setting up the multiple sister corporations may also be relevant to a finding of enterprise liability.

5. UNRESOLVED QUESTIONS REGARDING PIERCING: WHAT LAW GOVERNS? WHO DECIDES—JUDGE OR JURY?

Recall that the law of the state of incorporation governs the internal affairs of a corporation. Is piercing governed by the internal affairs doctrine? This question has not been given a great deal of attention by the courts because piercing claims typically involve small corporations, which are incorporated in the same state in which the corporation operates and incurs liability. Thus, choice of law questions do not frequently arise. When choice of law issues have arisen most courts have followed the law of the state of incorporation.

Another unresolved question is who decides whether there are grounds sufficient to pierce in a given case. More specifically, is this a factual issue for the jury or an equitable evaluation for the trial judge.   Plausible arguments can made in favor of allowing either the judge or the jury to decide this issue, and no majority rule has yet emerged.

6. PERSONAL LIABILITY ARISING IN CONNECTION WITH THE FORMATION PROCESS

a. Defective Incorporation

Recall in Chapter III we learned that when the state accepts the articles of incorporation for filing, corporate existence begins, even if the steps necessary to complete the organization—*i.e.*, adopting bylaws, issuing stock, holding organization meetings, etc.—are never completed and even if there is some minor defect in the articles of incorporation. In plain English, the corporation is born. In the jargon of corporate law it is a **de jure corporation**—an entity recognized by law as a corporation for all purposes.

Despite the simplicity of the statutory process of incorporation under modern statutes, people sometimes do not get it right. The party whose job it is to file the articles may simply forget to do so. Sometimes the individual who forgets is an attorney, in which case the issues discussed in this subsection might arise in a malpractice action against the forgetful attorney. In this situation, the persons who own or purport to act for the corporation, which was not formed, can be held personally liable for debts incurred by the business under agency principles or under specific provisions contained in some, but not all, of the governing corporate statutes.

More likely such persons may be held liable under a partnership theory. If two or more parties are carrying on a business for profit as co-owners and that business is not a corporation, what is it? As we learned in Chapter II, it is a general partnership—the default form of business structure, with more than one owner. One of the main consequences of partnership status is, of course, joint and several personal liability.[2]

There are two possible defenses to personal liability for the debts of a business that was defectively incorporated: (1) **de facto corporation** and (2) **corporation by estoppel**.

De facto corporation. A de facto corporation is a partially-formed corporation that provides a shield against personal liability of shareholders for corporate obligations. When a court invokes the de facto corporation doctrine, the court is saying it will treat the business as if it was a corporation for purposes of adjudicating the rights and duties of private parties, even though all of the statutory formalities for formation were not met.

---

2. If there is only one owner of a business that attempts to incorporate but fails, the result would be a sole proprietorship, rather than a partnership, but personal liability would still ensue.

Three elements must be established to invoke the defense of de facto corporation: (1) **colorable compliance:** the organizers of the corporation attempted to comply with the applicable statutes, but failed to do so; (2) **good faith:** the organizers were unaware of the defect that kept the corporation from being formed; and (3) **use of corporate power:** the company carried on as though they believed the corporation existed (they issued stock, held meetings, entered contracts, etc.). In most states, if all three elements are met, the alleged shareholders of the defectively formed corporation will be shielded against personal liability to the same degree as if they formed a de jure corporation.

Corporation by estoppel. If the owners of the business cannot prove one or more of the three elements necessary to sustain the defense of de facto corporation, they may still avoid personal liability for the debts of the business under the common law doctrine of corporation by estoppel. The concept behind corporation by estoppel is different from that behind de facto corporation. The general idea is so simple it sometimes trips up students. A third party who has dealt with an entity as though it were a corporation and without any expectation that the shareholders will be personally liable for the corporation's debt will be estopped from holding the shareholders liable when it is subsequently discovered that the corporation was not properly formed. Corporation by estoppel is an equitable defense. Therefor the party asserting the defense must have acted in good faith and not affirmatively misled the other party.

The classic illustration of the application of corporation by estoppel, is a 1964 Maryland case called *Cranson v. IBM*, which is in most law school casebooks. In *Cranson,* IBM sold eight typewriters on credit to Real Estate Service Bureau (the "company"), which was purportedly a corporation owned by Mr. Cranson. It turned out that the Company was not incorporated on the date it bought the typewriters. Unknown to Mr. Cranson, his lawyer forgot to file the articles and did not get around to filing the articles for seven months. However, the attorney advised Cranson that the corporation had been formed and showed him the corporate seal and minute book. Thereafter, the company carried on business as if it were a corporation (Cranson was elected President, he opened a corporate bank account, etc.). When the company failed to pay for the typewriters, IBM sued Mr. Cranson personally on the unpaid debt. The court refused to hold Cranson personally liable, reasoning that since the plaintiff IBM had relied solely on the credit of the supposed corporation when it entered into the transaction, it was estopped from using its later discovery of the defective incorporation as the basis for holding Cranson personally liable.

It is interesting how far this case carries the concept of estoppel. A famous contracts professor, Grant Gilmore, once defined "estoppel" as a word courts use when they want to hold a particular way and don't want to tell us exactly why. Usually estoppel is invoked against a party who makes a misrepresentation in favor of a party who relies on the misrepresentation. But in *Cranson* the party who made the misrepresentation was permitted to escape liability,   while   the   party   who   relied   on   the misrepresentation was estopped from disputing the misrepresentation.

Both de facto corporation and corporation by estoppel are common law defenses. Some modern corporate statutes specifically deal with defective incorporation by imposing statutory conditions for liability. However, the courts are not in agreement as to whether such statutes preempt the common law defenses of de facto corporation and corporation by estoppel.

b. Pre-Incorporation Transactions and Promoters' Liability

Recall that modern corporate statutes provide that a corporation's legal existence begins on the date the secretary of state issues a certificate of incorporation. The corollary to that rule is the corporation does not legally exist and thus has no capacity to make contracts prior to that date.

However, often before the certificate of incorporation is issued a lot of preliminary work must be done. Often the person planning the business to be carried on by the corporation makes contracts on behalf of the corporation he plans to form. For example, he might sign a lease for office space, hire employees, buy goods or services from third parties, etc.

These contracts are called **promoters' contracts** and the people who make them are called "**promoters**." In the vocabulary of corporate law, the word "promoter" has a more neutral and less negative meaning than in ordinary speech. Not some unsavory, fast talking character with "big hair," just a guy with plans for a new business to be operated by a corporation not yet formed.

Two issues often arise in connection with promoters' contracts: (1) the extent to which the promoters are personally liable under these contracts and (2) the extent to which the corporation is liable under such contracts after it is formed.

Promoters' liability. In dealing with cases involving promoters' liability to third parties on contracts made on behalf of corporations to be formed, most courts recite what has come to be the well-established general rule—the promoter is personally liable on such contracts. Most courts then go on to state the exception to the general rule, which is as well established as the general rule itself. Under the exception, if the other party to the contract, at the time she makes the contract, knows the corporation is not in existence but nevertheless agrees to look solely to the corporation, and not to the promoter for payment, the promoter is not personally liable under the contract.

This general rule and the exception (which is broad enough to swallow the general rule) are good examples of what sometimes happens when courts attempt to reduce factual distinctions to broad-based rules of law. Often we wind up with rules that confuse more than they clarify.

At page 47 of the *Hornbook on Corporation Law*, Professor Gevurtz explains that the traditional recitation of the rule is really upside down. The so-called exception, which basically tells us that this is a matter of intent, is really the general rule. And the so called general rule, which tells us that the promoter is liable, is really the default rule. The above analysis applies only to cases in which both the promoter and other party to the contract knew that the corporation did not exist. If the promoter misrepresents the status of the corporation yet to be formed and contracts on its behalf, the promoter can be held liable under a variety of contract or agency principles.

Obviously, the best way to avoid the problem discussed in this subsection is to first form the corporation and then have the corporation enter into the contract. If for some reason this is not possible, the attorney should recognize the difficulty courts have in applying tests based on the parties' presumed intent and spell out what is intended as clearly as possible in the contract.

Liability of the corporation. The corporation is not automatically liable on contracts made by the promoter on the corporation's behalf before the corporation was formed. The reason is grounded on the well-settled principle of agency law that one can not be an agent for an entity which is not in existence. Once the corporation is formed, the corporation may "adopt" the contract. Courts sometimes use the word "ratify." The terms "adopt" and "ratify" are often used interchangeably in this situation. Whatever term is used, the effect is that the corporation assumes the obligation.

Sometimes there is an issue as to whether the corporation has adopted a pre-incorporation contract. Obviously, there can be an express adoption (*i.e.*, the board of directors passes a resolution adopting the contract) as well as a clear and immediate rejection. A corporation can also adopt a contract by implication. For example, in *McArthur v. Times Printing Co.* the promoter made a one year employment contract with the plaintiff to work for a newspaper corporation. The contract was made prior to incorporation but the corporation's shareholders, directors and officers were aware of the contract. After it was formed the corporation did not expressly adopt the contract, but it allowed the plaintiff to continue working for six months. The court held that this inaction amounted to adoption of the one-year employment contract by implication.

C. THE SCOPE OF LIMITED LIABILITY PROVIDED BY UNINCORPORATED BUSINESS STRUCTURES

Recall that state legislatures have created three unincorporated business structures which provide full or partial limited liability—the **limited partnership**, the **limited liability company** and the **limited liability partnership**. This subsection discusses the scope of the limited liability provided by these business structures.

1. LIMITED PARTNERSHIPS

As we learned in § II.C.2, *supra*, a limited partnership (LP) is a partnership in which there are two classes of partners: (1) general partners, who manage the business and have unlimited personal liability and (2) limited partners, who have virtually no management authority but have limited liability, as long as they do not participate in the management or control of the business. The concept behind the LP was a trade-off to encourage capital-raising during the industrial revolution, when most limited partnership statutes were originally passed. The original statutes reflected a policy that limited partners, passive investors with no power to manage, should not be liable for the debts of the business over and above their original investment. Today, the original concept behind the limited partnership has been somewhat modified as reflected in the Revised Uniform Limited Partnership Act ("RULPA").

a. Statutory Safe Harbors

A major problem in the original Uniform Limited Partnership Act of 1916 was that the prohibition against participation in management or control gave no clue as to what specific acts violated the broad-based prohibition. The scope of this open ended prohibition against "participation in management" created uncertainty regarding the security of the limited partners' shield of limited liability. That problem was addressed in § 303(b) of RULPA, which creates a number of statutory "safe harbors" by defining a number of actions limited partners can take without being deemed to be participating in the management or control of the business. The list includes:

(1) being a contractor for or agent or employee of the limited partnership or a general partner;
(2) being an officer, director or shareholder of a corporation that is a general partner
(3) acting as a surety, guarantor or endorser for the limited partnership;

(4) serving on a committee of the limited partnership or the general partner; and

(5) participating (usually by voting) in a variety of decisions relating to the limited partnership, including removing a general partner, changing the nature of the business, dissolution, etc.

The above list is not exclusive and the listed safe harbors vary somewhat from state to state. Also, the listed safe harbors themselves are not exclusive. If a limited partner's activity falls within a safe harbor the activity is permitted without risking exposure to personal liability. If a limited partner takes part in activity not covered by any of the safe harbors, she does not automatically become liable for the debts of the limited partnership. Instead, the courts will consider whether her activity constitutes "participation in management" within the scope of the general prohibition.

b. Corporate General Partners

Today, it is well settled that a corporation (or other limited liability entity such as an LLC) can be the sole general partner of a limited partnership. Further, one of the safe harbors listed in the preceding subsection permits limited partners of the LP to be officers, directors or shareholders of the LP's corporate general partner. The practical result of combining the business structures in this way is limited liability for all concerned—creditors can only look for payment from the assets of the limited partnership itself and those of the corporate general partner, which are usually small in relationship to the enterprise as a whole.

It has been held in Delaware that directors of a corporate general partner owe fiduciary duties to the limited partners as well as to the corporation acting as the sole general partner. Whether or not a court might pierce the shield of limited liability of a limited partnership with a corporate general partner by analogy to the corporate piercing cases, discussed above, is still an unanswered question.

2. LLCs AND LLPs

As we have learned, the owners of closely held businesses often desire limited liability. And for many years the only business structure which provided owners of a business who wanted to be active in the management of the business with limited liability was the corporation. Today, as we have already learned, other choices are available and many closely held businesses are migrating to new unincorporated business structures which provide limited liability—primarily the LLC and LLP. This raises the question:

What is the scope of the limited liability provided by these unincorporated business structures compared to the scope of limited liability provided by the corporation?

That question has not yet been fully answered. The law regarding the scope of limited liability provided by LLCs and LLPs is largely undeveloped. There are very few cases and discussion by the scholars as to the scope of limited liability protection provided by these new unincorporated business structures has been relatively limited. Most writers, who have focused on the question, seem to assume that (1) there will be no significant difference in the scope of limited liability afforded by the LLC and LLP and (2) the scope of limited liability afforded by both these relatively new business structures will not significantly differ from that currently afforded by corporations.

Another issue likely to play out in this area in the coming years, which might arise in your practice, if not your law school class (unless your professor emphasizes the issue[3]), is:

Can the veil of an LLC be pierced?

What few cases there are suggest that some degree of veil piercing will likely be permitted with respect to LLCs. Despite uncertainties surrounding the piercing doctrine as applied to corporations, it seems highly likely that similar concepts will be applied to LLCs. While some of the concepts applied to corporations are not readily transferable to LLCs, indications are that courts will "pierce" the veil of an LLC under doctrines analogous to those currently applied in corporate piercing cases. See § IV.B.3, *supra*.

---

3. It is unlikely your professor will know the answer, but she may want to explore the issue.

CHAPTER V

HOW DO BUSINESSES RAISE MONEY?

A. INTRODUCTION

All businesses, large and small, need money (*i.e.*, capital) to operate and grow. The amount and source of the capital needed by a business may determine the business structure selected for that particular business. Recall in Chapter II an LLC was chosen as the business structure for the Taco Stand, a business with relatively modest capital needs, which were supplied by the people who would actually run the business. By contrast the High Tech Start-Up was a business that required substantial capital over a relatively long period of time. The bulk of the funds needed to start the business and operate until it began generating a positive cash flow were provided by a venture capital firm, whose exit strategy was to harvest value through a public offering. The business structure chosen for the High Tech Start-Up was a corporation.

In this chapter you will get a basic overview of a subject generally called "corporate finance" or "capitalization and financing," which deals with the process of **establishing a financial framework** and **raising funds** for the business. Many legal issues arise in connection with this process. This is one of the most confusing areas of corporate law to students without a business background because many of the concepts are unfamiliar and much of the language is new. We will limit our discussion to the basic issues related to corporate finance, most likely to be encountered in the basic business course. Most law schools offer an advanced course in corporate finance.

We will first discuss some of the major underlying concepts and define some of the basic terms related to corporate finance in as simple a way as possible. We will then discuss the following three substantive areas: (1) the authorization and issuance of stock, (2) preemptive rights and dilution and (3) the process of raising equity capital and how that process is regulated under the Federal Securities Laws.

B. SOURCES OF FINANCING

The three principle ways in which all businesses raise money are: (1) retained earnings, (2) borrowing and (3) selling equity in the business.

1. Retained Earnings. One obvious way for a business to finance its operations is through the use of profits from the business. This is the largest source of financing. It is also the source of financing that generates the fewest legal issues. How do the big drug companies fund their research and development? How does Microsoft pay all those bright computer types who develop their software? How does Exxon pay for all their oil wells, pipelines and refineries? Most of these operations are financed from the billions that these successful companies generate through operating profits and related cash flow. Using retained earnings does not create many legal problems or need for much further discussion.

Obviously the ability of a particular business to generate internal funds from operations depends on (1) the earnings of the business, (2) its stage of development, and (3) the amount needed to operate and grow the business. For example, in the hypothetical involving the Taco Stand in Chapter II, the business plan anticipated that the business would generate sufficient cash flow to finance its operations by the time the initial $100,000 raised from the sale of equity was depleted. The plan was to use the profits, over and above what was distributed to the principals by way of dividends and salaries, to operate and grow the business.

2. Borrowing. Businesses can, of course raise money by borrowing, which is called debt financing. The money borrowed must, of course, be repaid with interest. The problem with borrowing is that banks and institutional lenders like to make loans to borrowers who do not really need the money or who have unencumbered assets which they can pledge to secure repayment of the loan. For example, Southwest Airlines would likely have little trouble borrowing several million dollars to buy ten new commercial jets, given its strong balance sheet and demonstrated ability to generate profits. Also a mortgage on a commercial jet is good security for the lender. On the other hand the Taco Stand and High Tech Start-up, discussed in Chapter II, would have a hard time securing loans because they are in an early stage of development and have no proven track record of earnings.

3. Equity Financing. A business entity may obtain money from persons who buy interests in the business. In consideration for the money these buyers invest in the business, they acquire interests in (*i.e.,* become the owners of) the business. Depending on the business, these interest owners may consist of persons who will be actively involved in managing the business, passive investors, who are seeking a return on their investment, or a combination of the two.

Equity ownership in any business entitles the owners to a bundle of rights and powers. The three basic rights and powers are:

(1) The right to a share of the profits of the business,
(2) Ownership of a share of the assets of the business and
(3) The power to participate in the management of the business.

A distinction, critical not only to understanding this chapter, but also to understanding much of what the basic business course is all about, is understanding the difference in the manner in which this bundle of rights and powers (called the "attributes of equity ownership") are bundled and allocated among the various persons involved in the business. These attributes of equity ownership are allocated differently in the different types of business structures.

Unincorporated businesses. In a partnership the allocation of the attributes of equity ownership are usually fixed in a contract by and among the partners called a partnership agreement. The partnership agreement can specify what portion of the profits and distributions each partner is entitled to and what rights of management the various partners have. If the partnership agreement contains gaps, the state partnership statute provides the default rules.

The attributes of equity ownership are allocated in much the same way in an LLC. The allocation is usually fixed in a contract by and among the members of the LLC, which in most states is called an operating agreement. If the operating agreement contains gaps, the state LLC statute provides the default rules.

Corporations. In corporations the attributes of equity ownership are allocated differently. There is no contract among the owners which defines the attributes of equity ownership of each owner. Rather, ownership interests in the corporation are allocated through the issuance of shares of stock. The number of shares owned by a particular owner determines that owner's prorata share of the attributes of equity ownership (*i.e.*, dividend rights, distribution rights and voting rights). As more fully explained by Professor Gevurtz at pages 113 et. seq. in the *Hornbook on Corporation Law*, the basic idea behind shares of stock is to create fungible units of ownership, each with the same attributes of ownership.

The concept of specifying the rights of equity owners through their relative ownership of fungible shares of stock is useful, particularly in publicly held businesses (*i.e.,* where there is a market for the stock) which have a constantly changing group of owners. It avoids both the need for investors to read the governing partnership agreement or operating agreement before they invest as well as the need to amend these agreements each time a new investor invests or an owner transfers her interest to someone else. Further, in a corporation these different aspects of equity ownership can be bundled and packaged in different ways by creating different types of securities, such as common stock and preferred stock. This greatly facilitates the financing process by enabling the managers of the corporation to tailor a capital structure that fits the needs of the business, the desires of the various constituencies within the corporation, and the preferences of the marketplace. This flexibility of capital structure, along with limited liability, explains why virtually all publicly held businesses are organized as corporations, despite the disadvantage of double taxation imposed under Subchapter C of the Internal Revenue Code.

In summary, allocating the attributes of equity ownership in unincorporated business involves artfully drafting partnership agreements or operating agreements, an essential lawyering skill of the corporate lawyer, but probably beyond the scope of the basic business course (unless you have a professor who emphasizes drafting skills). On the other hand, allocating the attributes of equity ownership in a corporation is largely a matter governed by corporate law, which is within the scope of the basic business course. Since issues related to capitalization and financing most often come up in corporations, the remainder of this chapter will deal with corporations.

C. BASIC DEFINITIONS—TERMS AND CONCEPTS

We will now define some of the key terms used in the area of corporate finance. Many of the terms and concepts set forth in boldface type below may be unfamiliar to students without a prior business background. All need to become part of every student's basic business vocabulary.

Capitalization and financing. The process of raising capital (*i.e.* money) is called **financing**. **Capitalization** is a less precise term, the meaning of which varies depending on the context in which it is used. In this chapter we use the term capitalization in a broad sense—*i.e.*, in the sense of a corporation's **capital structure**. A corporation's capital structure usually consists of both ownership interests **(equity)** and obligations **(debt)**.

Debt. The most important thing to remember about debt is that it is an obligation which must be repaid. The most common form of debt is simply loans from friends or relatives, banks, private investors, venture capitalists, or shareholders. Debt, of course, is a liability on the balance sheet, where it is usually classified as long-term or short-term depending on whether the debt is due within a year of the balance sheet date.

Most loans are evidenced by **notes**. In larger corporations, debt may be evidenced by **bonds** or **debentures**. Bonds or debentures are usually issued in transactions in which a corporation borrows a large sum of money from numerous persons, each of whom make relatively small loans on identical terms, through the purchase of such bonds or debentures. For example, when a person buys a government bond, that person is making a loan to the government. Unless your professor makes a point of the distinctions, the distinctions between notes, bonds and debentures are probably outside the scope of the basic business course. All are instruments that evidence debt.

Equity. As stated above, equity means ownership. In a corporation equity is represented by shares. "Shares" are defined in Model Business Corporations Act ("MBCA") § 1.40(21) as the "units into which the proprietary interests in a corporation are divided." In plain English this means shares of stock are the units of ownership into which ownership of a business structured as a corporation are divided. MBCA §§ 6.01–6.03 contain additional information about shares of stock.

The same general statutory scheme relative to shares of stock found in MBCA is found in all state corporate statutes. Some state statutes use the terms "share" and "shareholder," while other use the terms "stock" and "stockholder." We use these terms interchangeably. A corporation can issue more than one type of stock (*i.e.*, class or series), if the articles of incorporation authorize it to do so. The most basic type of shares authorized in the articles of incorporation and issued by the corporation is called **common stock**. Most small corporations don't issue anything but common stock. If a corporation has more than one class of stock, typically it will have preferred stock in addition to the common.

What are the differences between common and preferred stock?

Common stock. Owners of common stock have the fundamental rights to vote and to receive distributions (*i.e.,* dividends or liquidating distributions) contingent upon earnings and claims of creditors and preferred stockholders. See, *e.g.,* MBCA § 6.01(b). Common stock can best be described as the residual interests in the corporation—what is left after all claims of creditors and preferred stockholders have been satisfied. Dividends are not guaranteed. They are payable only at the discretion of the board of directors. While common stock has the lowest priority and carries the highest degree of risk, it also enjoys the greatest potential for reward if the business is successful. Typically, common stockholders control the corporation through all or most of the voting power. Common stock has by far the greatest potential to appreciate in value.

Preferred stock. While legally classified as equity, preferred stock is, in fact a hybrid between debt and common stock. The best way to understand the essence of preferred stock is to consider the main differences between preferred and common stock. As the name implies, preferred stock has certain preferences over common stock, which are discussed in the next paragraph. On the other hand, preferred stock is usually nonvoting. Thus, preferred stockholders usually have no say in management. Also, since preferred shares are usually redeemable at a fixed price, they have little potential for appreciation compared to common shares.

While preferred stock may include numerous preferences, the two most common are dividend preferences and liquidation preferences. Since preferred stock is considered equity, preferred stockholders, unlike bondholders, do not have a right to be paid dividends and failure to pay dividends on preferred stock is not a default by the corporation. The decision whether or not to pay dividends on preferred stock, like dividend decisions as to common stock, is within the discretion of the board of directors. However, the preference requires that preferred stockholders be paid dividends (the rate of dividends on preferred stock is usually fixed) before any dividends can be paid to common stockholders. In addition, if the preferred stock is "cumulative," when a preferred dividend is not paid in any year it accumulates and all accumulated dividends on the preferred stock must be paid before any dividends can be paid on the common stock in later years. Dividend preferences generally benefit holders of preferred stock when the corporation succeeds.

Liquidation preferences generally benefit holders of preferred stock when the corporation fails. The liquidation preference is usually structured so that a fixed price must be paid to preferred stockholders before any amount is paid to common shareholders in the event of liquidation.

Securities. The broad term used in corporate law to encompass all of the various types of interests, both debt and equity, that a corporation may issue is "securities."

D. THE DEBT-EQUITY MIX AND LEVERAGE

Establishing the most appropriate mix of debt and equity for a particular company involves consideration of numerous business and legal issues by the business people charged with this task and the lawyers who advise them. Answering exam questions in the basic business course simply requires that you know four things:

First, the biggest disadvantage to borrowing is that the loans have to be paid back, with interest. If a corporation cannot meet its debt obligations as they mature that company will likely become insolvent. On the other hand dividends on stock are not fixed obligations. A company unable to pay dividends may have some unhappy stockholders, but it will not necessarily go under.

Second, there are tax advantages to debt. Interest on debt is deductible, while dividends on stock are not.

Third, leverage can be greatest advantage of debt financing or it can be the greatest disadvantage— depending upon how things work out. "**Leverage**" is an economic principle which explains how the use of debt in a capital structure may improve the owners' return on their investment. The greater the ratio of debt to equity, the greater the leverage.

For example, assume the capital structure of a business is \$100,000, all equity, and that business earns \$20,000 before interest and taxes in a given year of operation. That business has earned a return on equity of 20% (*i.e.*,

$20,000/$100,000). Now assume the capital structure of the business consists of $50,000 equity and $50,000 debt, bearing interest at 10% per year. The business earns $20,000, before interest and taxes during the year. Earnings must be reduced by the $5,000 in interest expense, however the $15,000 earned after payment of interest constitutes a return on equity of 30% (*i.e.*, $15,000/$50,000).

Leverage accentuates the negatives in unprofitable companies in the same way that it accentuates the positives in profitable companies. For example, again assume the capital structure of a business is $100,000, all equity. But assume the business loses $10,000 before interest and taxes during a given year. This is a 10% loss on equity. If that company's capital structure consisted of $50,000 in debt bearing 10% interest and $50,000 in equity the loss would grow to $15,000 reflecting interest costs. And the loss on equity would be 30% ($15,000/$50,000). The greater the leverage the more both good and the bad results are accentuated. Companies which are highly leveraged are sometimes referred to as being "thinly capitalized."

Fourth, while debt and equity constitute the generic components of capital structure, the distinction sometimes becomes blurred with respect to some hybrid securities. The corporate statutes allow great flexibility in designing securities. Some hybrids, such as preferred stock with a convertible feature have attributes of both debt and equity and are not easy to pigeon hole.

E. AUTHORIZATION AND ISSUANCE OF STOCK

Debt financing (*i.e.*, borrowing), is primarily governed by contract law and debtor-creditor law, both of which are outside the scope of this book. On the other hand, equity financing, which involves the authorization and issuance of stock, brings into play a number of concepts covered in the basic business course.

1. ISSUANCE OF SHARES

The power to issue the shares lies with the board of directors. "**Issuance**" simply means the sale by the corporation of its shares in a classic exchange transaction—the corporation obtains money, property or services in consideration for the shares and the buyers of the shares become stockholders—the owners of the corporation. Only the corporation can issue shares. A later transfer of shares by a shareholder is not an issuance.

The corporation only receives consideration for its shares at the time of original issuance. After original issuance, often a trading market develops in the outstanding shares. The trading market consists of one investor selling shares to another investor.   While corporations, for a number of reasons, like the price of their stock to be high, the corporation does not receive any consideration as a result of purchases and sales in the trading market nor, is it directly affected by the trading market transactions in either a legal or accounting sense.

2. AUTHORIZATION OF SHARES

Before the corporation can "issue" shares, the shares must be "authorized." The state corporate statutes do not dictate the number of shares that may be authorized. That number is set forth in the articles of incorporation. See, *e.g.*, MBCA § 6.01: "The articles of incorporation must prescribe the number of shares . . . the corporation is authorized to issue." All state corporate statutes contain similar provisions. Generally "authorized" is a word of art in corporate law which refers to authority granted by the articles of incorporation. When a corporation has issued all the shares authorized by its articles it must amend the articles to authorize the issuance of additional shares.

Usually, in the terminology of corporate law when one talks about shares they are authorized and something else. For example, "**authorized and outstanding**" means the shares are owned by the shareholders. "**Authorized but unissued**" means the shares have been authorized but not yet issued. They are available for future issuance. Corporations usually authorize more shares than they initially plan to sell to avoid having to amend the articles. If shares have been authorized and issued, but are subsequently reacquired by the corporation they are called "**treasury shares**."

In addition to fixing the number of authorized shares, the articles define the basic attributes of the shares. If there is only one class of shares—*i.e.*, common stock—the provision defining the attributes of the shares is quite simple. If, on the other hand, the articles provide for different classes of common stock or series of preferred stock with different rights, preferences and restrictions, the articles must indicate if different classes are authorized and, if so, the relative rights and preferences of the different classes. See MBCA §§ 6.01 and 6.02.

3. CONSIDERATION FOR SHARES

The basic rule under most modern corporate statutes is that a corporation can issue stock in exchange for whatever consideration the board of directors decides, subject, in most states, to two important limitations related to the amount and type of the consideration.

a. Type of Consideration

Traditionally, state corporate statutes (and in some cases state constitutions) limited the type of consideration corporations could receive in exchange for stock. Until the mid-1980s most state corporate statutes contained provisions similar to the following:

> the consideration paid for the issuance of shares **must consist of money paid, labor done or property actually received.**

In plain English such provisions did not allow stock to be issued in consideration for promises to pay money in the future (*i.e.*, promissory notes), promises to render future services, etc. In 1984 the MBCA was amended and today permits stock to be issued in consideration for any "tangible or intangible property or benefit to the corporation . . ., including . . . promissory notes . . . [and]

contracts for services to be performed. . . ." See MBCA § 6.21(b).

The current MBCA rule leaves it to the board to determine whether consideration is adequate and leaves it to shareholders to exercise their contractual and/or fiduciary remedies if it is not. Under the MBCA rule it is permissible to issue 100,000 shares to *A* in consideration for $100,000 cash, 100,000 shares to *B* in consideration for a promissory note for $100,000 and 100,000 shares to *C* as partial consideration for a three year employment contract.

However, many states still follow the old rule which limits the type of consideration. Those states would not allow the issuances to *B* and *C* because the type of consideration given in exchange for the shares would be deemed improper. The current rule varies from state to state, as does the emphasis placed on this issue by various professors.

b. Amount of Consideration

The traditional rules governing the amount of consideration a corporation is required to receive for its stock are more complex. They involve the so called "legal capital rules," which rest on the concepts of "par value" and "watered stock liability." The legal capital rules have been universally criticized by scholars and were abolished in the MBCA in 1984. However the legal capital rules are still the law in over half the states. Further, many professors want their students to understand the concepts of par value and watered stock liability.

Par value. Par value is simply a price per share which is specified in the articles. While par value is the lowest price for which the corporation can issue its shares, the drafters of the articles can make that dollar amount whatever they choose—it can be $1,000 per share, $.01 per share or any other number. It bears no relationship whatsoever to market value. Thus, if the par value is set in the articles as $100 per share, the corporation cannot, without potential liability to the recipients of the shares, issue shares for less than $100 per share.

Par value only constitutes a minimum issuance price. The corporation is free to charge more than par for its stock. Par value only has an impact on the price at which the corporation can originally issue its shares. It has no impact on the price at which shareholders may subsequently resell their shares.

If the notion that the minimum price a corporation may charge for issuance of its shares is a dollar amount selected from thin air and placed in the articles seems very strange, this is because it is strange. The rule is based on a 19th century primitive accounting system that was probably never valid and is certainly not valid today.

It is easy enough for lawyers to comply with the state's par value rule—simply specify a low par value (such as $.01 per share) in the articles and sell the stock for more ($10 per share, $100 per share or whatever) or issue shares "without par value" in states where this is permitted.

Watered stock liability. When stock is issued at less than par value the shareholders to whom the stock was issued incur what is known as potential "watered stock liability." The shareholders who receive the so called "watered stock" may be liable to the corporation or its creditors in an amount measured by the difference between par value and the amount they actually paid for the stock.

Casebooks often contain one or both of the following cases which illustrate watered stock liability. In *Hospes v. Northwestern Manufacturing & Car Co.* the promoters of a car company issued themselves preferred shares having an aggregate par value of $2.3 million in exchange for assets valued at $2.3 million. They also issued themselves common shares having an aggregate par value of $1.5 million for no additional consideration. In this famous 1892 case the court held that this transaction potentially created $1.5 million in watered stock liability on the part of the promoters. The opinion discussed two theories, the so-called "trust fund" and "holding out" theories as the rationale for the holding. Both of these theories have since been discredited.

Even though (1) the two main theories on which watered stock liability used to rest have been discredited and (2) the problem of potential watered stock liability can be easily avoided by simply establishing a low par value for the shares (and issuing the shares for consideration in excess of par), watered stock problems still sometimes occur, as illustrated by the 1988 case of *Hanewald v. Bryan's, Inc.*

In that case, Keith and Joan Bryan, the founders of Bryan's Inc., issued themselves a total of 100 shares of $1,000 per share par value stock for no consideration.

They personally loaned the corporation $10,000 and personally guaranteed a bank loan by the corporation of $55,000. The corporation than purchased the assets of plaintiff's retail store in consideration for cash and a promissory note. The corporation also signed a five year lease on the plaintiff's building. Later the corporation defaulted on the promissory note and the lease.

In a suit by plaintiff against the Bryans for watered stock liability, the court held the Bryans personally liable because they failed to pay par value for their shares. In other words they lost the shield of limited liability to the extent that the consideration they paid for their shares was less than par value. The court's rationale was simply that the governing North Dakota corporate statute required that the shareholders pay a minimum of par value for their shares. This case illustrates the so-called statutory liability theory, which is the rationale on which watered stock liability, if imposed, rests today.

The main teaching of this case is that it illustrates how par value and watered stock liability can be a trap for the unwary. By simply establishing a low par value for the stock and issuing shares to themselves at a price above par, the Bryans could have escaped liability without changing the underlying economics of the transaction.

The 1984 revision of MBCA eliminates par value and watered stock liability. About 20 states have adopted provisions in their corporate statutes dealing with par value modeled on the revised 1984 MBCA. Statutes modeled after the 1984 MBCA essentially create a new regime for issuing stock which eliminates the concept of par value and provides that shares issued for less than par do not create watered stock liability.

Fully paid and nonassessable opinions. Issues pertaining to the restrictions on both the type and amount of the consideration paid for shares on issuance often arise in the context of bringing new investors into a company. Usually when a company brings in new investors through a public offering or private placement, the investors require a legal opinion, that the new shares being issued are "**fully paid and nonassessable.**" The legal opinion is like something akin to an insurance policy—if the stock is not fully paid and non assessable and the new shareholders incur personal liability, they will have an action for malpractice against the law firm which rendered the opinion. Whether the stock issued is "fully paid and nonassessable" depends on the two legal questions discussed above, namely: (1) the **type** and (2) the **amount** of consideration.

F. ISSUING MORE SHARES— PREEMPTIVE RIGHTS AND DILUTION

When a corporation issues additional shares one of the main effects on existing shareholders of the corporation is that the issuance of the additional shares reduces the existing shareholders' percentage of ownership. For example, assume Alpha Corporation has 3,000 shares of common stock outstanding, which are owned by three shareholders *A*, *B* and *C*. Each owns 1,000 shares or 33.33%. If Alpha subsequently issues an additional 1,000 shares of common stock to *X*, the percentage ownership of

A, *B* and *C* is reduced to 25% each. This reduction of percentage of ownership is called **dilution**.

Shareholders can be protected against dilution under corporate law through a doctrine known as **preemptive rights**. A preemptive right is the right of a shareholder to subscribe to a pro rata portion of any new shares that the corporation proposes to issue that might operate to decrease the existing shareholders' percentage of ownership in the corporation. The basic idea is to protect the shareholders from dilution by giving them the opportunity to maintain their proportionate ownership in the company throughout the life of the corporation. They are not compelled to buy the additional shares, but they have a right to do so.

Preemptive rights began as a common law doctrine. Preemptive rights are no longer viewed as an inherent attribute of stock ownership. Today, the existence or nonexistence of preemptive rights is governed by the articles of incorporation. The answer to the question of whether a particular corporation has preemptive rights varies from state to state due to differences in the default rules under the corporate statutes of the various states. In some states preemptive rights do not exist unless they are specifically provided for in the articles (these are called "**opt in**" statutes). In other states, preemptive rights exist unless they are specifically rejected in the articles (these are called "**opt out**" statutes).

For example, § 6.30 of MBCA, which provides: "The shareholders of a corporation do not have a preemptive right to acquire the corporation's unissued shares except to the extent that the articles of incorporation so provide" is an **opt in** statute. Under an "opt in" statute if the articles of incorporation are silent there are no preemptive rights.

Preemptive rights do not attach to all new shares issued by a corporation. There are several transactions in which the issuance of new shares do not trigger preemptive rights, even in corporations where preemptive rights generally exist. Such transactions include the following: (1) shares issued to employees, when approved by a majority of the shareholders entitled to vote; (2) shares sold otherwise than for cash—*e.g.*, for property, to effect mergers, compromise indebtedness, etc.; and (3) shares of a different class—*e.g.*, holders of common stock don't have preemptive rights if the corporation decides to issue preferred stock; however preemptive rights may be triggered if the prefered shares are convertible into common shares. See, *e.g.*, MBCA § 6.30.

Several considerations enter into the decision whether or not to grant preemptive rights. They may serve as a useful device in close corporations, where each shareholder desires to be allowed to maintain her percentage of ownership. But even in close corporations a shareholders' agreement may offer a more efficient means of protection from dilution than statutory preemptive rights. If it is anticipated that the corporation may in the foreseeable future raise money through a private placement or public offering, preemptive rights will be a nuisance which might inhibit or delay such financing.

G. RAISING CAPITAL—REGULATION UNDER THE SECURITIES ACT OF 1933

1. INTRODUCTION

Often a company needs more money to operate and grow than it can generate from retained earnings and ordinary bank borrowing. When this is the case the business must raise money by selling additional equity securities. This is called equity financing, a process which raises several potential legal issues. Two possible sources of financing are: (1) individuals or other companies, who have some relationship with the company or institutional investors, who like the company's prospects for growth and profitability and are willing to invest and (2) venture capital firms, which are in the business of making equity investments in nonpublic companies. Raising money these sources will likely involve some type of "private placement."

The third possible source of financing is the public. When a company sells securities to the public the transaction is called a public offering. The first time a company sells stock to the public, it is called the "initial public offering" or IPO. The IPO is a transaction through which a company, almost always with the aid of an intermediatory called an "underwriter," transforms itself from a "closely held" to a "publicly held company."

What additional regulations come into play when companies raise money through the sale of securities?

Regulations under the **state** and **federal securities laws**.

State securities laws. All states have securities laws, which are often referred to as "Blue Sky Laws."[1] These statutes vary widely and are beyond the scope of this book. Beyond being aware of their existence, unless your professor, emphasizes these statutes, the state securities laws are beyond the scope of the basic business course.

The **federal securities laws** are a different matter. Today in some areas corporate law is so intertwined with securities law that they are virtually inseparable. Students in the basic business course are not expected to become full blown securities experts. All law schools offer one or more advanced courses in securities regulation. However, due to the overlap between the securities laws and general corporate law in certain areas, students must have some familiarity with the Federal Securities Laws and a general understanding of when and how they apply. The two most important of the federal securities Laws are the **Securities Act of 1933 ("33 Act")** and the **Securities Exchange Act of 1934 ("34 Act")**. Thus, while most of securities regulation is beyond the scope of this book (and beyond the scope of the basic business course), you need to learn about certain aspects of the 33 Act and the 34 Act. One of these aspect is the focus of this subsection—the impact of these laws on financing transactions.

---

1. They got this name from an early Kansas case in which the judge described the aim of these statutes as being to protect investors from schemes which have "no more basis than so many feet of blue sky."

What is the most important distinction students in the basic business course need to make in order to understand the 33 Act and the 34 Act at the most basic level?

The Federal Securities Laws recognize two distinct settings in which transactions involving securities occur:

Issuer transactions or primary market transactions involve capital raising by issuers. The company (called the "issuer") is raising money by selling newly issued securities, almost always with the help of an investment banker or underwriter. The net proceeds from such sale go to the company (*i.e.*, the issuer of the securities).

Trading transactions or secondary market transactions. After the company goes public, investors begin trading in the now outstanding securities and a so-called secondary market develops. The secondary market consists of trading transactions in which investor *A* sells outstanding securities of the company to investor *B*, and the seller, not the company, gets the proceeds from the sale Trading transactions have an impact the company, because higher stock prices increase overall market valuation of the company as a whole.

Both the primary or issuer market and the secondary market or trading market are regulated by the Federal Securities Laws but they are regulated differently.

The 33 Act regulates issuer transactions. The 33 Act comes into play only when the company sells its securities to investors. It is a highly integrated, narrowly focused statute that deals with this specific type of transaction—the type of transaction discussed in this chapter.

The 34 Act, primarily regulates trading transactions. The 34 Act regulates buying and selling outstanding securities after their original issuance. It contains a hodgepodge of provisions aimed primarily at regulating trading in outstanding securities and the institutions—such as the stock exchanges, broker/dealers, etc.—through which trading transactions take place. It also imposes certain continuing disclosure obligations on so-called "publicly held companies" whose securities are traded in the secondary market.

What is the policy behind these two statutes?

Most students instinctively answer—to protect investors. That answer is only partially right. Protecting investors is a policy of these statutes, but it is not the principal policy. The main purpose of the Federal Securities Acts is to protect the **integrity of the markets**. The 33 Act protects the integrity of the Primary Market; and the 34 Act protects the integrity of the Secondary Market. Recent events should help today's students appreciate this point. Mere mention of names such as Enron, WorldCom and Tyco illustrate the devastating economic effect that ripples through the economy when people lose confidence in the integrity of the markets.

Both the 33 and 34 Acts were passed in response to the stock market crash of 1929 and the Great Depression which followed. The speculative bubble we witnessed in the 1990s and the declines in market values during the first two years of the 21st century pale by comparison to the stock market bubble of the 1920s and the market crash of 1929. The hearings that preceded passage of these statutes found that $50 billion of new securities were issued in the United States in the 1920s and that fully half, or $25 billion, proved to be worthless. The hearings also revealed numerous instances of fraud and manipulation in the unregulated securities markets of the 1920s, which contributed to collapse of the market. Congress concluded that events leading up to the market crash of 1929 were a precipitating cause of the great depression of the 1930s.

We now turn to consideration of the 33 Act and the primary market transactions which that statute regulates. We will deal further with certain aspects of the 34 Act later.

2. THE SECURITIES ACT OF 1933

The 33 Act generally comes into play when companies raise money by selling securities. The 33 Act is a disclosure statute. Its basic purpose is to assure the availability of true, correct, reliable and complete information about the securities being offered to the public. In other words, after debate, Congress rejected a "merit regulation" approach and instead decided that investors should be provided full and accurate information about the securities being offered. It would then be up to the investors, based on such information, to make their own investment decisions.

a. The Registration Requirement

The 33 Act implements the policy of full disclosure through a **registration requirement** and an **antifraud requirement**. Most of the act is concerned with the registration requirement. Section 5 requires registration of public offerings of newly issued securities. It is helpful to think of § 5 as the heart of the 33 Act and to think of all other sections of the 33 Act, with the exception of § 17 and § 12(a)(2) which relate to the antifraud requirement, as limiting, implementing or qualifying § 5 in some way. The 33 Act is a complex statute with many subtle definitions and esoteric distinctions.

In addition, the 33 Act is written in a way that assumes the reader of the statute has an understanding of the process by which securities are sold to the public through underwriters—the so called process of "going public." In broad overview the process of distributing securities is comparable to marketing any other product. The issuer sells the securities to an underwriter who, sells some of the securities directly to investors and others to dealers who resell them to investors.

The 33 Act regulates the process of marketing these newly issued securities. The details, which are dealt with in the advanced course in securities regulation, are beyond the scope of the basic business course. However, students in the basic business course need to understand three questions: (1) What does registration entail? (2) What is the liability for failure to comply with the registration requirement? and (3) When is registration required?

(1) What Does Registration Entail?

Section 5 is the beginning point for virtually all questions under the 33 Act. It prohibits offers unless a registration statement has been filed with the SEC and prohibits sales until the registration statement has become effective. It also requires delivery of a prospectus to all purchasers of the securities. That statement raises as many questions as it answers—*i.e., What is a registration statement? What is a prospectus? What does filing and going effective mean?*

A **registration statement** is the disclosure document, required by the 33 Act, in which the company is legally required to bare its soul—tell investors all relevant material information about the securities being offered and the company offering the securities.

The major portion of the registration statement is the prospectus. The **prospectus** is the part of the registration statement delivered to investors. While the prospectus is a selling document, it is, first and foremost, a liability document, which must tell the whole truth in every material respect. If it does not there is potential for criminal penalty and draconian civil liability.

Filing and going effective relates to the process of preparing and filing the registration statement with the SEC; administrative review of the registration statement by the SEC staff and the eventual effectiveness of the registration statement. Section 5 divides the process of going public into three stages—the pre-filing stage; the waiting period (the period between filing and effectiveness) and the post-effective period. Both the ground rules for makings offers and sales as well as the work performed by the team of lawyers, accountants and business people involved in preparing the registration statement and verifying the accuracy and adequacy of the information contained therein vary during the three stages of the process. Details regarding the rules governing offers and sales during the registration process are beyond the scope of this book.

(2) What is the Liability for Failure to Comply?

Noncompliance with the registration provision of the 33 Act may result not only in criminal penalties and administrative sanctions, but also in civil liability for the company and various persons associated with the company. More specifically, § 11 imposes strict liability for any untrue statements or material omissions in the registration statement on the company (*i.e.*, the issuer), and on every person who signs the registration statement (the company's chief executive officer and chief financial officer are required to sign), every director, every person who provides an expert certification (such as the accountants who audit the financial statements in the registration statement), and the underwriters. See § 11(a).

Broadly speaking § 11 does away with the common law fraud requirements of scienter and reliance. It imposes strict liability on the company. The so-called individual defendants are liable unless they can meet the burden of showing that they exercised "due diligence." In general, due diligence requires that the individual defendants show that they made a reasonable investigation and that they were not negligent in failing to discover any material error or omission in the registration statement.   Specifics regarding the "due diligence" defense are beyond the scope of both the basic business course and this book.

Section 12(a)(1) complements § 11 by imposing liability for failure to register the securities or deliver a prospectus in accordance with the requirements of § 5.

In summary, the 33 Act regulates the process of going public through a three fold approach:

(1) Under § 5 the company can not make any offers unless and until a registration statement has been filed with the SEC and it can not make sales until the registration has been declared effective. If the company fails to comply—that is fails to register or deliver a prospectus as required—under § 12(1) the buyers have an absolute right of rescission (*i.e.,* get their money back).

(2) The 33 Act provides for a process of administrative review by the SEC but the statute clearly places ultimate responsibility for insuring the accuracy and adequacy of the registration statement on the issuer and certain others associated with the offering—*i.e.,* the potential defendants listed in § 11(a).

(3) Finally, if the offering documents are materially false or misleading the buyers have an absolute right of rescission under § 11. The issuer has no defenses. The other potential defendants named in § 11(a) must meet the burden of showing due diligence to escape liability.

(3)   When   is   Registration   Required?   (herein
Exemptions)

It would appear from § 5 that all offers and sales of
securities, including ordinary trading transactions, would
require registration. However, the apparent broad sweep
of § 5 is tempered by a number of exemptions found in § 3
and § 4 and by the definitions found in § 2.

Because of the way the 33 Act is structured, the statute
creates a rebuttable presumption that registration is
required.   In other words, the burden is on the party
claiming an exemption to establish his exemption.

Trading transactions. Recall, we noted earlier that the
most important distinction, students in the basic business
course need to understand in dealing with the 33 Act is a
distinction between so-called issuer transactions and so-
called trading transactions. Ordinary trading transactions
are exempt by § 4(1) which exempts transactions by any
person other than an "issuer," "underwriter" or "dealer," all
defined terms in § 2.   The net effect of this broad
exemption is to exempt all trading transactions from the
registration requirement imposed by § 5.   Stated
differently, subject to the exception noted in the footnote,
§ 5 only requires registration of securities offered by the
issuer.[2]

---

2. The strange and counterintuitive definition of "underwriter" in
§ 2(11) brings some sales of securities by persons in a control relationship
with the issuer and some sales by persons who hold so-called "restricted
securities" within the prohibitions of § 5. This complex topic is outside
the scope of this book.

Security defined. Application of the 33 Act (as well as the 34 Act as we will see later) hinges upon the thing offered being a "security." The term "security" is defined in § 2(1), which includes an extensive laundry list of all the things people normally think of as securities, including stocks, bonds, debentures, calls, puts, warrants, etc. Corporate stock is obviously a security. Section 2(1) has generally been interpreted expansively by the courts.

What is an investment contract?

One of the phrases included in § 2(1) is the term **"investment contract**," a term which had no particular meaning in the investment community, prior to adoption of the 33 Act. The drafters included "investment contract" in the statute as a "catch-all." They probably thought that if they missed something in their broad definition of "security" in § 2(1), this phrase might pick it up.

The landmark case defining investment contract is *SEC v. W.J. Howey Co.*, a case decided by the United States Supreme Court in 1946. The case involved the sale of specifically described tracts of orange trees in an orange grove in Florida. Under the test developed in *Howey,* as subsequently refined in later cases, the thing sold is an "investment contract" and thus a security if a person (1) invests his money (2) in a common enterprise (3) with the expectation of profit (4) from the efforts of others. The *Howey* test has been applied in hundreds of cases and has brought many things, not generally associated with the world of stocks and bonds, such as scotch whiskey receipts, self improvement courses, cosmetics, earthworms, beavers, cemetery lots, animal feeding programs, pooled litigation funds and computer modules, within the definition of "security" and thus, within the scope of federal securities regulation

Are partnership and LLC interests securities?

The application of the *Howey* test which is most important in the basic business course is its application to the question of whether interests in partnerships and LLCs are securities.

In analyzing partnership interests, the first question should be—was it a general partnership or a limited partnership. In a traditional general partnership (including an LLP) all of the general partners have a right of management, unless they have contracted away that right. Thus, the presumption is that general partnership interests are not securities. The traditional general partnership fails the part of the *Howey* test that requires "reliance on the efforts of others."

Limited partnership interests, on the other hand, have generally been held to be securities. By law the general partner has the exclusive authority to manage the enterprise and the limited partners are mere passive investors who rely on the efforts of the general partner to make them money. There have been a few exceptional cases where general partnership interests have been held to be securities. These cases generally involved situations where either under the terms of the partnership agreement or as a matter of practical reality, though the plaintiff was legally a general partner, she was in reality a passive investor relying on the efforts of others.

The applicability of the Federal Securities Laws to LLCs is not settled at this time. Some states have by statute mandated that LLC interests are securities. Others have statutorily decreed that LLC interests do not constitute securities. Most states leave the question to the courts and the Federal courts have not yet definitively spoken. It seems likely that as the law of LLCs develops, the question of whether LLC interests are securities will be analyzed under reasoning analogous to that presently applied to partnerships.

Exemptions generally. We now turn to the exemptions in §§ 3 and 4. Section 3(a) exempts certain securities from registration because of the nature of the securities. These include government securities, securities issued by banks and charitable institutions and short-term commercial paper. These exemptions are narrow and highly technical and their application is far outside the scope of anything likely to be encountered in the basic business course.

Section 3(a)(11), as qualified and defined by Rule 147, provides the so-called the "intrastate exemption." That exemption exempts securities offered and sold solely within the state in which the issuer is incorporated and does the principal amount of its business, provided that the distribution comes to rest in that state.

Section 3(b) is an enabling provision which gives the SEC power to create exemptions for offerings up to $10 million, which it believes are necessary or appropriate. An important exemption created under the authority of 3(b) is the so-called Reg. A exemption found in Rules 252–263 under the 33 Act. While technically an exemption, Reg. A is actually a simplified type of registration available to issuers offering securities valued at less than $5 million. The exemptions under Rules 504 and 505, discussed below, were also adopted under the enabling authority of § 3(b).

The private offering exemption and Regulation D. The exemption from registration most often used by issuers is some form of the "private offering exemption" found in § 4(2), which is by far the most important of the exemptions and the only exemption covered in depth in this book. Many of the casebooks on Corporations or Business Associations cover the private offering exemption and most professors discuss this exemption in the basic business course.

Today, most questions concerning the private offering exemption are resolved under Regulation D ("Reg. D"), a series of eight rules—Rules 501–508 under the 33 Act—adopted in 1982, and subsequently liberalized through amendment. It is difficult to understand how the current rules work without some understanding of the statutory enabling provisions and a little of the history that lead to adoption of Regulation D.

As previously stated the statutory authority for the "private offering exemption" is found in § 4(2). Section 4(2) exempts "**transactions by an issuer not involving a public offering.**" A lot of administrative and judicial gloss as well as a lot of history surrounds those nine words. The gist of what § 4(2) intended to exempt is simple. It permitted the issuers to issue securities in **close corporation offerings.** For example, a promoter starts a business which he intends to manage and raises the money to finance the venture by selling stock in his company to a small number of friends, relatives or business associates. There is clearly no reason to require registration in this situation. The investors are relying on a preexisting relationship and personal knowledge.

Another case where the private offering exemption is clearly available is the so-called **institutional private placement**. For example, a company goes to a small group of knowledgeable investors such as insurance companies, venture capital firms or pension funds and sells them either equity or debt securities. These investors can get whatever information they need directly from the company without a registration statement. Such private placements are an important sources of financing for both well established large companies and high tech startups.

No one has ever questioned the need or the desirability of having a private placement exemption. But for years there was a problem defining the scope of the exemption. The SEC tried to give us some guidelines through an early administrative release which essentially told us that (1) **numbers** are important—an offering to few is more likely to be private than an offering to many and (2) **relationships** are also important—if the offering is limited to people with a pre-existing relationship that is more likely to be private than an offering to strangers. While the SEC release made sense, it was too indefinite to give corporate planners the certainty they needed in structuring private placements.

The landmark decision on the scope of the § 4(2) private placement exemption, *SEC v. Ralston Purina*, was handed down in 1953 by the United States Supreme Court. But instead of giving us the certainty desired, *Ralston Purina* added significantly to the uncertainty.

The question in *Ralston Purina* was whether offers by Ralston Purina to certain "key" employees pursuant to an employee stock purchase plan without registration violated § 5. Ralston Purina claimed that the sales were exempt from registration as a "private offering" under § 4(2). The Supreme Court held that Ralston Purina had violated § 5 and the opinion attempted to lay down a test defining the scope of the private offering exemption.

The Court established two overriding requirements, both of which had to be present, for an offering to be "private" as opposed to "public":

(1)   "Do the offerees need the protection of the act or can they fend for themselves?" This has come to be known as the **Sophistication Requirement**.

(2)   "The offerees had to have access to the type of information that a registration statement would provide." This has come to be known as the **Access to Information Requirement**.

While the tests of *Ralston Purina*—sophistication and access to information—made sense and are still the law today, they are highly subjective standards and it is hard to determine prospectively whether the tests have been satisfied.

In addition, if one of the original purchasers turned around and sold the securities he bought too soon, he might be considered to be "purchasing with a view to distribution" and thus become a "statutory underwriter," as defined in § 2(11). This would destroy the exemption for everyone and subject the issuer to liability for failure to comply with the registration requirements of § 5. The original purchasers can not be used as mere conduits to effect a wider distribution.

That concept still applies today. Buyers in a private placement acquire so-called "restricted securities." This means resales of such securities are subject to restrictions (now governed by Rule 144, discussed later). Violation of those restrictions may destroy the exemption.

Regulation D. Most of the problems, which existed in the vague world of *Ralston Purina*, have now been resolved under Reg. D, a series of eight rules (Rules 501–508) under the 33 Act. Reg. D, first adopted in 1982 and subsequently liberalized through amendment, is an innovative amalgamation that combined exemptions which were adopted under the authority of two different statutory enabling provisions—§ 4(2) and § 3(b):

Reg. D creates **safe harbors**. If you meet the requirements of Reg. D, you do not have to register. But the reverse is not true. If you fail to meet the requirements of Reg. D, it does not necessarily mean you have violated § 5 of the 33 Act. It does mean that you have to sustain the burden of proof that you come within the § 4(2) exemption as defined by *Ralston Purina*. In other words, the case law may still provide an exemption in the rare, but not unheard of, case where an issuer does not completely comply with all of the terms and conditions of Reg. D. Obviously, structuring a deal so that it comes within a safeharbor provided by Reg. D is much safer.

The three Reg. D exemptions. Reg. D provides three exemptions—Rules 504, 505 and 506. The exemptions are qualified by the other five rules in Reg. D. Even though the three exemptions co-exist within a single regulation and contain a number of common conditions, it is important to understand that they are three separate exemptions, which rest on two separate statutory enabling provisions—§ 3(b) and § 4(2):

Rule 504. The gist of Rule 504, as amended, is simple. Essentially this exemption now says if you raise less than $1 million during a 12 month period, you are too small for the SEC to bother with. The SEC might come after you for fraud, but not for § 5 violations (failure to register).

Rule 505 is an exemption which allows issuers to raise up to $5 million by selling securities to up to 35 nonaccredited investors plus an unlimited number of accredited investors (defined below). The statutory authority for Rule 505, like Rule 504, is § 3(b) under which the SEC has authority to grant exceptions for offerings up to $10 million, subject to whatever conditions the SEC wants to place on the exemption. In the case of Rule 505, the number of purchasers is limited and the dollar amount of the offering, though larger than Rule 504, is still limited.

Rule 506 is an exemption under which the number of purchasers permitted are the same as under 505—*i.e.*, 35 nonaccredited investors plus any number of accredited investors. But there are two significant differences between Rules 505 and 506:

(1) **There is no dollar cap on the amount of money you can raise under 506**. You can raise $200 billion or more if you can find investors to buy that quantity of your securities and still comply with the other requirements of the rule.

(2) **Under 506 the nonaccredited investors have to be sophisticated**. In other words, if you have non accredited investors in a 506 offering, you must make subjective judgements about sophistication and access to information under the tests of *Ralston Purina.*

The reason for this distinction goes to the heart of understanding Reg. D. The statutory authority for Rule 506 is § 4(2) rather than § 3(b). Rule 506 is a definitional rule. It defines situations in which the § 4(2) private offering exemption, is available. The SEC has very broad rule making power under the 33 Act, but that power is not broad enough to allow it to ignore decisions of the United States Supreme Court. *Ralston Purina* said sophistication is the test and so any rule grounded on § 4(2) has to meet that test.

Rule 506 is structured so that accredited investors are conclusively presumed to be sophisticated, although, as discussed below, this is a fiction. Many accredited investors are not, in fact, sophisticated.

Conditions and requirements of Reg. D. Reg. D has substituted a detailed set of regulations for a broad based common law test. The Rule 505 and 506 exemptions are subject to a number of definitions, qualifications, conditions and requirements, which we will now discuss.

Accredited investors. Accredited investor ("AI") is the most important definition in Reg. D. Rule 501(a) sets out in detail and with a great degree of certainty the classes of persons that qualify as AIs. They include:

1.   **Institutional investors.**   Banks, insurance companies, broker/dealers, registered investment companies, savings and loan associations, and other institutional investors qualify as AIs.

2. **Directors, executive officers or general partners of the issuer or a parent**. High level people with the company or its parent qualify as AIs irrespective of meeting any other tests.

3. **Net worth of $1 million or more**. If the combined net worth of a husband and wife at the time of purchase exceeds $1 million, including their equity in their personal residence, they qualify as accredited investors.

An example will illustrate how far removed Reg. D is from the vague sophistication requirement of *Ralston Purina*. A widow, with her now deceased husband, in the 1960s bought a nice little house on an acre of land in a suburb near Los Angles for 10% down and a $50,000 mortgage. Now the widow owns that house free and clear and it is worth $1.5 million. Even though that widow may not have another asset to her name and no business or investment experience at all she is an AI because she meets the definition in Rule 501(a). The point is: One does not have to be sophisticated to be an AI. She just has to meet the test of Rule 501(a).[3]

4. **Income.** A person who had an individual income in excess of $200,000 or a joint income with his/her spouse of $300,000 in each of the last two years and reasonably expects income at the same or higher levels during the current year qualifies as an AI.

These are the main categories of AIs. The name of the game under Reg. D is to find AIs. Remember the rule: There is no limit on the number of accredited investors under either Rules 505 or 506. Under Reg. D, AIs are conclusively presumed to be sophisticated, though in fact, many are not sophisticated at all.

Integration. Integration is another important concept under Reg. D, as well as certain other exemptions. The concept is if two or more offerings are part of a **single plan of financing**, they are treated as a single distribution, even if they are broken up into different offerings. The effect of integration may destroy an exemption as illustrated by the following example.

---

3. Not only is Reg. D more certain and objective than *Ralston Purina*, it also has had the effect of broadening the exemptions. Many people who meet the 501(a) test of "accredited investor" would not come close to meeting the "sophistication" requirement of *Ralston Purina*.

Assume an oil company has a 640-acre development prospect under lease. The company wants to develop the property with a total of eight wells on the lease at a cost of $1 million per well—a total cost of $8 million. Can the company create 8 separate Limited Partnerships, raise $1 million in each and get a 504 exemption for each offering? The answer depends on whether the offerings are integrated—*i.e.*, considered a single plan of financing.

Prior to adoption of Reg. D it was often hard to determine what would trigger integration—an obviously fact-sensitive concept. The main factors considered are: (1) Were the sales part of a single plan of financing? (2) Did they involve the same class of securities? and (3) Were the sales made at about the same time, for the same consideration and for the same purpose?

It was hard to determine which of the factors might control and what mix might tip the balance in a given case. Reg. D provided certainty. Today, if the offerings are more than **six months apart**, they will not be integrated. The fact-sensitive pre-Reg. D integration tests now only apply if the offerings take place within 6 months of one another.

Information requirement. As previously stated, in addition to sophistication, *Ralston Purina* had a second requirement—access to information. The information requirement is carried forward into Reg. D.

Rules 505 and 506 have identical information requirements. The first is the issuer must prepare and deliver a disclosure document (usually called a "private placement memo") to all nonaccredited investors. No disclosure document is required for accredited investors. Thus, if a deal is limited to accredited investors no private placement memo is prepared; but if non-AIs are in the deal a private placement memo is usually prepared and copies are delivered to everyone.

Under Rule 502(b), the level of disclosure required depends on the amount of money the issuer is raising and whether or not the issuer is a 34 Act reporting company (*i.e.*, a company subject to the SEC's continuing disclosure requirements). Details regarding the type and level of disclosure required are outside the scope of this book. The important point to remember is that no disclosure document is necessary if the offering is limited to accredited investors.

The no general solicitation rule. The Rule 505 and 506 exemptions are subject to Rule 502 (c), the so-called no general solicitation rule. The no general solicitation rule clearly prohibits almost all forms of general solicitation of potential investors for a proposed offering of securities under Rules 505 or 506. Under the no general solicitation rule neither the issuer nor anyone raising money on its behalf can put ads in the paper, make cold calls or send direct mailings aimed at soliciting investors. Neither can the issuer or anyone associated with the issuer do an information seminar on its product, if a purpose of the seminar is to hype the stock as well as sell the product. Any of these acts will destroy the exemption.

An issuer who relies on a Rule 505 or 506 exemption may look for investors among: (1) people with whom it has a preexisting relationship and people referred by those people, through word of mouth contact and (2) venture capitalists or industry partners. Industry partners include customers, suppliers and other companies in the industry. That is about as far as an issuer can go without violating the no general solicitation rule.

Resales of restricted securities. The problem of resales by the original purchasers, a big problem under the pre-Reg. D case law, still exists. If one or more of the original purchasers turn around and immediately resell—*i.e.*, become conduits for a wider distribution—they become "statutory underwriters" and the exemption is lost. However, the uncertain tests under the old case law, which revolved around the buyers' subjective state of mind at the time of purchase and the "change of circumstances" doctrine have been replaced by a specific rule governing resales—Rule 144.

Rule 144 is a safe-harbor rule which regulates the sale of securities by control persons and holders of restricted securities. In essence Rule 144 more precisely defines the circumstances under which holders of restricted securities (*i.e.*, securities acquired in a private offering such as an offering exempt under Rules 505 or 506) and control persons (persons in a control relationship with the issuer referred to in the Rule as affiliates) can sell their securities without destroying the applicable exemptions. Rule 144 is discussed herein only insofar as it relates to resales of "restricted securities." Rule 144's restrictions on the resale of restricted securities, depend on how long one holds the restricted securities:

(1)   Securities held for less than one year—cannot be resold.
(2)   Securities held for more than two years—are freely saleable.
(3)   Securities held between one and two years may be sold in limited amounts and subject to a number of technical requirements set out in Rule 144, which are beyond the scope of this book.

After two years all of the detailed restrictions and limitations go away and the securities become freely saleable without destroying the exemption.

b. The Antifraud Requirement

In addition to requiring issuers to register securities (or find an exemption from registration) the 33 Act also prohibits fraud in the sale of securities by issuers. As noted earlier, § 17 and § 12(a)(2), the antifraud provisions in the 33 Act, prohibit false or misleading statements or material omissions in any prospectus or oral communication used to sell the securities. We will learn about fraud in the purchase or sale of securities in Chapter VIII, when we discuss Rule 10b-5, the broadest of the several antifraud provisions in the Federal Securities Acts. However two points related to fraud should be noted in the context of our current discussion:

(1)   If the issuer commits fraud in connection with its sale of securities (*i.e.*, an "issuer transaction"), it is subject to strict liability. But if the fraud is committed in connection with the resale of

outstanding securities (*i.e.,* a "trading transaction") there is no liability absent scienter.

(2)   While many sales of securities are exempt from the registration requirement of § 5, no sale of securities is exempt from the antifraud provisions of the 33 Act or Rule 10b-5.

CHAPTER VI

WHO DECIDES WHAT AS TO HOW BUSINESSES OPERATE?
(Governance)

A. GOVERNANCE OF UNINCORPORATED BUSINESS STRUCTURES

1. GENERAL PARTNERSHIPS

Partnership governance begins with the fundamental concept that each partner has equal rights to participate in the governance of the partnership. This fundamental concept is carried forward in the default rules under both UPA and RUPA that as to matters in the ordinary course of business, the decision of the majority of the partners controls. See RUPA § 401 (f) & (j) and UPA § 18(e) & (h). However, under both UPA and RUPA, the partners can contract around the basic rule in the partnership agreement and delegate governance authority to one or more partners.

In deciding whether a partner had actual authority to act on behalf of the partnership, look first to the partnership agreement. If the partnership agreement does not answer the question, you must look at the relevant partnership statute for an answer.

While the partnership agreement usually controls the actual authority of a partner, a partner may also have apparent authority. If the dispute is between the partnership and a third party, rather than between partners, the matter may be controlled by common law agency principles. The following examples illustrate how these rules play out:

1. Assume Dave, Joe and Lee, each contribute $10,000 and agree to start a Taco Stand, which they will own as equal partners. Joe and Dave want to lease a building owned by Robert, but Lee prefers another building owned by Jane. While relations among the partners are generally governed by the partnership agreement (RUPA § 103), in this case the oral partnership agreement does not speak to the question of who can make decisions on behalf of the partnership. Thus, we must look to the default rule under the partnership statute to resolve the issue. RUPA § 401(j) provides that matters related to the ordinary course of the partnership's business may be decided by a majority of partners. Therefore, Joe and Dave can direct the partnership to lease the building from Robert.

2. Assume the same facts as #1, but also assume that the parties signed a written partnership agreement, which provided that "Lee shall serve as managing partner and have authority to lease property on behalf of the partnership." In this case, the parties contracted around the default rule and Lee would have authority to lease the building on behalf of the partnership.

3. Assume the same facts as #2, but assume the provision in the partnership agreement read as follows: "Lee shall serve as managing partner and shall have authority to enter into agreements in the ordinary course of business on behalf of the partnership, provided, however, Lee shall not have authority to lease property on

behalf of the partnership without the express consent of her partners." In spite of this provision Lee signs a lease on Jane's building, without consulting Dave or Joe. In spite of the fact that Lee violated the partnership agreement and might be liable for breach of contract to her partners, the partnership would be bound by the lease with Jane under the agency principle of apparent authority. A partnership agreement can not extinguish apparent authority. See RUPA § 103(b)(10).

These examples illustrate that partnerships begin with the basic concept that partners have equal rights in the management of the partnership's business. That basic concept finds value in the default rules that govern disputes among partners. The default rules provide that the partners can contract around most of these rules in a partnership agreement. However, the partners can not change their basic status as co-principals and co-agents of the partnership and often when rights of third parties are involved, the agency principles of actual and apparent authority control.

2. LIMITED PARTNERSHIPS

As previously discussed, general partnerships consist of two classes of partners (1) general partners, who have the authority to govern and (2) limited partners, who have "**no authority** to participate in the management or control" of the business. If a limited partner violates the "no participation rule" he becomes a general partner and loses the shield of limited liability.

The original Uniform Limited Partnership Act (1916) offered no statutory guidance as to what constituted "participation in management or control." However § 303 of the Revised Uniform Limited Partnership Act (1976), as amended, provides a number of safe harbors (*i.e.,* things a limited partner can do without being deemed a general partner). These include:

(1) being an agent or employee of the limited partnership or a general partner;

(2) being an officer, director or shareholder of a corporate general partner;

(3) advising a general partner with respect to the business of the limited partnership;

(4) guaranteeing or assuming specific obligations of the limited partnership;

(5) requesting or attending a meeting of partners; and

(6) approving or disapproving, by vote or otherwise, several enumerated matters including dissolution, sale or exchange of assets, change in the nature of the business and the admission or removal of general or limited partners.

3. LIMITED LIABILITY COMPANIES

The rules governing the management of LLCs are flexible and vary from state to state. Today, most state LLC statutes afford the owners (called "members") the option of electing:

(1) To manage the business themselves—called a "**member-managed LLC**"; or

(2) To elect managers to manage the business—called a **"manager-managed LLC."**

The governance structure in an LLC is set forth in the operating agreement. The decision-making authority of the members of a member-managed LLC is similar to that of partners in a general partnership. The decision-making authority of the managers of a manager-managed LLC is similar to that of the board of directors of a corporation. See § VI.B.3.a.(1), *infra,* for additional discussion on the governance of LLCs.

B. GOVERNANCE OF CORPORATIONS

1. THE STATUTORY SCHEME OF CORPORATE GOVERNANCE

In contrast to the direct democracy scheme of governance followed in partnerships, corporations follow a so-called republican (or representative) scheme of governance. The owners of the corporation (shareholders) elect a group of individuals (called the board of directors) who are in charge of the corporation and set the policy for operating the corporation. The board appoints officers to carry out the policies dictated by the board and monitors the officers' performance.

This simple description of how corporations are governed reflects the basic governance model mandated by the corporate statutes of all states, to wit:

All corporate power shall be exercised by or under the authority of, and the business and affairs of the corporation shall be managed by or under the direction of the board of directors. Cf. MBCA § 8.01(b); Del. § 141(a).

These statutory provisions reflect the fundamental idea that in a corporation **ownership of the business is separated from control**. Although the shareholders "own" the corporation they have virtually no decision making power (in their capacity as shareholders) with respect to how the business is run. They only have the right to elect and remove directors and to vote on certain matters proposed by directors.

In broad overview, issues concerning the governance and decision making process in corporations largely revolve around the following questions pertaining to the actions and interactions of (1) shareholders, (2) the board of directors and (3) officers:

(1) *Which of these groups has authority to decide what?*
(2) *How do they go about deciding?*
(3) *How do the three groups interact?*
(4) *When will their actions bind the corporation?*

The **shareholders** elect directors and usually they can remove directors. Their vote is also required to approve certain so called "fundamental" corporate transactions. Otherwise, even though they own the corporation, shareholders do not participate in management, nor do they have any authority to act for or bind the corporation.

The **board of directors** is the center of management authority. Under the corporate statutes, all corporate power and authority flows from the board. However, the board does not run the day to day operations of the corporation. It delegates that function to the officers, who it appoints. The board typically meets on a regular basis and monitors performance. The board does not derive its authority from the shareholders, who elect them, but from the corporate statute. The directors have fiduciary duties to the corporation and they are subject to liability if they violate those duties. See Chapter VII, *supra.*

The **officers** perform the day to day management of the corporation. This function has been delegated to them by the board of directors and they are answerable to the board not the shareholders. Officers can bind the corporation as to matters within the "ordinary course of business," but must get board approval as to "extraordinary" matters.

Scholars have described the traditional corporate governance model as an inverted triangle. The shareholders, who own the business, elect the board. The board, which is described as the "center of corporate governance," appoints the chief executive officer and other officers, determines corporate policies and monitors the management of the corporation by the officers and rank and file employees.

Numerous issues relating to corporate governance play out within the broad based framework described above. But once the basic framework is understood the specific issues become much easier to resolve.

a. Authority of the Board of Directors to Make Decisions on Behalf of and Bind the Corporation

As an artificial entity a corporation can only act through individuals. As previously noted all modern corporate statutes vest the authority to act for and bind the corporation in the board of directors. The same corporate statutes place certain requirements on the manner in which the board must act in order to bind the corporation.

The board must act as a body. Except in one-person corporations and a few other exceptional situations, the board of directors is a **body**—more than one person. Some corporate statutes require a minimum size, often three. The size of the board is always set forth in either the articles of incorporation or the by-laws. The key point to remember is that all power vested in the board is vested in the board of directors as a body. The corporate statutes vest no power in the individual directors, when they are acting as individuals.

Formal requirements for board action. Certain formal requirements which govern board action flow from the fundamental concept that the board must act as a body. The board can only validly act at **meetings duly called, pursuant to proper notice, at which a quorum is present.** Usually a majority vote of the directors present is required to pass a resolution, but the bylaws may require more than a mere majority.

Generally, directors, unlike shareholders, must vote **in person**. Most corporate statutes permit meetings to be held by conference telephone calls provided the corporation's by-laws authorize this procedure. Also most modern corporate statutes provide for **unanimous written consent,** if authorized by the by-laws.   Under this procedure, resolutions circulated to all directors and unanimously adopted by all directors (not merely a majority) constitute valid board action even though there was no meeting.

If the formal requirements described above are not followed—*e.g.,* there is lack of quorum, improper notice, or no meeting, then whatever action the board purported to take is **invalid.** In other words, if the formal requirements are not followed, the action taken is simply action by a bunch of individuals; it is not the action of the "board" and therefore is of no force and effect.

Ratification, estoppel and waiver. When third parties, whose rights are adversely affected by improper board action, justifiably relied on the improper action, particularly if the board knew the action was improper, a court may uphold the transaction on the basis of estoppel, waiver or ratification, concepts with which all students in the basic business course should be familiar.

A case in many casebooks, *Mickshaw v. Coca-Cola Bottling Co.* illustrates this point. In *Mickshaw* the plaintiff was an employee of Coca-Cola Bottling Co. ("Coke") prior to World War II. Coke had only three directors, one of which, in an interview by a local newspaper, stated that any Coke employee who went into military service would be paid the difference between his salary at Coke and his military pay (at that time quite low). The newspaper published the director's promise to make up the pay differential. The other directors read the article and did not object.

Two years after the article appeared, Mickshaw went into the service. When he returned to work for Coke after the war, Coke refused to pay him the difference between his military salary and his Coke salary. Mickshaw sued and won. The court said even though the action had not been formally approved by the board of directors, the board's inaction under the circumstances was tantamount to a ratification.

b. Authority of Officers to Make Decisions for and Bind the Corporation

Unlike the board of directors, which derives its authority to manage the corporation and bind it by its actions from the corporate statutes, corporate officers do not have any special status under the corporate statutes.

While some corporate statutes contain broad provisions describing the functions of the officers (see, *e.g.*, MBCA § 8.41), **generally, the scope of an officer's authority is determined under the law of agency. In a corporate setting, the corporation, acting through its board, is the principal and the officers (as well as other employees) are the agents**. Thus, most answers to the question—is the corporation bound by a particular transaction authorized by an officer—are determined under the agency rules of actual and apparent authority.

Actual authority. Under agency principles, actual authority can be **express** or **implied**. The clearest example of express actual authority arises when the board, acting in a proper manner (*i.e.*, as a body, at a meeting, etc) adopts a resolution authorizing an officer to carry out a specific transaction. This sort of authority is frequently granted for bigger deals—*i.e.*, buy a competitor, build a new major plant, have a stock offering, etc.

Another common source of actual authority is a bylaw provision, such as the following:

> The President shall be the principal executive officer of the Corporation and shall, subject to supervision of the board of directors, make all decisions relating to the ordinary course of the company's business and otherwise control the business and affairs of the company.

Actual authority can also be implied. Several techniques—all based on common sense and the common law of agency—are used by the courts.

One judicial technique for finding implied authority is to interpret the scope of the express grant broadly. For example, a bylaw provision gives the president authority to "manage the day-to-day affairs of the company." That is a broad-based open ended grant, which a court might interpret broadly or narrowly to include or exclude various specific acts.

A second judicial technique is to look at the board's reaction to similar actions taken in the past by the officer. If the board did not object to such action in the past, a

court might infer that the board would not object to the
action in question.

Apparent authority. Even when there is no actual
authority, if a third party justifiably relies on action taken
by an officer, a court might hold that the corporation is
bound under the concept of apparent authority. A court
might conclude that by virtue of his office the president of
the corporation has the "inherent" power to authorize a
particular act. Apparent authority issues often turn on
whether a particular transaction is an ordinary course of
business transaction or whether it is an "extraordinary"
transaction outside the ordinary course of business.

Ratification, estoppel and waiver. Finally, even when
an officer exceeds the scope of both his actual authority
and apparent authority, the corporation may still become
bound by his actions retroactively if the board, having
knowledge of a transaction, does not question or reverse
the action. In that type of a situation a court might
conclude that because of the board's inaction, the
corporation ratified the action or that it is estopped or
waived its right to question the act.

c. Uncertainty as to the Scope of the Power of Directors and Officers to Bind the Corporation—the Problem and the Solution

As the above discussion makes clear, application of the
rules regarding the authority of directors and/or officers to
bind the corporation is unclear. The cases often turn on
minute factual distinctions or on equities on one side or the
other. More specifically, these cases usually turn on

factual questions such as: (1) What is "ordinary course of business" as distinguished from an "extraordinary transaction"? (2) Did the particular officer act within the scope of his "actual" or "apparent" authority? (3) Did the board comply with the requisite formalities of "meetings," "notice" and "quorum"? (4) Was the board acting as a "board" rather than as a group of individuals? (5) Do the facts support a "ratification," "estoppel" or "waiver"?

There is a simple and effective way to eliminate these questions. **Ask for a certified copy of the board resolution authorizing the transaction.**

In re Drive-In Development Corp., a case found in many casebooks, illustrates this procedure. In that case Drive-In delivered to a lending bank a certified copy of a resolution of the board of directors, authorizing Drive-In to guarantee a loan made by the bank to Drive-In's parent corporation. The resolution was duly certified by Drive-In's corporate secretary.

Later, in a bankruptcy proceeding, the bank's claim for payment under the guaranty was disallowed by the referee in bankruptcy because Drive-In's minute book did not show that the board of directors had authorized Drive-In to guarantee the loan, despite the secretary's certification to the contrary. The court reversed the referees finding and held that even if Drive-In exceeded its authority by delivering the guarantee, without board approval, the secretary's certification is apparent authority that Drive-In acted pursuant to board authority, regardless of whether or not the authorizing board resolution was actually adopted.

d. The Shareholders' Role in Corporate Governance

Can shareholders participate in management or make decisions that bind the corporation?

The answer is "**no**." And the rule is clear: **Shareholders, even a majority of them, though they own the corporation cannot (in their capacity as shareholders) manage the corporation, nor can they act for or bind the corporation.**

The corporate statutes do give shareholder authority to vote on certain so called fundamental corporate actions. These include mergers, sales of substantially all the corporation's assets, dissolution and amendments to the articles of incorporation. But even in these areas the shareholders can not initiate any of these transactions. For example, shareholders can not initiate a merger or negotiate the terms. The transactions are initiated by the board and all the shareholder can do is vote yes or no to transactions proposed by the board of directors. The shareholders' vote is like a power to veto certain transactions proposed by the board.

Does this mean that, as a practical matter, the owners of the corporation—the shareholders—have no ability to influence the way the corporation is managed?

The answer to that question is also "**no**." Shareholders have a right to vote, and through their right to vote indirectly exercise a great deal of influence on the board. In most corporations, shareholders elect directors

annually.   And   under   most   corporate   statutes,
shareholders can remove directors.

In general, the law protects shareholders by providing
them with three principal rights: (1) the **right to vote**,
(2) the **right to information** and (3) the **right to sue both
directors and officers for breach of fiduciary duties**. In
this section we will focus on shareholders right to vote We
will examine shareholders' rights to information and to sue
for breach of fiduciary duties later.

e. Mechanics of Shareholder Voting

General.   The   broad   parameters   which   govern
shareholders voting are set out in all the state corporate
statutes. See, *e.g.*, § 7.01–§ 7.25 of MBCA. Except for
variations found in so called "Integrated Close Corporation
Statutes," a topic we will discuss later, the statutory rules
for shareholder voting are the same for close and public
corporations. However, the rules were clearly written with
public corporations in mind, and the rules are applied
differently in public and close corporations.   More
specifically: (1) in close corporations many of the rules are
often ignored and (2) in public corporations voting is
governed, not just by state law, but also by the SEC's proxy
rules. We will discuss these refinements and others later.
This section provides a basic overview of the mechanics of
shareholder voting dictated under the state corporate
statutes.

Shareholders exercise their voting rights at meetings.
State corporate statutes specify how meetings are called,
notice, quorum, the manner of voting, the vote required to

pass a resolution, how votes are counted, etc. The rules governing shareholder voting are generally straight forward. Most modern corporate statutes are broad enough to enable corporations to authorize a wide variety of voting procedures in their bylaws.

Annual and special meetings. There are two kinds of shareholders meetings: (1) **annual meetings**, held once a year, at which directors are elected and other regular business is conducted and (2) **special meetings**, called when shareholder action is required. The bylaws typically specify the timing of annual meetings and how and by whom special meetings may be called. Generally, either the board or shareholders holding a specified number of shares can call a special meeting. Any meeting other than the annual meeting is a special meeting.

Notice, quorum and voting. All statutes require that shareholders be given written notice of both annual and special meetings. The statutes further require that the board set a **record date**. Only shareholders "of record" as of the record date are entitled to notice and to vote at the meeting. See MBCA § 7.07. The statute usually specifies a time for notice. For example, § 7.05(a) of MBCA requires notice be given no less than 10 days or more than 60 days prior to the meeting.

There must be a quorum and the statutes typically set the quorum as a majority of the shares entitled to vote. This may be altered by provisions in the articles or bylaws in most states. Usually each share has one vote. Generally shareholder approval requires a majority of the shares that actually vote.

Shareholders can vote either in person or by proxy. A proxy is simply a grant by a share-holder of the power to vote his shares to someone else. In effect, the proxy creates an agency relationship in which the proxy holder acts as the shareholder's agent. Unless "coupled with an interest" proxies are revocable. "Coupled with an interest" means the proxy holder has some interest in the shares other than the mere right to vote such shares. If, for example, X borrows money from Y and pledges his shares as collateral for the loan and gives Y a proxy to vote the shares until the loan is repaid, then Y has a proxy coupled with an interest.

Action without a meeting. Most modern corporate statutes allow shareholders to act without a meeting by giving their written consent. But the statutes vary as to percentage of shareholders necessary for a valid consent. Compare MBCA § 7.04(a) with Del. § 228.

f. Who Decides How a Large Public Corporation Like McDonald's Runs Its Business?

Since all of you are probably familiar with McDonald's Corporation, we thought we would illustrate how some of the basic rules of corporate governance play out by considering the following hypothetical questions, which relate to the operation of McDonald's business:

We should all know that the question—*Who decides how McDonald's runs its business*—is too broad to be answered. We must break the question down into a series of more specific questions:

*Who decides: (1) Where the next store will be located?
(2) Whether a new type of sandwich will be added to the
menu? (3) Whether McDonald's will begin operating in
China? (4) Whether McDonald's will buy a large
competitor, Wendy's? (5) Whether McDonald's will
liquidate its business?*

Where the next store will be located?

This is clearly an ordinary course of business
transaction and an officer, probably the vice president in
charge of that particular aspect of McDonald's business,
will decide. There will likely be a provision in the bylaws
governing this question.

The menu question?

Again, probably an officer. Maybe in the case of
McDonald's, after performing and analyzing test market
results, the CEO would decide. It is a little closer question
but still likely an ordinary course of business decision.
Board approval would not be necessary.

Of course, the answer to this question would be
different if the menu change were something more
fundamental then merely adding a new type of sandwich.
For example, replacing french fries with refried beans.

Whether McDonald's should begin operations in China?

Expanding into a new market like China is clearly an
extraordinary undertaking, which will probably entail
spending millions to create the appropriate infrastructure

as well as high-level research on Chinese people's tastes in food. This is not ordinary course of business. Thus, board approval would likely be required.

Whether McDonald's will buy its competitor Wendy's?

Obviously the board must authorize a transaction of this magnitude. Further this is the sort of fundamental corporate change that must be submitted to a vote of shareholders for approval. Under a body of law we haven't yet discussed, since both McDonald's and Wendy's are publicly held companies, this matter would fall within the SEC proxy rules, which would entail furnishing shareholders with a massive disclosure document describing the transaction. We will discuss the proxy rules later. See § VI.B.4.b, *infra.*

Liquidation of the company?

Obviously this is a transaction that must be initiated by the board of directors and approved by a vote of shareholders.

2. GOVERNANCE PROBLEMS DIFFER IN "CLOSE" AND "PUBLIC" CORPORATIONS

If you merely read the state corporate statutes, you would conclude that the same statutory scheme of corporate governance applies to all corporations. However, this **statutory scheme does not reflect how corporations are governed in the real world.** In the area of corporate governance, the types of problems likely to be encountered and the way the rules play out vary significantly depending on whether the corporation is a **close corporation** or a **public corporation**.

Recall that a close corporation is owned by a few shareholders who are usually all active in the management of the business and there is no ready market for their shares. By contrast, public corporations are owned by numerous shareholders, the vast majority of whom are passive investors, in no way involved in management and their shares are freely marketable. The only important decision most shareholders of a public corporation have to make is when to sell their shares.

In the next section, B.3, we will discuss the principal issues facing shareholders of close corporations and in the succeeding section, B.4, we will discuss the principal issues that impact shareholders of public corporations.

3. GOVERNANCE OF CLOSE CORPORATIONS

How and why does governance of a close corporation differ from the statutory scheme?

In a close corporation the shareholders, directors and officers are usually the same people. The controlling shareholders typically elect themselves as directors of the corporation. And then the shareholder-directors typically appoint themselves as officers. Thus, the same people usually occupy all three tiers of the hierarchy.

In this environment, the controlling shareholders view themselves much the same way as partners view themselves—namely, as running a businesses they own.

They tend to ignore corporate formalities associated with the three-tier-hierarchy imposed by the statutory scheme. and often pay little attention to the role in which they are acting at any given time.

In a close corporation, **the seat of power is in the controlling shareholders**. But under the statutory scheme of corporate governance, controlling shareholders (in their capacity as shareholders) have no power to manage the corporation. That power is vested in the board of directors. This need not be a problem because in the overwhelming majority of cases the controlling shareholder is usually a director and often controls the board. It can become a problem when persons acting in multiple roles act in the wrong capacity in a given transaction.

What are the main governance issues that arise in close corporations?

(1) Controlling board decisions;
(2) Controlling voting by other shareholders;
(3) Controlling the transfer of shares; and
(4) Abuse of minority shareholders by majority shareholders.

We will discuss these issues in the order listed.

a. Attempts to Control Board Decisions

The typical fact situation. The cases in your casebook involve aspects or variations of the following fact situation. The controlling shareholder of a close corporation (who is a member of and typically controls the board), in his capacity as a shareholder, enters into a contract either with other board members or a third party. Later one of the parties to the contract alleges the contract is not enforceable because it usurps the authority granted to the board of directors under the corporate statute. This basic fact situation, which arises in an infinite number of variations, raises the following question:

Should the law allow a person to avoid a contract because the contract was made in a corporate setting, even though that contract could not be avoided if it were made in a partnership or LLC setting?

We will examine how both the courts and legislatures have dealt with this question.

(1) Judicial Solutions

In *McQuade v. Stoneham*, Stoneham, the controlling shareholder of the corporation that owned the New York (now San Francisco) Giants baseball team, McGraw (the hall of fame manager of the Giants) and McQuade entered into a contract. They all agreed to use best efforts to (1) elect each other as directors and (2) elect each other as officers at specified salaries.

Later McQuade fell into disfavor with Stoneham, and Stoneham caused McQuade to be replaced as a director and officer. McQuade sued for breach of contract. The lower court found a breach and awarded McQuade damages. On appeal, the court reversed on the grounds that the contract was void as against public policy because it impinged on the authority of the board of directors to manage the corporation mandated by the New York corporate statute.

While the broad holding of this case probably no longer reflects the law, *McQuade v. Stoneham* appears in most casebooks and effectively makes the point that in a corporation a person can act in several roles simultaneously. The three men, as shareholders, could agree to elect each other directors, but they could not, in advance, agree what they would do in their role as directors.

Our students are often uncomfortable with *McQuade.* They tend to ask who was harmed by this agreement and why should the parties be condemned for doing something in a corporate setting, which would be allowed (and likely applauded as good planning), if done in a partnership setting. The New York court itself apparently had some misgivings about its holding in *McQuade* because in *Clark v. Dodge*, a case decided only two years later, the court narrowed the scope of its holding in *McQuade.*

Clark v. Dodge dealt with an agreement between Clark, who owned 25% of the stock of a company that produced certain medicines and Dodge, who owned the remaining 75% of the stock of the company. Under the agreement Dodge, the majority shareholder, agreed that he would vote as either a stockholder or a director to retain Clark, the minority shareholder, as general manager of the company and pay him 25% of the company's profits in the form of either salary or dividends, so long as Clark remained "faithful, efficient and competent."

Dodge breached the agreement, and Clark sued for specific performance. Despite *McQuade*, the court refused to void the agreement and granted Clark specific performance. The only apparent distinction between these two cases was that in *Clark*, all the shareholders were parties to the agreement, while in *McQuade* there were a few minority shareholders who were not parties to the agreement.

In a subsequent case, *Long Park v. Trenton-New Brunswick Theaters Co.*, under facts similar to those in *Clark*, the court struck down an agreement among all three shareholder of the company that provided that one of the shareholders would manage the company for 19 years. The rationale was that the agreement impinged on the board's authority to manage the company. The court distinguished *Clark* on grounds that *Clark* involved only a "slight impingement," while the impingement in *Long Park* was more than slight.

These three cases provide a common law rule for the governance of close corporations in New York, namely—slight impingements to the statutory norm that do not damage anyone who is not a party to the agreement are acceptable. However, this rule fails to give sufficient guidance to corporate planners as to how much variation from the statutory norm courts will allow.

Judicial decisions outside of New York have been equally ambivalent and have laid down equally murky rules. *Galler v. Galler*, decided by the Supreme Court of Illinois, is the example found in most casebooks.

The *Galler* case, like the *McQuade* case, illustrates the multiple roles individuals often play in closely held corporations. The two brothers, Isadore and Benjamin Galler, each owned 47.5% of the outstanding stock of a successful closely held corporation in the wholesale drug business. A key employee of the company owned the remaining 5% of the outstanding stock. The brothers were also two of the three members of the company's board of directors and officers of the company.

The brothers entered into an agreement, which was intended to provide financial security for their respective families if one of the brothers died. The agreement contained several provisions, such as agreements to (1) amend the bylaws, (2) to vote for certain persons as directors and (3) restrict the sale of the stock, which were clearly enforceable because they related to actions Isadore and Benjamin could take in their capacity as shareholders. But two of the provisions in the agreement were objectionable. These provisions required the corporation to (1) pay a pension to the widow of either of the contracting shareholders in the event of his death and (2) pay dividends at a specified rate. These provisions were objectionable on the grounds that they impinged on the directors' authority to manage the corporation.

Following Benjamin's death, Isadore's widow and son repudiated the agreement and Benjamin's widow sued to enforce the agreement. The court upheld the agreement and in so doing, announced the following rule: **An arrangement concerning management of a close corporation, if the arrangement is agreeable to all of the**

shareholders and if there is no fraud or injury to creditors or the public, should be upheld.

The *Galler* opinion discussed the need for special statutes for close corporations. State legislatures responded—how and with what effect will be discussed in our next two subsection.

(2)   Legislative Solution #1—Integrated Close Corporation Statutes

The legislatures in 17 states responded to the suggestion made by the *Galler* Court that there should be special statutes for close corporations by adopting special provisions in their general corporate statutes designed specifically for close corporations. These provisions have come to be known as "Integrated Close Corporation Statutes."

The Integrated Close Corporation Statutes vary widely from state to state. The common characteristic they all share is that they are opt-in statutes, meaning that close corporation status must be specifically elected by eligible corporations and a statement of such election must be included in the articles of incorporation. If an eligible corporation opts to be governed by the special rules contained the state's Integrated Close Corporation Statute, that corporation will be treated as a special subset of corporations and will be allowed to dispense with some of the formalities associated with the shareholder, director and officer hierarchy of corporate governance.

Relatively few corporations have elected to opt for special close corporation treatment. Therefore, we will only give you a broad overview of the Integrated Close Corporation Statutes, using the Delaware statute as our model.

In general, key provisions of the Delaware Close Corporation Statute (Del., Subchapter XIV, § 341–§ 356) provide the following:

Eligibility and election. Only corporations with fewer than 30 shareholders and whose stock is subject to transfer restrictions can opt for close corporation treatment. To opt-in, a close corporation's articles must state that the corporation is a close corporation. Del. §§ 341, 342. Opting for close corporation treatment requires a two-thirds vote of shareholders. Del. § 344.

Termination of close corporation status. By a two-thirds vote of shareholders and the filing of an amendment to the articles of incorporation, close corporation status can be terminated.

Restricting the discretion of or eliminating the board of directors. By written agreement, a majority of the shareholders of a close corporation entitled to vote can "restrict . . . the discretion or power of the board of directors. Del. § 350. The shareholders may also eliminate the board of directors entirely and manage the corporation themselves. Del. § 351.

Resolving deadlocks. The statute provides for a number of deadlock breaking devices for businesses managed by shareholders which opt for close corporation status. Del. §§ 352, 353.

The Integrated Close Corporation Statutes had their heyday in the 1980s, the decade in which most of such statutes were adopted. None have been adopted since that decade and it is unlikely that more will be adopted in the future due to the advent of the LLC, discussed in the next subsection, which came into wide spread use in the 1990s.

(3) Legislative Solution #2—the LLC Statutes (herein governance of LLCs)

Recall that we previously described an LLC as a business structure which provides its members with limited liability (similar to that traditionally provided by corporations) and pass through taxation (similar to that traditionally provided by partnerships). In addition, the LLC also provides more management flexibility than any other business structure available today. There are no statutory requirements for a corporate-like hierarchy of shareholders, directors and officers, as in corporations.

The governance rules of an LLC are usually incorporated in a document called an "operating agreement" in most states. The LLC statutes merely establishes "default rules" that govern, if, but only if, there are no controlling provisions in the operating agreement.

The operating agreement can be described as a combination of corporate bylaws and a partnership agreement. It governs the internal operation of the LLC and defines the relationships among the members of the

LLC, establishes the process for admitting new members, sets forth the requirements for contribution, governs voting rights, provides for the dissolution and windup of the LLC, provides for the allocation of profits and losses, etc. There are few restrictions on how an LLC can be governed. It can operate like a corporation, a partnership, or something in-between.

The Delaware LLC statute, specifically incorporates a policy of giving maximum effect to **freedom of contract** in LLC agreements. See Del. § 18-1101(b). Thus, an artfully drafted operating agreement can structure the management of the LLC in accordance with the owners' (called "members" in an LLC) desires. The LLC borrows from both corporate law and partnership law but in reality **LLCs are governed by contract law**.

State LLC statutes give the members the option of electing to manage the business themselves, more or less, the way partnerships are managed. These LLCs are called "**member managed LLCs**." Alternatively, under the LLC statutes of most states, the members may elect one or more managers to manage the business. These, LLCs are managed more like a corporation and are called "**manager managed LLCs**."

The use of LLCs is in large part tax driven. It is important to the owners that the LLC be taxed like a partnership. Until 1997, the manner in which LLCs were taxed was determined by a set of rules under the internal revenue code called the "Kintner Regulations." They were used by the IRS to determined which unincorporated business entities would be taxed as corporations and which would be taxed as partnerships. The basic test under the Kintner Regulations was whether a particular business structure had more corporate or noncorporate attributes. This fact-dependent test created uncertainty as to LLC's tax status and, for a time, inhibited the use of LLCs.

Effective January 1, 1997, the IRS repealed the Kintner Regulations and substituted an elective scheme of taxation called "**check the box**." Under "check the box," some unincorporated entities such as publicly traded partnerships are automatically taxed as corporations. Others, including the vast majority of LLCs, can choose to be taxed either as partnerships or corporations on an elective basis simply by checking the appropriate box, the first time they file a tax return.

With the elimination of the uncertainty as to their tax status brought about through repeal of the Kintner Regulations, the LLC has emerged as a widely accepted business structure. Today, every state has an LLC Statute. (In 1990, only two states, Wyoming and Florida, had LLC statutes.) The LLC has obviously enjoyed far greater acceptance than the Integrated Close Corporation statutes. Today, the LLC is a widely accepted alternative to the corporation for closely held businesses. In the last few years it has emerged as the business structure of choice of thousands of closely held businesses throughout the country.

b. Control of Voting by Shareholders

Recall that if a closely held business is organized as a corporation, absent an election to be treated as a "close corporation" under an integrated close corporation statute, ultimate management authority rests with the board, which derives authority from the corporate statute, rather than from the shareholders who elect the board. Consequently, in a closely held corporation having a say in management means having control of, or at least having representation on, the board of directors.

The most important decisions shareholders make are decisions about directors. Shareholders elect directors (see Del. § 211(b); MBCA § 8.03(c)) and shareholders can remove directors (see Del. § 141(k); MBCA § 8.08). Thus, shareholders of close corporations frequently form coalitions and authorize various arrangements, agreements or devices to control voting. We will discuss the most common of these devices.

(1) Cumulative Voting

If a single individual (or an allied group) owns a majority of the stock of a corporation, that individual (or group) will be able to elect all the directors unless there is **cumulative voting**. Cumulative voting, unlike straight voting, allows shareholders to accumulate all of their votes and allocate the votes to one or more candidates for the board. Cumulative voting increases the chances of minority shareholders having board representation. Cumulative voting only applies to the election of directors.

Distinguish straight and cumulative voting. You need to understand the difference between cumulative voting and straight voting. Under straight voting each shareholder gets to cast her number of shares for each

director running for election. For example, assume Dave's
Tasty Tacos, Inc. has three directors on its board and it
has three shareholders—Dave, who owns 60 shares, Joe,
who owns 30 shares and Lee, who owns 10 shares. Under
straight voting Dave has 60 votes, Joe has 30 votes and Lee
has 10 votes for seats 1, 2 and 3 on the board. Thus, a
shareholder owning the majority of the stock (like Dave)
will be able to elect every director.   And minority
shareholders (like Joe and Lee) will be unable to have any
representative on the board.

With cumulative voting, however, directors are not
elected seat-by-seat.   Rather, there is one "at large"
election, in which the shareholders cast votes. In our
example, the top three vote getters would be elected to the
board.   In casting their votes, the shareholders get to
"cumulate" their votes. This means each shareholder gets
to multiply the number of shares times the number of
directors to be elected. In our example Dave has 180 votes
(60 shares times 3 directors), Joe has 90 votes (30 shares
times 3 directors) and Lee has 30 votes (10 shares times 3
directors). Each shareholder can allocate her votes, as she
sees fit, and the top three recipients are elected.

Application. Consider how cumulative voting would
work in our example. Cumulative voting would allow the
minority shareholders to vote all their shares for a single
candidate.   The following formula can be used in
determining the number of shares needed to elect one
director:

$$S \div (D + 1) + \text{(some fraction or 1)}$$

S = number of shares voting
D = number of directors to be elected

In our example the numerator would be 100 (shares to be voted). The denominator would be 4 (3 directors to be elected plus 1). Thus 25 shares is the minimum needed to elect one director.[1]   No rounding is necessary in our example.

If Joe cumulates his 90 votes for a single candidate there would be no way that Dave could spread his 180 votes in a way that would defeat Joe's candidate. But Dave has enough votes to elect two directors or a majority of the board. Lee, on the other hand, does not have enough votes to elect even one candidate. This illustrates the point that cumulative voting does not guarantee minority representation on the board. It simply makes minority representation easier to obtain.

What must be done for shareholders to have cumulative voting? In most states cumulative voting is permitted but not required. Only a few state corporate statutes still require cumulative voting. In the states where cumulative voting is permitted but not required, whether or not cumulative voting exists is controlled by a provision in the articles of incorporation. In a majority of states for shareholders to have cumulative voting the articles must contain a provision stating that shareholders

---

1. The part of the equation that says "some fraction or 1" merely requires rounding to the next full number of shares if the answer is a fraction—*i.e.,* if we were electing 5 directors and the answer came out to 16.67, 17 shares would be needed to elect a director.

may vote cumulatively. These statutes are called "opt in" statutes. See, *e.g.,* MBCA § 7.28(b). A significant minority of states, however, allow shareholders to vote cumulatively unless the articles contain a provision denying shareholders the right to vote cumulatively. These statutes are called "opt out" statutes.

Other observations about cumulative voting. As our example indicated, cumulative voting requires planning and doing the math. If a shareholder casts her votes in an inefficient way she may not get the directorships she is entitled to.

The lower the number of directors standing for election, the higher the percentage of stock required to elect a director by cumulative voting. Thus, the majority shareholder may mitigate the effect of cumulative voting by reducing the size of the board or by creating a staggered board.

A staggered board means that not all of the directors stand for election each year. For example, a board may consist of nine directors, each elected for a staggered term of three years. Thus, only three directors would stand for election in any given year. Staggered boards have been challenged in states in which cumulative voting is mandatory and in most cases the courts have upheld the validity of staggered boards despite their adverse effect on cumulative voting.

Finally, the main effect of cumulative voting is that it increases minority representation on the board. Whether this is good or bad depends on one's point of view. In general, studies have shown that in corporations with very few shareholders, cumulative voting is usually meaningless. Sometimes it fosters deadlocks, a problem discussed later. Public corporations seldom have cumulative voting because it complicates the voting process and rarely alters the results. Cumulative voting is most effective in medium-sized corporations, that have between 20 and 200 shareholders, where ownership is sufficiently concentrated for cumulative voting to have the desired effect and where factions are likely to exist.

(2) Supermajority Requirements

Another means by which a corporation's usual control structure can be modified to give minority shareholders a greater voice in governance is through so called "Supermajority" requirements. Supermajority requirements modify the usual rule that the vote of the majority controls. Typically a majority of the shares entitled to vote is needed for a quorum and a majority of the shares voting is necessary to carry a particular resolution.

The general notion behind imposing a requirement is that instead of a mere majority, a vote of $\frac{2}{3}$, $\frac{3}{4}$ or whatever is necessary to constitute a quorum or to carry a resolution. This gives a significant minority something akin to a veto power. A Supermajority requirement makes it hard for most corporations to act without the the assent of at least a significant portion of the minority. Supermajority requirements can be imposed at the shareholder level, the board level or both. They can be applicable to all matters or to specific matters such as approving mergers, fixing dividends, etc. And they may alter quorum as well as voting requirements. See, *e.g.*, MBCA § 7.27 (shareholders) and MBCA § 8.24 (directors).

Most states permit Supermajority requirements. Some state statutes require that the enabling provisions be in the articles of incorporation; others allow the provisions to be in either the articles or the bylaws. Supermajority requirements have generally been upheld by the courts on the basis that while they add to the risk of deadlock, they provide a bargained-for benefit to minority shareholders.

(3) Shareholder Voting Agreements

Shareholder voting agreements, sometimes called vote-pooling agreements, are contracts between shareholders to vote their shares in a manner prescribed in the contract. Today voting agreements are generally controlled by ordinary rules of contract law and are specifically authorized by most state corporate statutes. See, *e.g.*, MBCA § 7.31.

Historically, courts were reluctant to enforce shareholder voting agreements. Courts were concerned about the separation of voting power from ownership. The 1947 case of *Ringling Bros. Barnum and Bailey Shows, Inc. v. Ringling* was a watershed event in the changing of this mind set. Though now somewhat dated, this case has a great set of facts and tells us a lot about the concept of voting agreements and how they are used. The case is in almost all of the casebooks.

At the time the *Ringling* case arose, the original founders who created the famous circus had long since died and ownership of the closely held corporation, which owned the circus was vested in three sets of heirs: (1) Edith Ringling (and her son Robert) with 315 shares; (2) Aubrey Haley (and her husband) with 315 shares and (3) John North Ringling with 370 shares. The board of the Ringling corporation consisted of 7 directors, who were elected annually by cumulative voting.

For several years, John North Ringling ran the circus, but as often happens in close corporations, sometimes personalities get in the way, factions develop and vie for power. In 1943 Edith and Aubrey joined forces and signed a voting agreement. Under the terms of their agreement, the two ladies agreed to vote their shares together. By so doing, they were able to elect 5 of the 7 directors and seize control of the corporation from John. Mr. Haley, Aubrey's husband and Robert, Edith's son, took over control of the business from John.   However, in 1944 during a performance of the circus in Connecticut the circus tent caught fire. One hundred eighty people died and over 500 were injured. Mr. Haley, who was in Connecticut, running the circus, was prosecuted, convicted of manslaughter (failure to have sufficient staff, etc.), and forced to spend some time in prison. Robert ignored Mr. Haley, while he was in jail, but John visited him.   The experience embittered Mr. Haley, who after his release from prison persuaded his wife Audrey to end her alliance with Edith. At the 1946 annual meeting, Aubrey refused to vote with Edith (or per the instructions of the arbitrator) and litigation ensued. On appeal there were two issues:

(a) Was the voting agreement a valid agreement the court would enforce?

The Delaware Supreme Court held yes. The agreement was not void as against public policy. The court reasoned that it was analogous to a proxy coupled with an interest.

(b) Would the court grant specific performance?

The court refused to grant specific performance. Instead it ordered that the Haley votes be ignored.

As a result of this litigation John regained control of the board. Through control of the board, he controlled the circus, which he managed for several years following the decision until the circus was sold.

The *Ringling* case illustrates a turn around in judicial hostility toward voting agreements. Today, most courts would go further than the *Ringling* court and enforce the agreement by specific performance. Further, most states, today, have statutes validating shareholders' voting agreements and most of those statutes provide that such agreements are enforceable by specific performance. See, *e.g.,* Del. § 218(c); MBCA § 7.31. The model act does not impose any special requirements on voting agreements, but many state statutes do impose special requirements, such as that they be in writing, limited in duration, etc.

(4) Voting Trusts

The voting trust is another legal device used to vest control in the hands of a particular person or faction. Its effect is similar to the effect of voting agreement. However, the differences between a voting trust and voting agreement outweigh their similarities and law professors often focus on these differences.

Self-enforcing. Unlike voting agreements, which are not self-enforcing and are grounded on contract principles, voting trusts are self enforcing and they are grounded on trust principles. In a voting trust, shareholders transfer legal title to their shares to one or more voting trustees. The voting trustees, for a defined period, have exclusive power to vote the transferred shares. Other attributes of ownership, such as rights to dividends, remain with the former shareholders, who become beneficiaries of the trust. Typically the beneficiaries are issued voting trust certificates as evidence of their beneficial ownership of the shares transferred to the trust. Because the voting trustees become the legal owners of the shares, their right to vote such shares is not dependent upon a court order of specific performance. Rather, the voting trust is self-executing. The voting trustee does owe the former shareholder/beneficiaries fiduciary duties.

Creatures of statute; express requirements. Unlike voting agreements, which have common law roots, voting trusts are strictly creatures of statute. The statutes authorizing voting trusts typically impose a number of formal requirements, which in general must be strictly complied with to insure validity of the voting trust. The requirements for creating a voting trust vary from state to state. MBCA § 7.30 is typical. It requires that: (1) the trust agreement be in writing, (2) the shares be specifically transferred to the trustee, (3) the trust be limited in duration to not more than ten years and (4) the trust agreement be on file at the corporation's principal office.

Termination. Once a particular shareholder transfers her shares to a voting trust, the shareholder is in for the duration of the trust. She can not revoke her transfer during the life of the voting trust. Voting trusts can only be terminated early if all the beneficiaries of the trust agree to terminate the voting trust.

Uses of voting trusts. Voting trusts can be used for the same purpose as voting agreements—*i.e.,* to enable a coalition of minority shareholders to control the board. However, voting trusts are used for a variety of other purposes—in public as well as close corporations. They are often used in corporate financings, including bankruptcy reorganizations. A voting trust can insure a management acceptable to creditors for an extended period of time. Similarly, an elderly controlling shareholder, who wants to pass ownership to younger family members, can use a voting trust to permit management free of family rivalry for a period of time.

In sum, voting trusts are consensual. They bind only the parties who agree to participate. But once a shareholder agrees by transferring her shares to the voting trustee, that person is bound for the duration of the trust. The trustee is a fiduciary, who owes the beneficiaries of the voting trust (the former shareholders) fiduciary duties similar to those owed by any trustee to the beneficiaries of an express trust. Voting trusts are devices by which the power to vote is temporally, but formally and irrevocably, separated from the other incidents of stock ownership.

c. Stock Transfer Restrictions and Buy-Sell Agreements

In theory, the shares of all corporations are freely transferable. The concept of free transferability reflects reality in publicly held corporations. A shareholder of a public corporation, whose shares are traded daily in the organized securities markets, can sell her shares by merely calling her stockbroker with a sell order. But the reality is very different for owners of shares of closely held corporations. By definition there is no active market for these shares.

Majority shareholders, who control the close corporation, may be able to sell their shares based on an evaluation of the company. But even controlling shareholders have problems finding buyers willing to pay a fair price. Minority shareholders have a much harder time finding buyers. Few people are interested in buying a minority interest in a close corporation. The only likely buyer is the majority shareholder and he is usually only willing to buy at a favorable price.

Moreover, shareholders of a close corporation, who are often active in the business, often want to restrict their fellow shareholders from selling their shares to outsiders. They want to promote harmony by excluding outsiders.

For these reasons free transferability of shares, while said to be a fundamental attribute of a corporation, is often not a practical reality in close corporations. Nor is free transferability an absolute right. The law allows reasonable restrictions. The types of restrictions which the law allows may serve a dual purpose, namely: (1) provide minority shareholders with a greater degree of liquidity and (2) give shareholders the ability to restrict sales to outsiders.

Transfer restrictions must be reasonable. Under the modern rule, stock transfer restrictions must be reasonable under the circumstances. See, *e.g.,* MBCA § 6.27. The approach of the courts in applying this rule is to balance the competing considerations of fostering free transferability of ownership, on the one hand, and giving shareholders some power to exit and/or to limit ownership to persons the remaining shareholders know and trust, on the other. Thus, while an outright prohibition against transfer would be invalid, the following types of restrictions have been upheld: (1) purchase options, (2) rights of first refusal and (3) buy-sell agreements.

Purchase options and rights of first refusal. A purchase option is an agreement which requires a shareholder (or the estate of a deceased shareholder) to offer his shares to the corporation or to the other shareholders of the corporation at a specified price.

A right of first refusal obligates a shareholder to offer her shares to the corporation (or to the other shareholders) at the same price and on the same terms offered by an outsider for such shares, before selling the shares to an outsider. The main difference between a purchase option and a right of first refusal is that in the former the price is set by agreement, while in the latter the price is what- ever the outsider offers for the shares. Both are generally valid and enforceable. See, *e.g.,* MBCA § 6.27(d)(1); Del. § 202(c)(4).

Buy-sell agreements. As the name suggests, a "buy-sell agreement" is simply a contract that requires the corporation, the majority shareholder or all remaining shareholders pro rata to purchase the shares of a selling shareholder in specified situations at a specified or ascertainable price. Buy-sell agreements are the most widely used types of stock transfer restrictions. They are valuable and effective tools in closely held corporations. A properly drafted buy-sell agreement should answer the following questions: (1) what triggers an obligation to buy or sell, (2) what the purchase price will be and (3) where the money is to come from. Most of the law pertaining to such agreements comes from the law of contracts and is beyond the scope of this book.

Third parties. Restrictions on the transfer of shares which are valid and enforceable between the parties to the restrictions (*i.e.,* the parties to a buy-sell agreement) may not be binding against third parties. The restrictions are valid and enforceable against the third party only if the third party (1) knows of the restriction or (2) the restriction is "conspicuously noted" on the stock certificate. See MBCA § 6.27(b).

d. Deadlock and Oppression in Close Corporations— Avoidance and Remedies

There is no need for shareholders in public corporations to get along. Usually shareholders in public corporations do not even know who their fellow shareholders are. Shareholders in public corporations have no expectation of participating in management, beyond voting for directors. And, most importantly, shareholder of public corporations know that if they do not like the way the corporation is being run they can "take the Wall Street walk"—sell their shares in the public market.[2]

(1) The Potential for Deadlock and Oppression in Close Corporations

The situation is quite different in a close corporation. In close corporations the shareholders are usually involved in running the business. Often they depend on the business for their livelihood. These shareholders are likely to be linked by family ties or close personal relationships. And the Wall Street walk is not an available option.

What happens if the shareholders of a closely held corporation have a falling out and can no longer agree on how the company should be run?

Generally speaking that depends upon the division of stock ownership among the shareholders. The two problems most likely to result are **deadlock** or **oppression**.

Deadlock. Assume a corporation has two shareholders each owning 50% of the stock. The two shareholders would normally elect themselves and perhaps one crony each to the board. As board members, the two shareholders would elect themselves officers and would run the company. If the two shareholders can no longer agree, there is potential for "**deadlock**." Deadlock refers to fundamental

---

2. Also, partners in a partnership can usually withdraw, and through the dissolution process, force the redemption of their interest. In an LLC, redemption will be provided for in the operating agreement.

disagreements among equal shareholders that can virtually paralyze the corporation's ability to operate. Deadlock can destroy the ability to reach agreement at either the shareholder or the director level.

Recognizing the potential for deadlock and avoiding it by effective planning. In real life, while deadlock sometimes occurs as a result of a falling out between the original shareholders, it occurs more frequently when one of the original shareholders of a successful closely held business dies and the deceased shareholder's shares pass to the next generation. Students (particularly those that have a professor who emphasizes planning) should be able to recognize environments with the potential for deadlock and be aware of the tools available to avoid deadlocks.

Anytime two shareholders or two factions have an equal ownership of a corporation's voting shares, particularly if there is an even number of directors on the board, a potential for deadlock exists. Various mechanisms are available for dealing with deadlocks. They include: (1) pre-dispute arbitration agreements such as the ones found in the *Ringling* case, discussed in § VI.B.3.b(3), *supra,* and (2) buy-sell agreements, structured to resolve deadlocks. See § VI.B.3.c, *supra.*

Another effective device for avoiding deadlock is a deadlock-breaking director. An example of how deadlocks arise and how they can be avoided by effective planning is found in the case of *Lehrman v. Cohen.* In that case Lehrman and Cohen founded a company, Giant Food Stores, Inc., which at the time of this litigation had became the leading grocery store chain in the Washington, D.C.

area. The two founders had no trouble getting along, but at the time the case arose, one of the founders had died and the other was elderly. Giant Foods was equally owned by the Cohen and Lehrman families—each family owned 50% of the stock. Recognizing an environment ripe for deadlock, counsel for the company caused the company to be recapitalized. He creating a class of common stock called AL—owned by Lehrman family and a class of common stock called AC—owned by Cohen family. Each of those classes could elect two directors to a five-person board. The counsel created a third class of stock called AD and issued one share of AD stock to himself. The AD stock could elect one director, but it had none of the other attributes of ownership, except the right to elect one director (*i.e.,* a deadlock-breaking director).

The court upheld the deadlock-breaking director arrangement. Today, a deadlock-breaking director, whether chosen by agreement, arbitration, or built into the capital structure of the corporation, is an effective deadlock preventing device.

Oppression. Assume three shareholders *A, B* and *C,* each own 33.3% of the voting stock of a company they founded and each is a director. Assume there is a disagreement and *A* and *B* remove *C* from the board. Through control of the board *A* and *B* can take actions against *C.* These actions, commonly referred to as "**oppression**," may include terminating *C*s employment with the company, refusing to pay dividends and siphoning off corporate earning through high compensation to themselves. Such techniques are referred to as "freeze-outs" or "squeeze-outs." Often these techniques, which can be used in combination, force a minority shareholder such as *C* to sell her shares to the majority shareholders *A* and *B* at an unfairly low price.

(2) Remedies for Deadlock or Oppression

What remedies are available to equal or minority shareholders in the event of deadlock or oppression?

The principal judicial remedies available to equal shareholders, trapped in a dysfunctional corporate marriage, by deadlock and minority shareholders, similarly trapped by oppression and the absence of any meaningful power to exit, are **involuntary dissolution** and actions based on **violation of fiduciary duties.** We will defer discussion of claims based on violation of fiduciary duties until next chapter. See § VII.A, *infra.* Involuntary dissolution and related remedies will be discussed herein.

Involuntary Dissolution and Related Remedies. The principal statutory remedy available to shareholders who want a corporate divorce is "involuntary dissolution." All states have statutes authorizing involuntary dissolution, but the specifics of both wording and application of such statutes vary significantly from state to state. MBCA § 14.30 is as good an example as any for considering the issues that might arise in a proceeding for involuntary dissolution.

Historically, courts were reluctant to grant involuntary dissolution. The Official Comment to MBCA § 14.30 advises courts to be "cautious" in granting this remedy and some state statutes provide that courts should grant this

remedy "only if . . . all other remedies available either at
law or in equity . . . are determined by the court to be
inadequate."

In recent years: (1) many courts have become less
reluctant to order involuntary dissolution and (2) some
courts have ordered majority shareholders to buy out the
oppressed minority shareholders, even when the applicable
corporate statute does not contain specific language
empowering the court to order a buy-out.

The MBCA was amended in 1991 to permit majority
shareholders in a close corporation to elect to buy out the
petitioning shareholder in an involuntary dissolution
proceeding at fair value. See MBCA § 14.34(a). Obviously,
what constitutes "fair value" can be a significant issue
when this remedy is elected or ordered by the court.
Courts ordering dissolution typically allow and encourage
the shareholders to agree on a price. If they fail, the court
will set the price.

Grounds for involuntary dissolution. MBCA § 14.30(2)
specifies the following grounds for involuntary dissolution:

(a) deadlock at either the board or shareholder level;
(b) illegal, oppressive or fraudulent conduct by directors
or control shareholders; and
(c) misapplication or waste of corporate assets.

Alternative remedies short of dissolution. Many
courts are hesitant to order dissolution, even when
dissolution is specifically authorized by the statute.
Sometimes courts order remedies, short of dissolution,

which include: (1) awarding damages to the oppressed shareholder, (2) ordering a buy-out—even where the statute does not expressly empower them to do so—based on the court's inherent equity powers and (3) appointing a "receiver" or "custodian." "Receivers" generally liquidate the business, while "custodians" generally preserve the assets and operate the business for an indefinite period. See, *e.g.,* MBCA § 14.32.

4. GOVERNANCE OF PUBLIC CORPORATIONS

Recall that the same statutory scheme of corporate governance applies to all corporations, both "public" and "close." We have discussed how and why the statutory scheme fails to reflect reality in "close" corporations. The statutory scheme also fails to reflect reality in "public" corporations.

a. How Does the Governance of Public Corporations Differ From the Statutory Scheme?

The difference was explained in an irreverent, but understandable way in a management book entitled *Up the Organization*, written by Robert Towsend, former President and CEO of Avis Corporation, in 1971. Mr. Towsend wrote:

The huge, successful company is a dinosaur, but it has one decisive advantage over the middle-sized outfit that is trying to grow. . . . [M]ost big companies have turned their boards of directors into non-boards. . . . This achievement has to be understood to be admired. . . .

While ostensibly the seat of all power and responsibility, directors are usually friends of the CEO put there to keep him safely in office. They meet once a month, gaze at the financial window dressing, provided them by the managers who run the business, listen to the chief and his team talk superficially about the state of the operation, ask a couple of dutiful questions . . . and adjourn until next month.

Over their doodles around the table, alert directors spend their time in silent worry about their personal obligations and liabilities in a business they can't know enough about to understand. . . .

In his *Hornbook on Corporation Law*, page 230, Professor Gevurtz describes the difference in a more scholarly and traditional way, as follows:

The divergence between the corporate governance model and reality in a public corporation does not involve the melding of shareholders, directors and officers into the same few people, but instead involves the flow of power between these three groups. The model perceives power will flow from shareholders, who decide who will be the directors, to directors who select the corporate officers. The reality in most publicly held corporations has been almost the reverse. The officers, particularly the CEO, decides who will be the directors and what policies the corporation will pursue.

Professor Gevurtz refers to the difference he described above as an "inversion." Governance problems in public corporations resulting from this inversion in the last couple of years, starting with the Enron scandal, have emerged as the most serious and hotly debated problem in corporate law today. While we cannot tell you how this problem will be resolved, the following discussion should help you understand the problem. Many corporate law professors are currently debating this problem in the legal journals and are likely to discuss the problem in class.

What is the problem?

The best way to understand the problem is to start by going back to basics—all the way back to basic agency concepts. The principal has the authority to control the agent, and the agent is supposed to act in the principal's interest. But there are situations in which agents and principals have different interests. For example, assume the taco stand, which we have used as an example through out this book is owned by Dave, as a sole proprietorship. While Dave is the sole owner of the business, he has several employees, the people who make the tacos and ring up the sales. The employees are, of course, agents of the owner Dave.

Dave, the principal, wants his employees (the agents) to work hard for as little money as possible. The employees prefer the exact opposite. They would like to get paid as much as possible for as little work as possible. This divergence of interest is not a serious problem for Dave since he is personally managing his taco stand—keeping control of his agents' performance and an eye on the purse strings.

In a public corporation the officers are agents of the corporation. In this situation, the shareholders, who own the corporation are not physically able to watch what is going on. Moreover, under the statutory scheme of corporate governance, the shareholders, though they own the business, have no authority to manage the business.

In the corporate scheme of things, who is supposed to look out for the shareholders' interest?

The obvious answer is the board of directors. The shareholders elect the directors. The directors, like the officers have fiduciary duties to the corporation. One of the main roles of the board of directors, at least in theory, is to keep an eye on the CEO and his team as well as on the cash much like Dave does in managing the employees and the cash at the taco stand.

How do situations like Enron occur?

The answer should be obvious. A corporation's agents, its officers, control the corporation, and they are in a position to siphon off value from the business. They can do this in a number of ways, both obvious and subtle. They can grant themselves lavish compensation packages (including massive option grants), and expensive executive perks, like corporate jets, company apartments and country club memberships. They can engage in pet projects that do not benefit shareholders, such as building a corporate art gallery or giving massive amounts of money to the CEO's favorite charity. They can engage in corporate empire-building activities that increase the CEO's power and influence but do not benefit the corporation's bottom line. And in a few cases, they may even steal the money or engage in self dealing to the detriment of the corporation and its shareholders as some have allegedly done in companies such as Enron, Tyco and World Com.

The board has a legal duty to see that none of this happens and they can be held legally liable to the corporation for violating their fiduciary duties if it does happen (as we will discuss in detail in the next chapter). But the board's job is not easy. If the board is too intrusive and tries to micro manage or second guess the CEO's every move, this will hurt morale and drive away good managers and employees. Organizations function best when the various constituencies within the organization operate with a high level of trust and confidence. Too much intrusion and suspicion can damage the enthusiasm, loyalty, and performance of the CEO and his team So the board has the awkward job of being simultaneously the cop and head cheerleader, fostering team spirit, while keeping an eye on the till.

The board's job is further complicated by other factors. First, officers are in a much better position to make important business decisions than the board. Officers work full-time at their job (often much more than full-time, or they wouldn't have become officers) and they usually have years of relevant experience in the company and the industry. Outside directors (board member who are not also officers of the company), while usually experienced business executives (often retired CEOs), ex-public officials, etc. serve only part time. They usually meet only once a month. One recent survey found that the average board member of public companies spends about four or five hours a week on board work.

Second, directors depend to a large extent on the officers for their information. The CEO makes the business decisions and is at the nerve center of the corporation's information network. No one in the company has more access to information than the CEO, and the CEO controls what information is presented to the board.

Third, the board is usually friendly toward the CEO. In many public corporations, most of the board members were selected to serve on the board by the CEO. There is usually a high level of respect among the CEO and the board members. Thus, boards tend to to back their CEO. They tend to generously compensate CEOs who perform and they are often reluctant to fire non performing CEOs.

So for a variety of reasons, most of the time (though not always), the board finds itself simply trusting the decisions made by the CEO and his team. This is not necessarily bad, if it has the right CEO in place. But experience shows that sometimes a board which puts too much trust in a CEO finds that it has allowed the corporation to be mismanaged (and sometimes even looted). When that happens, the members of the board may find themselves defendants in a shareholders' derivative suit, which we discuss in the next chapter.

This brings us to the bottom line questions: How much board governance is desirable? How independent should the board be? Should there be more governmental regulation?

These very questions are currently being debated in the halls of congress, the state legislatures and regulatory agencies, such as the SEC. The current debate was in large part fostered by recent corporate scandals. The complexities of the problem are such that there are no definitive answers to those questions at this time. There seems to be a discernable trend toward more independent boards, which better protect shareholder interests and provide greater oversight of corporate officers. Currently it appears that this trend will accelerate, in large part due to the outrage and loss of confidence resulting from the recent corporate scandals noted above.

b. Voting by Shareholders in Publicly Held Corporations and the SEC's Proxy Rules

The "inversion" problem discussed above notwithstanding, shareholders elect directors and, in most states, can remove directors. As previously noted, a shareholder does not have to be present to vote his shares at either an annual or special meeting. All state corporate statutes provide that the shareholder may vote by "**proxy**." Cf. MBCA § 7.22; Del. § 212(b). In this section we discuss how the process of shareholder voting by proxy is regulated under the federal securities laws.

What is a proxy?

A proxy is simply a grant by a shareholder of the power to vote her shares to someone else. The person who grants the power is called a proxy giver. The person who receives the power is called a proxy holder.

A proxy is basically a form of agency. The proxy giver consents to the proxy holder's voting the share for her. Under basic agency principles, the proxy holder must vote the shares in accordance with the proxy giver's instructions and the proxy is revocable, unless it is coupled with an interest.

Why do publicly held companies solicit proxies?

Shareholders of publicly held companies are a dispersed, disorganized and largely disinterested group. Seldom will voting for directors at the company's annual meeting be a matter of high priority for the overwhelming majority of shareholders. Assume a company's annual meeting of shareholders is to be held in New York City and a shareholder lives Fort Worth, Texas. It is highly unlikely that this shareholder or other shareholders, living all over the country, would consider taking the time or spending the money to attend that meeting.

Thus, the overwhelming majority of shareholders in publicly held corporations vote by proxies solicited by management, if they vote at all. Management must solicit proxies in order to obtain a quorum so that business can be transacted at the meeting. The quorum requirement under most state corporate statutes is a majority of the shares entitled to vote. Cf. § MBCA 7.25(a).

Who regulates the proxy solicitation in publicly held corporations?

The process is regulated under federal law. Specifically, it is regulated under § 14(a) of the Securities Exchange Act of 1934 ("34 Act") and the rules thereunder. These rules are called the "**Proxy Rules**." If you think about this, it might seem strange that the process is regulated under federal rather than state law. People casually acquainted with the federal securities laws know that these laws are about buying and selling securities—protecting the integrity of the securities markets. The proxy rules are not per se about the securities markets—raising money or buying and selling stock. They are about corporate governance, which is part of general corporate law.

There is no such thing as federal corporate law. So why did the federal government get involved and impose a significant additional layer of regulation in this area? The answer is that the Congressional hearings which preceded passage of the 34 Act showed that there were significant abuses in the process and that state law was virtually void of any regulation of the shareholder voting process. Federal law, or more specifically the proxy rules, were passed to fill the gap As a result, in publicly held companies—the GMs, Exxons and IBMs of the world—voting at shareholder's meetings are governed by federal law, rather than by Delaware or other state law. It is obviously more efficient to regulate proxy solicitations by large companies at the Federal level, since the activity obviously crosses many state borders.[3]

How did Congress choose to regulate the solicitation of proxies?

Section 14(a) of the 34 Act gives the SEC the authority to regulate the proxy process. Section 14(a) of the 34 Act is strictly an **enabling provision**. The statute itself does not prohibit or require anything. It simply gives the SEC the authority to regulate and mandates that the SEC adopt rules governing this process. In other words, Congress basically said to the SEC (the agency which it created under the 34 Act), we have a problem. We don't know how to fix it. Develop a solution by adopting rules that govern the proxy solicitation process.

Our point is you must to look to the **rules** to find the substantive regulation—what is required and what is prohibited. Specifically, Regulation 14A, a series of 14 Rules and two schedules that govern the solicitation of proxies. These rules have the force of law.

Do the proxy rules apply to all companies?

No. The proxy rules only apply to a sub-set of companies known as "companies registered under the 34

---

3. The proxy rules illustrate that while the federal securities laws are primarily aimed at regulating the securities markets, in some areas these statutes spill over and regulate other corporate activities. In this case the voting process related to corporate governance.

Act," "reporting companies" or "publicly held companies"—
synonymous terms.

Do not confuse our use of the term "publicly held
companies," which we used in this section to refer to
companies subject to the proxy rules, with our use
elsewhere in the book of the similar term "public
company," a term we used elsewhere to distinguish "public
companies" for which there is a market for the shares from
"close corporations," which have no market for their
shares.

The term "publicly held company," as used in this
section, is a word of art—a defined term under the § 12 of
the 34 Act—which means a company that either:

(1) has a class of securities listed on a national
securities exchange—§ 12(b) or

(2) at the end of a fiscal year has 500 or more
shareholders and assets of $10 million or
more—§ 12(g).

If a company meets either of the above tests it must
register under the 34 Act and, as a result of that
registration, it becomes a "publicly held company" for 34
Act purposes. That status subjects the company to a
number of obligations and requirements, one of which is
the proxy rules.

The proxy rules come into play in two very different fact
patterns: (1) contested elections and (2) noncontested
elections. Contested elections involve a proxy fight for

control of the corporation. In a contested elections, not only the incumbent directors but also an insurgent group, trying to kick out the incumbents and elect its own slate of directors, is soliciting proxies. Noncontested elections involve the usual annual meeting of shareholders (or sometimes a special meeting), where the shareholders, are required by state corporate law meet to elect directors and sometimes approve other matters. In this situation only management is soliciting proxies.

Contested elections are relatively rare and beyond the scope of a basic business course. We will only discuss the application of the proxy rules to routine noncontested proxy solicitations.

How do the proxy rules affect a routine noncontested solicitation of proxies?

The Federal proxy rules do three things: (1) require that the party soliciting proxies file the proxy material with the SEC in advance of soliciting proxies, (2) regulate the type of information that the proxy material can contain as well as the format in which the information is presented and (3) impose liability if the proxy soliciting material is materially false or misleading.

In basic concept and approach, the proxy solicitation process is regulated in much the same way as the process of going public, because the proxy rules were modeled after the 33 Act registration requirements which govern public offerings. Both require the preparation and delivery of a comprehensive disclosure document. In public offerings the disclosure document is called a prospectus. In the solicitation of proxies the disclosure document is called a proxy statement.

A **proxy statement** is a comprehensive written disclosure document which must accurately and truthfully provide all of the information relevant to the matters to be voted on at the meeting, called for in Schedule 14A of the proxy rules. Details regarding the information called for by Schedule 14A are beyond the scope of this book.

The linchpin of proxy regulation is Rule 14a-3, which provides that no one may solicit a proxy unless the solicitation is accompanied or preceded by a proxy statement. Solicitation is broadly defined as the first step in a campaign to solicit votes. Rule 14a-3 also requires that the proxy statement be accompanied or preceded by an annual report to shareholders, containing specified financial data. And Rule 14a-4 regulates the form of the proxy card on which shareholders indicate their approval or disapproval of each matter voted on at the meeting.

Pursuant to Rule 14a-6, definitive copies of the proxy statement and form of proxy must be filed with the SEC at or before the time they are first mailed to shareholders. If the proxy solicitation relates to any matters other than the election of directors, approval of accountants or shareholder proposals, preliminary copies of the proxy statement and form of proxy must be filed with the SEC at least ten days prior to mailing. The SEC staff often comments on, and insists on changes, in the proxy material before it is mailed.

What happens if the proxy statement is false or misleading?

Rule 14a-9 makes it unlawful to solicit proxies by means of any proxy statement or other communication "containing any statement which is . . . false or misleading with respect to any material fact or which omits to state any material fact. . . ."

The SEC can enforce this rule through civil, criminal or injunctive actions. And since the 1964 Supreme Court decision in the case of *J.I. Case v. Borak*, violations of Rule 14a-9 can be the basis for a suit by private shareholders.

The *Borak* case held that a shareholder, whose vote to approve a merger was obtained by means of a misleading proxy statement had an implied right of action for damages or other relief. The rationale for the court's decision in *Borak* was the general tort principle that violation of a statute creates an implied right of action in favor of the persons for whose benefit the statute was enacted. Recognition of the so called "implied right of action" has been an important development not only with respect to litigation under Rule 14a-9, but also with respect to litigation under Rule 10b-5, which we discuss in Chapter VIII.[4]

---

4. There is significant overlap in the elements necessary to state a cause of action under Rule 14a-9 and the broader and more widely used general antifraud rule, Rule 10b-5, which is discussed in depth in Chapter VIII, *infra*.

What are the elements of a cause of action under Rule 14a-9?

A plaintiff must show the following elements to state a cause of action under Rule 14a-9:

1. **Jurisdiction**.—The company soliciting the proxies must be a company which is subject to proxy rules (meets the tests of § 12(b) or §12(g) of the 34 Act, discussed above)—*i.e.*, a "publicly held company."

2. **Misstatement or omission of fact**.—Obviously the statement or omission must be shown to be false or misleading.   This includes lies, half truths and deception—in general the same kinds of misconduct prohibited by Rule 10b-5. See § VIII.B.2, *infra*.

In the case of *Virginia Bankshares, Inc. v. Sandberg* a key issue was not whether the statement was false or misleading but rather whether the statement was a "fact" as opposed to a mere opinion.   The proxy statement soliciting shareholders approval of the proposed merger of a majority owned subsidiary into the parent company, included the following statement: "The Plan of Merger has been approved by the board of directors [of the subsidiary bank] because it provides an opportunity for the bank's shareholders to achieve a high value for their shares."   The jury at trial found that the directors of the subsidiary did not really believe that statement was true, but made the statement under coercion from the parent company. the Supreme Court held that this statement as to motive was a statement of fact (as opposed to mere opinion) which if false (or if the directors did not believe the statement) could be the basis for a cause of action under Rule 14a-9.

3. **Materiality.**—A Rule 14a-9 plaintiff must prove not only that a statement or omission is false or misleading but also the materiality of the misstatement or omission.

Materiality is a controlling concept, under both the 33 and 34 Acts. The linchpin of the entire disclosure-based system is that anything material must be disclosed and conversely anything not material need not be disclosed. This is critical whether we are talking about liability for false and misleading statements in a 33 Act prospectus, violation of the proxy rules or violation of the general antifraud rule, Rule 10b-5. See § VIII.B.3, *infra.*

While materiality is a threshold issue under all three of the areas of the federal securities laws that we touch on in this book, the most frequently cited test of materiality comes from a case involving the proxy rules, *TSC Industries, Inc. v. Northway, Inc.* In that case the United States Supreme Court held that:

> an omitted fact is material if there is a substantial likelihood that a reasonable shareholder would consider [the omitted fact] important in deciding how to vote . . . . Put another way, there must be a substantial likelihood that the disclosure of the omitted fact would have been viewed by the reasonable investor as having altered the total mix of the information made available.

This is a common sense, jury oriented test. The question is: *Would the reasonable prudent investor in light of the total mix of information provided consider the questioned information significant in making her decision* as to how to vote (or, in the context of the 33 Act or Rule 10b-5, whether to buy or sell the securities).

4. **Level of fault.**—Rule 14a-9 merely prohibits the solicitation of proxies by proxy statements or other communications which contain false or misleading statements or omissions. It does not expressly provide a remedy if the rule is violated. This has raised a question as to the level of fault required.

Does plaintiff have to show that the materially false or misleading statement or omission was made recklessly or intentionally (i.e., some level of scienter); is negligence enough; or is it enough just to show falsity?

The Supreme Court has not yet spoken to this question, and so far, the lower federal courts are split on the issue. The current majority rule seems to be that the **level of culpability required depends on the remedy sought**.

If the remedy sought is merely an **injunction**—some sort of prospective relief—*i.e.,* postpone the meeting until we can work the matter out—**no level of fault is required**, not even negligence. If the remedy sought is rescission or damages—*i.e.,* undo a done deal, give plaintiff $100 million in damages, etc.—all courts seem to agree that some **level of fault is required**. But the courts are split as to whether the level of fault required is negligence or scienter.

5. **Reliance/causation**.—Difficult questions can also arise as to the level of causation a complaining shareholder must establish between a misstatement or omission in the proxy statement and approval of the transaction complained of, particularly in cases where it is likely or certain that the transaction would have been approved, irrespective of how the complaining shareholder would have voted. In your course, you may be asked to consider the following Supreme Court cases which speak to this issue.

In *Mills v. Electric Auto-Lite Co.*, the court held that all the plaintiff had to show to establish the necessary causation was that that the proxy solicitation was an "essential link" in the consummation of the transaction complained of. In other words, plaintiff was only required to show that he would have considered the omitted fact in voting, not that the omission would have had a decisive impact on whether or not the transaction was approved.

Virginia Bankshares, Inc. v. Sandberg also involved a proxy solicitation seeking shareholder approval of a merger. The transaction challenged was a "freeze-out" merger, pursuant to which, the parent corporation, which owned 85% of subsidiary's stock, was seeking to acquire the interest of the minority shareholders. Since only an 80% vote was required to approve the merger, approval was assured. Nevertheless, the parent submitted the proposal to a vote of the minority shareholders, and the proxy statement was found to contain a material misrepresentation. The Supreme Court reversed a lower court judgment for the plaintiff, holding that the fact that the parent corporation had the votes necessary to approve the merger, regardless of how the minority shareholders voted, broke the chain of causation.

6. **Remedies.**—The remedies available for violation of the proxy rules include injunctions, rescission and damages or a combination of these remedies.

CHAPTER VII

WHAT ARE THE LEGAL DUTIES OF THE DECISION MAKERS AND HOW ARE THOSE DUTIES ENFORCED? (herein Fiduciary Duties)

In the last chapter we identified the individuals who make decisions for the business structures. With legal power goes legal responsibility. The decision makers for a business, whether the business is structured as a corporation, a partnership or an LLC are said to have "**fiduciary duties.**" And they may be exposed to liability if they violate those duties.

The word "fiduciary" comes from the law of trusts and, broadly speaking, involves acting for the benefit of someone else. However, fiduciary is a context oriented word which defies explicit definition and applies to a variety of relationships. Just as trustees owe fiduciary duties to beneficiaries and agents owe fiduciary duties to their principals, directors and officers of a corporation owe fiduciary duties to their corporations. The individuals who control the governance of other types of business structures also owe fiduciary duties to the owners of those businesses.

While the label "fiduciary" applies to a wide variety of relationships, the scope of the duty imposed may vary depending on the nature of the relationship. Justice Frankfurter made this point in an often quoted statement from his opinion in *SEC v. Chemery Corp.* He wrote: "Directors are fiduciaries . . . but to say that a man is a fiduciary only begins analysis; it gives direction to further inquiry .... What obligations does he owe as a fiduciary?"

This chapter is about the nature and scope of the fiduciary duties of the decision makers in the various types of business structures. We will also explore the manner in which fiduciary duties are enforced.

A. FIDUCIARY DUTIES OF CORPORATE DIRECTORS AND OFFICERS

1. IN GENERAL

The state courts, rather than the legislatures, have primarily defined the scope of the fiduciary duties owed by directors and officers to their corporations. The courts have attempted to strike a balance between giving managers the flexibility to run the business and holding the managers accountable to the owners of the business. This is not an easy balance to strike. As a result, the rules are often imprecise and often vary from state to state. The specific standard will vary depending upon the nature of both the relationship and the questioned transaction.

In general, the scope of the duties owed by directors and high-level managing officers, such as the CEO, to their corporations are the same. Lower level employees owe a lesser degree of duty, but all officers and employees are agents of the corporation and owe the principal certain duties within the scope of their agency. In certain situations, control shareholders may also owe their corporations fiduciary duties.

The law groups the fiduciary duties owed by directors and officers to their corporations into two basic categories: (1) **the duty of care** and (2) **the duty of loyalty**.

2. THE DUTY OF CARE

The standard which generally governs the scope of the duty of care required of corporate fiduciaries rests on the reasonable prudent person standard familiar to students of tort law. There are two major subsets of the duty of care: (1) cases involving **action** by the directors or officers that turns out to be wrong and (2) cases involving **inaction** resulting from inattention or lack of vigilance.

a. Breach of the Duty of Care by Action

In these cases the directors or officers typically make some type of decision or take some action which, with the benefit of hindsight turns out to have been wrong and results in a loss to the corporation. In this type of case, courts give great deference to the business judgment of the directors or officers. The so-called "**business judgment rule**" reflects a judicial "hands off" attitude toward acts or omissions of directors and officers. A good judicial statement of the fundamental notion underlying the business judgment rule is found in *Joy v. North*:

> While it is often said that corporate directors and officers will be liable for negligence . . . all seem agreed that such a statement is misleading. Whereas an automobile driver who makes a mistake in judgement as to speed or distance injuring a pedestrian will likely be called upon to respond in

damages, a corporate officer who makes a mistake in judgement as to economic conditions, consumer tastes or production line efficiency will rarely, if ever, be found liable for damages suffered by the corporation. . . . [T]he fact is that liability is rarely imposed upon corporate directors or officers simply for bad judgement and this reluctance to impose liability for unsuccessful business decisions has been labeled the business judgement rule.

Shlensky v. Wrigley, which appears in almost all the casebooks, is a classic example of this type of case. The case essentially involves a dispute over how a business should be run.

Phillip K. Wrigley owned over 80% of the stock of the corporation which owned the Chicago Cubs baseball team, a team which last won the World Series in 1917 and last appeared in the World Series in 1945. Mr. Wrigley and the directors believed that baseball was meant to be played in the daytime and they refused to install lights at Wrigley Field, even though at the time this case arose, every other major league team had installed lights and had been playing the majority of their weekday games at night for years.

Shlensky, a minority stockholder, brought a shareholders' derivative suit against Mr. Wrigley and the other directors, to force them to install lights. Shlensky presented evidence that night baseball was more profitable than day baseball. Mr. Wrigley and the other directors believed that night baseball might have a detrimental effect on the neighborhood around Wrigley Field. They argued that in the long run, neighborhood deterioration might hurt attendance at Cub games.

The court dismissed Mr. Shlensky's complaint and held that the court would not second guess decisions of the directors if there was a rational basis for their decision and there was no fraud, illegality or conflict of interest, even when, with the benefit of hindsight, it is shown that the decision was wrong.

The approach in the *Wrigley* case reflects the approach of almost all courts prior to the 1980s. Many courts still adhere to this approach, which is based on a policy of leaving business decisions to business people. As the *Wrigley* opinion said, courts do not have the training or expertise to second-guess business decisions made by disinterested business people who are acting without fraud or other taint.

In 1985 in *Smith v. Van Gorkom*, the Delaware Supreme Court rendered a "famous" but controversial decision which narrowed the protection afforded directors' decisions by the business judgment rule. The *Van Gorkom* court took a different approach than that found in *Wrigley,* which reflected a judicial attitude far less deferential to the board's business judgment. The *Van Gorkom* court was willing to second guess many aspects of the board's judgment and discretion.

The facts, set out in great detail in the opinion, involved a friendly cash-out merger and a fast-moving series of events which culminated in board approval of the merger at a two hour board meeting. On September 13, 1980, Van

Gorkom, the CEO of Trans Union Corp., a publicly traded company, met with Jay Pritzker to explore whether one of Mr. Pritzker's companies might have an interest in acquiring Trans Union at $55 per share. At the time Trans Union was trading on the New Stock Exchange at around $38 per share. The $55 per share price was based on an earlier informal study which concluded that the intrinsic value of the Trans Union stock for leveraged buy out purposes was $55-$60 per share.

Following further conversations, on September 18, Pritzker offered to buy Trans Union for $55 per share, the price suggested by Van Gorkom at their initial meeting. He gave Van Gorkom three days to accept or reject the offer. Since this was a transaction which required board (as well as shareholder) approval, Von Gorkom called a special meeting of the Trans Union board on Saturday, September 20, 1980.

The board meeting, described in great detail in the opinion, lasted two hours. Only two of the ten directors knew prior to the meeting that the purpose of the meeting was to consider selling the company. Van Gorkom made a 20-minute oral presentation in which he outlined the terms of the deal. There was no written summary and the merger documents were not available for review.

A Trans Union attorney, who attended the meeting, advised the board that "they might be sued if they did not accept the deal." ($55 per share represented a premium of about 45% over the market price of the stock.) The deal was structured in a way that allowed Trans Union to solicit other bidders, who might top the Pritzker offer for a period of 90 days.   No other bidders made offers during this period.

The board unanimously approved the merger.   Later, Trans Union shareholders approved the merger by a margin of 10 to 1.

Plaintiff brought a class action law suit against the members of the Trans Union board, which consisted of five inside and five outside directors.   The chancellor (trial court) entered summary judgment for the defendants.   In a 3-2 decision Delaware Supreme Court reversed and remanded.   The majority opinion stated that the directors had a duty to inform themselves adequately of the terms of the merger prior to approval of same and that failure to do so amounted to gross negligence, which is not protected by the business judgement rule.

As the dissenting opinion suggests, the majority in *Van Gorkom* went to great length to emphasize a litany of things that the Trans Union board did or failed to do:

(1) inquire into Mr. Van Gorkom's role in suggesting the terms of the merger;

(2) accept, without question, the chief financial officer's opinion that $55 per share was within the fair range of intrinsic value established by the company's internal leveraged buy out study without adequately inquiring as to the basis for his opinion;

(3) did not get a "fairness" opinion from an outside investment banking firm;

(4) acted too quickly, without proper notice or deliberation; and

(5) did not review the merger documents.

And the majority ignored a number of facts, which under prior decisions, such as *Wrigley,* would have supported the lower courts verdict under the business judgement rule:

(1) the $55 per share price represented a 45% premium over the $38 per share market price;

(2) the $55 was within the range of intrinsic value established by an internal leveraged buy out study;

(3) the advice by the Trans Union attorney that the directors might be sued if they did not accept the Pritzker offer;

(4) the pressure on the board created by Pritzker's deadline for acceptance;

(5) the knowledge and experience of a well qualified board;

(6) the fact that no competing bidders topped the Pritzker offer during the period in which competing bids were invited; and

(7) the overwhelming approval of the deal by shareholders.

Almost all law schools cover *Smith v. Van Gorkom* in great depth in the basic business course and almost all law professors are critical of the decision. For example, one highly respected scholar described *Smith v. Van Gorkom* as "one of the worst decisions in the history of corporate law."

Despite the abundance of scholarly analysis, the impact this case has had on the scope of the business judgment rule is still not fully understood. The following two points about *Smith v. Van Gorkom* might get you points on your exam. First, the Delaware Supreme Court got much more involved in reviewing the directors decision making process than had been the judicial practice prior to this decision. Recall, in *Wrigley* the court stated judges do not have the training or expertise to second-guess business decisions made by the board. The *Wrigley* court implicitly said it did not want to get involved. In *Smith v. Van Gorkom* the court got totally involved. The court gave us a whole litany of director oversights. It seemed to be second guessing every aspect of the board's decision. Second, the *Van Gorkom* case, particularly when read with subsequent Delaware decisions, seems to require the board to more closely scrutinize mergers, acquisitions and other end- game transactions than ordinary operating decisions such as day or night baseball.

Impact of *Van Gorkom* on board behavior.   *Van Gorkom* has had a major impact on board behavior and procedures, particularly in the area of mergers and acquisitions. Today, before a board authorizes a major acquisition, they get a third party to render a "fairness opinion," which values the company being acquired. The board goes through elaborate decision making procedures scripted by their lawyers—*i.e.,* numerous meetings, a voluminous paper trail, etc.

Impact of *Van Gorkom* on state legislatures.   *Van Gorkom* has also had an impact on state legislatures. Following this decision, premiums for directors' and officers' liability insurance (D&O insurance) increased dramatically. Today, few qualified people would serve as directors unless they are provided adequate D&O insurance.

Delaware quickly responded to the so-called "D&O insurance crisis" by adopting a statutory provision that enabled corporations to amend their articles to include a provision which shields directors from personal liability for breach of their duty of care. See Del. § 102(b)(7). Notice that Del. § 102(b)(7) only applies to duty of care (not duty of loyalty) violations; only applies to directors (not officers); and only applies to actions for damages (not injunctive relief). MBCA § 202(b)(4) provides similar protection against liability for duty of care violations. Some states have also adopted provisions in their corporate statutes that codify the standards of director behavior. See, *e.g.,* MCBA § 8.30(a).

b. Breach of the Duty of Care by Inaction

Directors are expected to monitor the performance of the CEO and other senior managers to whom the directors have delegated the day-to-day management of the company. They face potential liability if they go "to sleep at the switch" while officers and other managers harm the corporation. This aspect of the duty of care has been described as follows:

> Every director has an affirmative duty to inform himself/herself about the performance of the company, to attend meetings regularly, to be

vigilant, to make an appropriate degree of inquiry
and to act for the general welfare of the corporation.

However, the scope of a director's duty to monitor is not
clear and courts have been reluctant to impose liability for
director inaction. The following two cases are illustrative.

In *Barnes v. Andrews*, the corporation, Liberty Starters
Corp., was formed to make starters for Ford automobiles
and aircraft. Liberty had raised a substantial amount of
money through a stock offering (and many investors,
including the defendant Mr. Andrews, lost money when the
company subsequently went into receivership). Due to
technology problems and in-fighting among the managers,
Liberty never produced a single starter.

About a year after the company was formed
Mr. Andrews, a wealthy investor and personal friend of
Maynard, the promoter and president of Liberty Starters
became a director at Maynard's request. Andrews later
resigned about a year prior to Liberty's going into
receivership. Andrews and Maynard frequently drove into
the city together. The opinion states that (1) Andrews
attended all but one of the board meetings during the time
he served on the board, (2) his "integrity was
unquestioned" and (3) he did from time-to-time inquire in
a general way of Maynard how things were going at
Liberty, but he was content to accept general answers
(such as "everything is going fine" or "it looks promising").
He never pressed Maynard for any details, even though the
company was producing nothing and "slowly bleeding to
death." Barnes, the receiver, sued Andrews for breach of
his duty of care.

In this famous opinion, Judge Learned Hand addressed both the duty of care and causation. First, he held that a director's duty of care encompasses a duty to inform himself of what is going on with some particularity and that Mr. Andrews breached that duty. Second, Hand held that Andrews was not liable because the plaintiff failed to show that Andrews' breach of duty was the proximate cause of the injury to the corporation. In other words, plaintiff failed to show that even if Andrews had made the inquiry required of a diligent director, he could have prevented Liberty Starter from going into receivership.

In *Francis v. United Jersey Bank*, Mrs. Pritchard inherited 48 percent of the stock in a closely held business from her husband, the founder of the business. The couple's two sons (who owned the rest of the stock) took over management of the business after Mr. Pritchard's death. The sons and other employees allegedly misappropriated large sums of the company's clients' money and the corporation filed for bankruptcy.

Mrs. Pritchard and her two sons were the only directors. Mrs. Pritchard knew nothing about the business and did nothing to learn about it. She rarely attended board meetings or went to the office. In fact, following her husband's death, she became depressed and drank heavily. The trustee in bankruptcy sued Mrs. Pritchard's estate, alleging that she violated her duty of care.

The court held that Mrs. Pritchard breached her duty of care. More specifically, the court found that Mrs. Pritchard failed to discharge her duty as a director and that such failure caused harm to the corporation. In other words, in this case the plaintiff prevailed on the causation issue as well as on the duty of care issue.

What is the distinction between Andrews and United Jersey Bank?

Andrews involved operating problems. If, as in *Andrews*, the problem the director fails to discover as a result of her lack of vigilance is a general operating problem, it will usually be difficult for plaintiff to show that if the director had discovered the problem she would have been able to correct it.

In contrast, if, as in *United Jersey Bank*, the conduct the director fails to discover as a result of her lack of vigilance is improper conduct, such as embezzlement, improper loans, self-dealing, etc., it is obvious that had she caught the improper conduct she could have prevented further wrongdoing by threatening to expose the wrongdoers, calling the authorities, etc.

What is the scope of the directors' duty to inquire or monitor the activities of the executive officers or other employees of the corporation?

MBCA § 8.30(b) and the case law suggests that except in special situations, which require "due diligence," such as, a company about to go public or do a merger, the directors can rely on information provided them by officers and other employees. For example, directors can rely on the CEO as to how the company is doing overall, they can rely on figures supplied by the CFO as to financial condition and profitability, etc.

Despite MBCA § 8.30(b) and the case law, the recent Delaware case of *In re Caremark, Inc.* suggests that a board may have a duty to install a monitoring system. It should be pointed out that the *Caremark* statements are dicta because, in the case before it, the court was merely approving an agreed settlement in which the directors promised to do a better job of monitoring in the future.

3. THE DUTY OF LOYALTY

On page 321 of the *Hornbook on Corporation Law*, Professor Gevurtz describes the cases we have just covered as cases in which the complaint is that the directors or officers breached their **duty of care**—in other words, the directors were "lazy or dumb." He than describes the cases, which we will cover next as cases in which the complaint is that the directors breached their **duty of loyalty**—in other words, they were "greedy and put their own financial interests ahead of the interests of the corporation or its shareholders."

Duty of loyalty cases involve conflicts of interest. There are many ways in which a director or officer can breach the duty of loyalty. Stealing company assets or competing with the company, while employed by the company are two examples, which are probably too obvious to be on your test. We will focus on the two duty of loyalty problems most likely to be tested: (1) **interested director transactions** and (2) **usurping corporate opportunities**.

You should be note at the outset that **duty of loyalty cases do not involve the business judgment rule**. Duty of loyalty cases involve some level of conflict of interest, which precludes application of the business judgment rule.

a. Interested Director Transactions

Conflicts of interest occur in a variety of ways. For example, officers or directors of a company may own property that they sell or lease to their company, they may enter into contracts with their company to provide goods or services, etc. These are examples of direct conflicts of interest. A close relative of an officer or director or an entity in which the officer has a significant financial interest might enter into a similar transaction with the officer's or director's company. These are examples of indirect conflicts of interest. Most situations where one or more directors or officers are on both sides of the transaction, are now resolved under statutory rules discussed herein.

History—The early common law rule of automatic voidability. In the 19th century the rule governing interested director transactions was simple. All transactions between directors or officers and their corporations or between corporations with common directors were voidable at the election of the corporation. In other words, at early common law, a mere showing that a director or officer had a financial interest on both sides of a transaction was enough to void the transaction. It did not matter whether the corporation benefitted from the transaction or that other directors, who had no financial interest in the transaction, approved the transaction. This was called the "rule of voidability per se."

Modern conflict of interest statutes. Beginning in the early part of the 20th century, the various states began enacting statutes (called conflict of interest statutes) which changed the common law rule of voidability per se. Nearly all cases involving interested director transactions are now governed by these statutes.

The approach of these statutes is that even if there is a conflict of interest, the transaction or contract it is **not voidable** if certain statutory tests are met.

Analyzing an interested director transaction under a modern conflict of interest statute. While the particulars of the various conflict of interest statutes vary, the overall approach followed by most is similar. See, *e.g.,* Del. § 144. Most modern conflict of interest statutes incorporate a three step process of analysis:

(1) Is the transaction within the statute?
(2) What does the statute require?
(3) What is the effect of satisfying the statute?

(1) *Is the transaction within the statute (i.e., is there a conflict of interest)?*

The transaction falls within the statute if it is a transaction between the corporation and an officer or director of the corporation, who has a **direct or an indirect interest in the transaction.**

If a transaction falls within the statutory definition , you have a conflict of interest. It does not matter that the transaction might have benefitted the corporation or been eminently fair. Under the statutes conflict of interest is a neutral term in the sense that it does not mean the transaction is voidable. In fact, the transaction is not voidable if you comply with the statute.

(2) *What does the statute require?*

First, full disclosure of all material facts concerning the conflict of interest and the transaction.

Second, ratification of the transaction by a majority of the disinterested directors (or if it is not practical to get board ratification, ratification by a majority of the disinterested shareholders).

Third, if she can not get director of shareholder ratification, the interested party, under some, but not all state conflict of interest statutes can still defeat voidability if she can meet the burden of proving that the transaction was fair. The statutes are state-specific on whether fairness will suffice in situations where neither board or shareholder approval is obtained.

You do not need all three requirements, any one, coupled with full disclosure, will suffice.

(3) Finally, the conflict of interest statutes specify the effect of compliance.

If the statute is satisfied, the transaction is not voidable, even though there was a conflict of interest.

b. Usurpation of Corporate Opportunities

Another major subset of the duty of loyalty problem arises when directors or officers take for themselves business opportunities, that might be of interest to the corporations they serve. **Usurping a corporate opportunity violates the basic rule that directors and officers cannot utilize their positions with a corporation to whom they owe fiduciary duties to profit personally at the expense of the corporation.** While easy enough to state, this rule has been difficult to apply, primarily because the courts in deciding specific cases attempt to strike a balance between two conflicting policies:

(1) Discouraging disloyal behavior by officers and directors toward the corporations they serve; and

(2) Permitting entrepreneurial activities by directors and officers, as individuals.

The courts have not developed a clear test to determine what opportunities belong to the corporation and what opportunities directors and officers may take for themselves. Rather, over the years, the courts have applied several different tests. The various tests, applied by the courts, are as follows:

The interest or expectancy test. The interest or expectancy test restricts a director or officer from taking property or a business opportunity for himself where the corporation has an existing interest in the property or opportunity or has an expectancy growing out of an existing interest. While generally the least restrictive of the various tests in terms of the scope of the opportunities it allows officers and directors to pursue, the scope of the restriction imposed under this test has varied considerably from case to case depending on how various courts interpret "interest" or "expectancy."

The line of business test. Under this test, an officer or director must turn over to the corporation any opportunity which is in or relates to the corporation's business. In general the prohibition placed on officers and directors usurping opportunities under the line of business test has been broader in scope than the prohibition under the interest or expectancy test. However, the scope of the prohibition may vary substantially under this test depending on how a particular court in a given case interprets the scope of a particular corporation's business.

The Delaware courts use the line of business test. Many casebooks include *Guth v. Loft*, a 1939 Delaware case. The defendant, Guth was the president of Loft, Inc., a manufacturer of candy, syrup and beverages. Megargel, who at the time controlled the National Pepsi-Cola Company ("Old Pepsi"), informed Guth of the opportunity to buy the assets of Old Pepsi, which was than in bankruptcy. The assets of Old Pepsi at the time consisted mainly of its secrete formula for making Pepsi-Cola and the Pepsi trademarks.

Guth and Megargel formed a new company ("New Pepsi") which bought the assets of Old Pepsi and produced and marketed the soft drink now known as Pepsi-Cola. Guth also used Loft's facilities, employees and credit to improve the formula of the soft drink, which is now known

as Pepsi-Cola. Loft sued claiming that Guth had usurped
a corporate opportunity.

The Delaware Supreme Court held that Guth had
breached his fiduciary duty to Loft and ordered him to
transfer his stock in New Pepsi to Loft. The opinion stated
that since the opportunity acquired by Guth was so close to
the business of Loft, its acquisition by Guth was
prohibited, even though the opportunity originally came to
Guth in his individual, rather than his corporate, capacity.
The court also indicated that it would have so ruled even
if Guth had not used Loft's facilities and resources in
developing the opportunity.

The fairness test. Some courts have stated that the test
as to whether an officer or director usurped a corporate
opportunity is simply a test of basic fairness under the
circumstances.   Courts applying the fairness test to
corporate opportunities look to a variety of factors, such as:
(1) how the defendant learned of the opportunity (*i.e.*, did
the information come to him by reason of his position with
the company), (2) how important the opportunity was to
the corporation, (3) was the corporation seeking this or a
similar opportunity, (4) whether the defendant used
corporate funds or facilities in acquiring or developing the
opportunity, (5) whether the defendant resold or attempted
to resell the opportunity to the corporation and (6) whether
the corporation had the resources to develop the
opportunity.

The two-step test. The two step test combines the line
of business test with the fairness test. Under the two-step
test the court first considers whether the opportunity was

in the corporation's line of business. If so, the court then considers whether it was nevertheless fair for the defendant to pursue the opportunity. The burden of proof as to the first question is on the plaintiff. If the plaintiff meets this burden, the burden shifts to the defendant to show that despite being in the same line of business, the defendant's taking the opportunity was fair based on equitable considerations.

The ALI approach. The American Law Institute's Corporate Governance Project ("ALI") has formulated a new approach to corporate opportunity. The ALI formulation was extensively discussed in *Northeast Harbor Golf Club, Inc. v. Harris*, a 1995 case which appears in many of the casebooks. In that case the Maine Supreme Court rejected the line of business test followed in Delaware and adopted the ALI test.

In *Northeast Harbor*, Nancy Harris was president of a corporation which owned and operated a golf club in Bar Harbor, Maine. She personally purchased two parcels of land near the club and informed the Club's board of directors of both purchases. She purchased the first parcel, the Gilpin property, in 1979. She learned of the availability of that property because she was the president of the club. She learned of the availability of the second parcel, the Smallidge property, in her individual capacity (the postmaster of the town told her about it).

Although the board voiced no objection when originally told of the purchases, a few years later, when Ms. Harris announced that she and some of her children planned a housing project on these purchased properties, the board concluded that the housing project was not in the club's best interest and sued Ms. Harris for usurping a corporate opportunity by buying the two parcels of land.

The trial court held that Harris had not usurped a corporate opportunity because buying land was not in the corporation's line of business and the corporation lacked the financial resources to buy the properties. The Supreme Court of Maine reversed and remanded. It rejected the Delaware "line of business" test and instructed the lower court to apply the ALI test.

ALI Principles of Corporate Governance § 5.05(b) defines a corporate opportunity as a business opportunity that:

(1)   the director or officer becomes aware of in his corporate capacity or through the use of corporate information or property, which the director or officer should reasonably know is being offered to the corporation or reasonably believes would be of interest to the corporation; or

(2)   the director or officer knows is closely related to a business in which the corporation is engaged or expects to engage.

If there is a corporate opportunity, then the question becomes whether the taking of the opportunity was approved in the manner fixed by § 505(a), which generally requires the officer or director to make full disclosure and give the corporation the chance to take or reject the opportunity.

Defenses. *Is financial inability of the corporation to take advantage of the opportunity a defense?*

A majority of the courts seem to hold that a defense based on the corporation's financial inability to undertake the corporate opportunity presented can only be raised in cases where the corporation is legally bankrupt or at least de facto insolvent.

A significant minority of the courts apply a less restrictive test and allow any form of financial inability of the corporation to be used as a defense. Recall that in the *Northeast Harbor* case, the trial court cited the lack of the club's financial wherewithal to buy the real estate as one of its reasons for holding in favor of Ms. Harris.

What if the officer or director gives the corporation a chance to acquire the opportunity but the corporation declines?

If the corporate opportunity is offered to the corporation—that is made available to the corporation with full disclosure—and an impartial board declines to take the opportunity, that is a **complete defense**. If you see these facts on your exam, check to determine (1) whether the board was, in fact, **impartial**; and (2) whether **full disclosure** was in fact made.

This rule significantly lessens the impact of the corporate opportunity doctrine because it **merely requires that the opportunity be offered to the corporation** before being taken advantage of by the officer or director.

Remedy. *What is the remedy of the corporation if a corporate opportunity is usurped?*

The usual remedy is to place the property or opportunity wrongfully acquired and any profits derived therefrom in a **constructive trust** for the corporation Usually the corporation must reimburse the officer or director for his acquisition costs. This remedy is not much of a determent because the defendant does not end up much worse for having attempted to usurp the corporate opportunity even when the effort fails. A few courts have allowed punitive damages in cases involving bad faith.

B. FIDUCIARY DUTIES OF CONTROL SHAREHOLDERS

Recall we learned earlier that the fiduciary duties of directors and officers are generally the same in both nature and scope. Control shareholders also owe certain fiduciary duties to their corporations and its minority shareholders; however, the fiduciary duties of control shareholders differ from those of directors and officers in both nature and scope.

1. DEFINING CONTROL AND SITUATIONS IN WHICH CONTROL SHAREHOLDERS HAVE FIDUCIARY DUTIES

What is a control shareholder?

The definition of a control shareholder is a shareholder or affiliated group of shareholders **with demonstrated ability to influence a majority of the board**.

The clearest evidence of control is someone who owns a majority of the outstanding stock—*i.e.,* 51% or more. And in certain close corporations majority stock ownership may be required.   On the other hand, in publicly held corporations with widely dispersed shareholders, far less than 51% would likely constitute control. A control person may be a parent corporation, an individual or a so called control group—*e.g.,* closely aligned family members, the CEO and his top lieutenants.

The test of control is **de facto control**. If, as a practical matter, a person can walk into the board room and say, "I want this done" and it gets done, without argument, that person is a control person.

Once a person or group is identified as a control shareholder, the question becomes does she owe fiduciary duties to the corporation and its other shareholders?

Control shareholders owe fiduciary duties to the corporation and its minority shareholders. However, the fiduciary duties of control shareholders do not parallel those of directors and officers. The nature and scope of a control shareholder's fiduciary duties vary depending on the nature of the transaction, whether the corporation is a public or closely held corporation, and other factors.

2. DEALINGS BETWEEN A PARENT AND A MAJORITY OWNED SUBSIDIARY

A parent corporation, by definition a control person, dictates how the subsidiary operates and usually executives of the parent control the board of the subsidiary. This situation creates multiple conflicts of interest and potential for abuse by the parent. **The threshold question is usually whether the questioned transaction should be given a presumption of propriety under the business judgment rule or whether the transaction should be viewed as a conflict of interest transaction and made subject to fairness review.**

Sinclair Oil Corp. v. Levien, a case found in almost all the casebooks, considers this question. The Delaware Supreme Court held that transactions between parent and subsidiary companies are subject to fairness review only if the minority shareholder shows "self-dealing" in which the controlling parent preferred itself at the expense of minority shareholders. Another way of stating the test is **whether through the exercise of influence by the parent (*i.e., "self-dealing"*), the parent received a benefit and the subsidiary's minority shareholders suffered a determent.**

The *Sinclair* case illustrates the application of the **benefit and determent** test by distinguishing between two sets of transactions challenged by minority shareholders of Sinven, Sinclair's 97% owned Venezuelan subsidiary:

(1) Sinclair caused Sinven not to enforce certain contracts for the sale of oil at specified prices made with wholly owned subsidiaries of Sinclair. The

court treated the non enforcement of these contracts as self-dealing transactions (*i.e.*, Sinclair received a benefit and Sinven suffered a determent). The burden than shifted to Sinclair to show that its decision not to enforce the contracts was intrinsically fair, and Sinclair did not meet that burden.

(2) Sinven had a policy of paying high dividends. Over a seven year period the subsidiary had paid $38 million more in dividends than it had earned. The burden was on the minority shareholders to show self-dealing—a burden the minority shareholders failed to meet. Since all of Sinven's shareholders (minority and majority) received the same proportionate share of dividends plaintiffs did not meet its burden of showing self-dealing. The dividend policy was thus afforded the presumption of propriety under the business judgment rule.

While the Delaware benefit and determent test is now the majority rule many professors also discuss the minority rule, sometimes called the "California rule" and the distinction between the two rules. In *Jones v. H.F. Ahmanson & Co.*, the California Supreme Court imposed the burden of showing intrinsic fairness on the majority if the transaction (1) causes harm to the minority shareholders or (2) enables the majority shareholder to obtain an exclusive benefit.

In sum, the distinction is that in Delaware minority shareholders must show **both** a benefit and determent to impose the burden of proving intrinsic fairness on the controlling majority shareholder, while in California the minority can impose this burden on the controlling majority shareholder by showing **either a benefit** to the majority **or a determent** to the minority.

3. FIDUCIARY DUTIES IN FREEZE OUT MERGER TRANSACTIONS

Statutory mergers are one of three ways in which two or more corporations may combine. The corporate statutes of every state contain provisions which allow two or more corporations to merge into a single corporate entity. In general, statutory mergers are accomplished by the formulation of a plan of merger) which is approved by the boards and shareholders of both parties to the merger. We will learn more about mergers in Chapter X.

For now, we need to learn how merger statutes can be used to eliminate the interests of minority shareholders. Such mergers are called "freeze out," "squeeze out" or "cash out" mergers. In these freeze out mergers, the majority typically has enough votes to approve the transaction even if the minority objects.

The end result of a "freeze out" merger is that the minority shareholders receive cash for their interests and the majority shareholder ends up owning 100% of the equity. Obviously, whenever the minority interest is eliminated through a freeze out merger, minority stockholders are entitled to receive a fair price for their shares.

Freeze out mergers present a clear conflict of interest and have obvious potential for abuse, because the majority shareholder (usually though not always a parent corporation) wants to pay the minority shareholders as little as possible for their interests. Thus, freeze out mergers frequently generate litigation. While these transactions have been challenged in Federal courts under the SEC's proxy rules (as we learned in Chapter VI—see, *e.g., J.I. Case v. Borak*) and under Rule 10b-5 (as we will learn in Chapter VIII—see, *e.g., Sante Fe v. Green),* today the minority shareholders' most likely remedy will be an action in state court for violation of fiduciary duties.

Weinberger v. UOP, Inc., a decision handed down by the Delaware Supreme Court in 1983 and found in most casebooks, is a major decision in this area. Signal, which owned 50.5% of UOP's outstanding stock, decided to acquire the remaining 49.5% of the stock held by minority shareholders in exchange for cash.

Arledge and Chitea, two Signal employees who sat on the UOP board, did a feasibility study in which they concluded that acquiring the remainder of the UOP stock at up to $24 a share would be a good investment for Signal. Signal offered $21 a share for the minority interest based on a fairness opinion prepared by Lehmann Brothers. At the time the UOP stock was trading in the range of $14 to $15 per share. The 6 non-Signal directors met and approved the plan of merger (the 7 Signal directors abstained). Later the merger was also approved by a majority of the minority shareholders of UOP.

Weinberger, a minority shareholder of UOP, sued Signal, UOP and various directors for breach of fiduciary duty toward minority shareholders. He alleged in a class action that he and other minority shareholders were not paid enough for their shares.

The lower court held for the defendants, but the Delaware Supreme Court reversed and remanded. In its opinion the Delaware Supreme Court established what has come to be known as the "**entire fairness test**." The two prongs of the entire fairness test are: **fair dealing** and **fair price**. The court held that this acquisition failed both prongs of the test.

In holding that the UOP acquisition failed the fair dealing prong of the entire fairness test the Delaware Supreme Court considered:

■ The unreasonable time constraints placed on the UOP board (the deal initiated by Signal was presented to and approved by the UOP board in four business days).

■ Lehman's fairness opinion, which was prepared on a hurry up basis at the request of Signal

■ Less than full disclosure, because Arledge and Chitea's feasibility in which they concluded a price of $24 per share would have been feasible, was not shared with the UOP board or shareholders.

The court also held that this deal failed the fair price prong of the test. The lower court used the so called "Delaware Block Method" for assessing the value of the UOP shares. That method uses weighted averages of various elements (including earnings and assets) in arriving at per share value of the minority shareholders shares. While the court criticized the Delaware Block Method as too rigid and outmoded, it did not suggest an alternative method of valuation. The court did, however, hold that the Delaware Block Method was no longer exclusive and that any method of valuation generally considered acceptable in the financial community, including the discounted cash flow method used by investment bankers, could be considered.

Today the entire fairness test is not limited to freeze out merger cases. In Delaware, it is used in other cases involving transactions subject to fairness review. This test has also been adopted by courts in a number of other states.

4. SALE OF CONTROL

Another type of transaction in which issues relating to a control shareholder's fiduciary duties arise is the sale of control. For example, assume that the stock of ABC Corporation is trading at $12 a share. Harry owns 51% of ABC's stock. The remaining 49% is owned by numerous public shareholders. Joe wants to buy control of ABC. Joe agrees to pay Harry $20 a share for his controlling interest in ABC. The $8 per share over and above the market price is called a **control premium**.

A control premium is the excess over and above the market value of a block of stock that comes with controlling the corporation's business.   Control is a valuable commodity. It is the key to the corporation's treasury, assets and earning power. Common sense tells us that control may be worth a premium.

The question raised by the example is: Does Harry have to share the $8 a share he received as a control premium with the minority shareholders?

As a general rule, the answer to the question is **no**. The mere fact a control shareholder gets a premium for his control stock does not in and of itself create a cause of action in favor of the corporation or the minority shareholders. A shareholder can sell his stock for whatever price he can get for the stock, including a control premium, subject to certain exceptions.

The exceptions are situations recognized by the case law, where the sale of control may violate fiduciary duties owed by the controlling shareholder to the corporation or the minority shareholders. Violations of those duties may result in the minority shareholders becoming entitled to share pro rata in the control premium or having a cause of action against the control shareholder.

What are the three main exceptions to the general rule?

(1)   A control person cannot sell to a person he has reason to believe will loot the corporation;
(2)   A control person cannot divert a corporate opportunity to himself; and
(3)   A control person cannot improperly sell corporate offices to the buyer.

a. Sale to Looters

A control person cannot sell control of the corporation to persons she has reason to believe will loot the

corporation.   Since there are not many buyers who
announce that they want to buy control of the company so
they can loot it, the issue in these cases usually boils down
to a question as to the scope of the duty of reasonable
inquiry.

DeBaun v. First Western Bank & Trust Co. is a classic
example of a looting case, found in most of the casebooks.
Johnson, the founder of a successful close corporation,
owned 70 of the 100 outstanding shares. When Johnson
died, the Bank, as Johnson's executor, sold his shares to a
company controlled by Mattison, who looted the
corporation. In about a year he turned a corporation with
a positive net worth of $220,000 into one with a negative
net worth of $218,000—a negative turn-around of about
$450,000.

The bank failed to adequately investigate the buyer,
Mattison. Public records in Los Angeles County revealed
a mass of information on Mattison, including 38
unsatisfied judgements (some for fraud). An investigation
would have revealed that Mattison could not pay the
purchase price for the shares without dipping into the
corporation's assets and retained earnings. The bank
simply failed to adequately investigate.

The minority shareholders DeBaun and Stephans, who
owned 20 and 10 shares, respectively, sued the bank. They
recovered $473,836 from the Bank on a derivative theory
(in favor of the corporation). The manner in which
damages were computed is interesting. They recovered the
net asset value of the Corporation when Mattison bought
in, plus an amount equal to anticipated after-tax earnings

and the sum required to pay existing claims incurred while Mattison was running (looting) the company. In a looting case, if the plaintiff can prove specific damages she can recover either from the looter or the former controlling shareholder, who sold to the looter. Here, since the Bank sold to a looter without making a reasonable investigation, it was liable for all damages proximately caused by its breach of duty.

b. Diverting a Corporate Opportunity

A control shareholder who diverts a corporate opportunity, in which all shareholders might have shared, to himself violates his fiduciary duties and may have to share the control premium with minority shareholders.

Logic and basic notions of fairness support this rule. So does the case law. The case included in most of the casebooks to illustrate the application of this rule is the widely cited case of *Perlman v. Feldmann*. The opinion is less than a model of clarity, and scholars have been debating the exact basis for the holding for years.

The relevant facts were that Feldmann and members of his family owned approximately 37% of the outstanding stock of Newport Steel Corporation, a publicly held company. Feldmann was also the president and chairman of the board of Newport Steel. His status as a control person was not disputed in the case.

Newport manufactured steel, which during the Korean war was in short supply. The buyer, Wilport Company, a syndicate of end users of steel products, wanted to acquire a dependable new source of supply. There was evidence that Wilport or another potential buyer had proposed to acquire Newport through a plan of acquisition in which all of Newport's shareholders (majority as well as minority) would have participated. For purposes of this discussion we assume that the original proposal was tantamount to an offer to acquire all of Newport's outstanding stock.

Feldmann rejected that proposal. He made a counter proposal, under which he agreed to sell Wilport his 37% controlling interest in Newport for $20 per share. That price included an $8 per share control premium over and above the than current market price of about $12 per share. Minority shareholders, who did not participate in the deal brought a shareholders' derivative suit. Reversing the Federal district court, the Second Circuit held that Feldmann had violated his fiduciary duty to the minority shareholders and required him to share his control premium with the minority shareholders.

The opinion contains several broad statements, some of which, as pointed out in the dissent, do not accurately express the law of fiduciary duties and there has been lively scholarly debate over just what the grounds for this decision were. However, if one characterizes the facts as supporting the premise that Feldmann, a control person, in some way diverted a corporate opportunity to his own benefit, the decision appears sound, irrespective of its confusing language.

c. Sale of Directorships

All courts give lip service to the rule that it is unlawful for directors to sell their seats on the board. However, it is quite common following the sale of control for directors to resign from the board and appoint persons nominated by the buyer of control to succeed them. Often, such resignations are an express condition to closing the sale. This is not surprising because control of the board is usually a big part of what the buyer has bought.

Often following the sale of control, the change in the composition of the board occurs through the process of seriatim resignations. A current member of the board resigns, and the remaining board members (using their power to fill vacancies) appoints one of the buyer's nominees to fill the vacancy. Then a second director resigns and so on until all of the buyer's nominees have replaced the existing board members. Most courts allow this process, which clears the way for the new controlling shareholder to take charge of the company. Otherwise, the new controlling shareholder would have to either wait until the next annual meeting of shareholders or call a special meeting of shareholders to replace the old board.

Such arrangements are generally upheld unless the plaintiff can show an obvious sale of directorship such as: (1) an agreement to resign in exchange for cash, (2) an agreement to buy the resigning director's stock at a higher price if she will resign from the board or (3) that the buyer did not acquire sufficient control to elect his own slate of directors, absent agreements by the present directors to resign, for which the buyer in some way paid.

C. FIDUCIARY DUTIES OF PARTNERS

The scope of the fiduciary duties owed by partners to the partnership and to each other is broader than the scope of the fiduciary duties owed by directors, officers or control shareholders to their corporations and its shareholders. The common law foundation on which partners' fiduciary duties rest was established in 1928 in the landmark decision of *Meinhard v. Salmon.*

In that case, in one of the most frequently cited and influential passages in partnership or corporate law, Justice Cardozo described the scope of a partner's fiduciary duties as follows:

Copartners, owe to one another, while the enterprise continues, the duty of finest loyalty. Many forms of conduct permissible in a workaday world for those acting at arm's length, are forbidden to those bound by fiduciary ties. . . . Not honesty alone, but the punctilio of an honor the most sensitive, is then the standard of behavior. . . .

Today, Cardozo's famous "punctilio of an honor" statement is viewed by many scholars as a bit too extreme and indefinite to represent a workable standard for defining the duties of persons in a partnership relationship. Such duties are now generally characterized as duties of "utmost good faith," "loyalty" and "care." The scope of these duties is further refined in § 404 of RUPA. Under § 404, the duty of loyalty prohibits misappropriation of partnership property, usurpation of partnership opportunities, having an interest adverse to the partnership or competing with the partnership. The standard imposed by the duty of care is gross negligence. And partners have an obligation of good faith and fair dealing in the discharge of all of their partnership duties. Finally, these duties may not be waived or eliminated in the partnership agreement, but the partnership agreement may set standards which can be used in defining the scope and evaluating the performance of these duties.

D. FIDUCIARY DUTIES IN CLOSE CORPORATIONS

Directors, officers and control shareholders of close corporations are obviously subject to at least the traditional fiduciary duties of corporate directors, officers and control shareholders discussed in § VII.A and B, *supra.* The overarching question in this section is:

Are directors, officers and control shareholders in "close corporations" subject to stricter fiduciary duties than those imposed on directors, officers and control shareholders generally?

An analysis of the differences in the way "close" and "public" corporations are governed (See generally § VI.B.2, *supra*) and the differences in the nature of the problems typically faced by shareholders of close and public corporations, leads to the conclusion that the answer to this question should be yes. As discussed in the preceding chapter, the primary dangers faced by minority shareholders in close corporations are (1) the **liquidity problem** (no ready market for their shares) and (2) the

threat of **oppression** and **freeze out** (minority shareholders
are usually employed by the corporation and often depend
on that employment for their livelihood).

For example, assume *A*, *B* and *C* start a business which
they incorporate as ABC, Inc. *A*, *B* and *C* each own 33.3%
of the corporation's voting stock and each is employed by
the corporation. As is typical of close corporations ABC,
Inc. pays no dividends, but most of the company's current
earnings are distributed to the owners through payment of
salaries and perks, such as retirement benefits. There is
a disagreement and *A* and *B* remove *C* from the board.
They then fire *C* as an employee of ABC, Inc. Following
*C*s termination of employment, *A* and *B* continue their
policy of paying no dividends and distributing most of the
company's earning to themselves through salaries and
perks. In this situation, *C* would have a hard time making
a case that *A* and *B* violated the traditional duties of care
or loyalty, which do not prohibit *A* and *B* from doing what
they have done[1].

If the parties had organized their business as a
partnership, *C*s removal would have triggered an action
for accounting of partnership profits and payment for his
partnership interest. Neither the MBCA or state corporate
statutes contain provisions which obligate a corporation to
repurchase stock form a shareholder similar to the
provisions applicable to partnership dissociation contained

1. *C*'s principal remedy would be a proceeding for involuntary dissolution,
discussed earlier in §VI.B.3.d.(2). Also, absent an employment contract, under the
employment at will rule an employee (including an employee-shareholders) may be
dismissed at any time with or without cause.

in § 601 of RUPA, which we will learn about in Chapter X. In recent years some courts have recognized partnership-like fiduciary duties among participants in close corporations.

A case, which is in most casebooks because of its discussion of the similarities between close corporations and partnerships is *Donahue v. Rodd Electrotype Co.* In *Donahue*, the plaintiff was the widow of a long-time employee of the company, who over the years had acquired 50 shares of the company's stock. The remaining 198 shares were owned by Harry Rodd and his three sons.[2] The sons had taken over management of the company, Harry, age 77, was ready to retire, but he wanted some money. The corporation agreed to buy 45 of Harry's shares for $800 per share (the book value of the shares). The widow Donahue tendered her 50 shares to the corporation, demanding that it buy her shares at the same price as it bought Harry's shares. When the corporation refused, she sued, alleging breach of fiduciary duty to a minority shareholder.

The lower courts, noting that the purchase of Harry's stock was in good faith and at a fair price, held for defendant. The Supreme Court of Massachusetts reversed, and in so doing, established what is known as the "**equal access rule**." The court specifically limits application of the equal access rule to close corporations, as defined in its opinion. Under the equal access rule controlling shareholders owe a fiduciary duty to minority shareholders

---

2. Harry owned 81 shares and the sons owned 36 shares each.

to give them an equal opportunity to sell their shares to the corporation on the same terms as the controlling shareholder.   As a remedy the court allowed the corporation to choose between buying Donahue's shares at $800 per share or rescinding the agreement to buy Harry's stock at that price.

Shortly after *Donahue,* the Supreme Court of Massachusetts rendered another important decision on the scope of fiduciary duties in close corporations. In *Wilkes v. Springside Nursing Home, Inc.* the court both affirmed the general concept underlying *Donahue* and, at the same time limited its application.

Wilkes involved a classic close corporation squeeze-out. Four individuals were equal owners of a corporation that owned and operated a nursing home.   All four were directors and employees of the corporation.   The corporation paid no dividends, but paid equal salaries to each of the four owners for work performed at the nursing home.   Wilkes had a falling out with the other three shareholders.   They removed Wilkes from the board and fired him as an employee.   Wilkes sued for breach of fiduciary duties.

The Massachusetts Supreme Court tempered the scope of its ruling in *Donahue* by fashioning a balancing test. The court stated that in certain "legitimate spheres" such as employment matters, dividends, etc., the majority has discretion to manage the business in the way it sees fit, even if minority shareholders are harmed in the process. The *Wilkes* holding requires that the majority must show a legitimate business purpose for its action (*i.e.,* firing

Wilkes). If the majority meets its burden, the burden than shifts to the minority to show that the objective sought to be achieved by the majority in taking the action it took could have been accomplished in a manner less harmful to the minority's interests.

Under *Wilkes*, it is then up to the court to balance the majority's business objective against the practicality of accomplishing the objective in a manner less harmful to the minority's interests. In *Wilkes* the controlling shareholders were unable to show a legitimate business purpose for firing Wilkes, and thus the court never reached the balancing issue.

Not all jurisdictions agree with the view that shareholders in closely held corporations owe one another expanded fiduciary duties in the nature of those owed by partners to each other. The Delaware Supreme Court rejected this notion in *Nixon v. Blackwell*, a case with facts similar to those in *Donahue.* In *Nixon,* a closely held corporation through its employee stock ownership plan and key man life insurance provided employee-shareholders the opportunity to cash out their ownership interests in the corporation on death or retirement. Non-employee shareholders, who lacked any market for their shares sued. The trial court held that providing liquidity for employee-shareholders, while not providing similar liquidity to non-employee shareholders, constituted a breach of fiduciary duty. The Delaware Supreme Court reversed stating that it would be inappropriate for courts to create ad hoc rules to protect minority shareholders, which were not provided for in the statute or otherwise contracted for.

Bottom line. Some states have embraced the notion of expanded fiduciary duties in close corporations, as reflected in *Donahue* and other cases, while other have not. Most states have not yet ruled one way or the other. This is an emerging issue and the depth to which you will be required to understand this issue in your basic business course will depend on the emphasis placed on same by your professor.

Professors who emphasize this area may be trying to make a point about basic process. Historically, the law of fiduciary duties was developed (and as a work in progress is being developed) by the courts under two separate models: (1) The **corporate model** where the main concern was the scope of the duties of care and loyalty owed by directors and officers to the corporate entity and (2) the **partnership model** where the main concern was with the way the partners treat one another. The close corporation is a hybrid and the courts are trying to develop workable rules that govern relationships in this hybrid by borrowing from both the corporate and the partnership models.

E. FIDUCIARY DUTIES IN AN LLC

If, as suggested in the last section, the scope of fiduciary duties in close corporations are not yet fully developed, by comparison, the scope of fiduciary duties owed by members and managers of LLCs could be described as being in an embryonic stage. It is beyond the scope of this book to speculate on how this embryo will develop in the years to come. We can identify the principal issues likely to play out as the courts and legislatures go through the difficult process of defining the scope of fiduciary duties in LLCs. Key issues will likely involve:

(1) The diversity of the LLC statutes;
(2) The impact of provisions in the operating agreement on the scope of fiduciary duties; and
(3) Whether the courts choose to follow a corporate or partnership model in defining the scope of fiduciary duties in LLCs.

Diversity of LLC statutes. LLC statutes vary widely in the way they describe the fiduciary duties owed by members and managers of LLCs. And because LLCs are so new there are no definitive judicial decisions that establish clear cut criteria for defining the scope of such duties.

The Uniform Limited Liability Company Act ("ULLCA") in § 409 expressly provides for fiduciary duties in a manner similar to § 404 of RUPA. ULLCA § 409(b) limits the duty of loyalty to (1) accounting to the LLC for any property or profit derived in conducting or winding up the business, (2) refraining from dealing with the LLC while having an interest adverse to the LLC and (3) refraining from competing with the LLC. In § 409(c) the duty of care is limited to gross negligence or reckless conduct, intentional misconduct or a knowing violation of the law. Members in member-managed LLCs and managers in manager managed LLCs are both subject to these duties. Finally, ULLCA § 103 limits the manner in which the scope of fiduciary duties may be limited or modified in the operating agreement.

In sharp contrast to the ULLCA, the Delaware Limited
Liability Company Act ("DLLCA") does not specify any
fiduciary duties for members or manager and expressly
states that maximum effect will be given to freedom of
contract.   See § 18-1101(b).   Section 18-1101(c)(2)
specifically states that "[t]he member's or manager's or
other person's duties may be expanded or restricted by
provisions in a limited liability agreement." While we
know of no Delaware case law interpreting this provision,
a recent Delaware Supreme Court decision, *Elf Atochem
North America v. Jaffari*, suggests that under DLLCA the
parties may be able to eliminate fiduciary duties.

Delaware and the ULLCA represent opposite ends of a
wide spectrum of ways the in which the LLC statutes of
the various states define the scope of fiduciary duties. The
ULLCA has not been widely accepted and there is much
variation in the way the state LLC statutes deal with the
scope of fiduciary duties. Obviously, a higher degree of
uniformity would be desirable.

The impact of the operating agreement. Over half the
state LLC statutes provide that the scope of fiduciary
duties may be modified or eliminated by provisions in the
operating agreement.   This is in sharp contrast to
partnership law. Recall that in partnerships, the partners
can contract around most of the default rules in the UPA
or RUPA, but they cannot eliminate their fiduciary duties
by provisions in the partnership agreement.

A number of state LLC statutes contain provisions,
similar to Delaware § 18-1101(c), which allow the
operating agreement to modify or define the fiduciary

duties of members or managers without restriction. If read literally and fully enforced by the courts, provisions such as Delaware § 18-1101(c) would permit LLCs to operate free of any fiduciary duties. Your authors, being part of a generation of lawyers steeped in the tradition of *Meinhard v. Salmon*, have some difficulty with the concept of allowing the parties unfettered ability to restrict or eliminate fiduciary duties in situations where such duties are necessary to prevent injustice.

The model applicable to LLCs. Finally, the question raised in § VII.D., *supra*, relative to the scope of fiduciary duties in close corporations, is equally applicable to LLCs. That question is: *If fiduciary duties are imposed by the courts in LLCs, will they be modeled after the fiduciary duties imposed on officers and directors of a corporation or on those imposed on partners?*

Some writers have suggested that corporate-type fiduciary duties should be imposed on managers of manager-managed LLCs while partnership-type fiduciaries should be imposed on members of member-managed LLCs. This suggestion seems over simplistic, particularly in view of the fact that virtually all LLCs are closely-held businesses. More importantly, it seems premature to discuss this issue until the two other issues, previously discussed, are more clearly defined.

Bottom line. Since your professor is not likely to know what the scope of fiduciary duties in LLCs is, it is not likely that she will expect you to know. However, she may well expect you to understand the issues and see the analogies between LLCs and the older forms of business structures because the courts and legislatures are likely to draw from corporation and/or partnership law in developing rules for LLCs.

About all we can say at this stage of development is that the scope of fiduciary duties in a specific LLC will depend on two questions:

(1) what does the governing state statute say and
(2) what does the governing operating agreement say?

F. HOW ARE VIOLATIONS OF FIDUCIARY DUTIES ENFORCED?
(herein Shareholders' Derivative Suits)

1. THE GOVERNANCE DILEMMA

We have seen that directors and officers owe fiduciary duties to the corporation, the breach of which gives rise to a cause of action in favor of the corporation. We have also seen that the power of management, vested in the directors and officers, includes the power to bring law suits to redress injuries suffered by the corporation.

Most derivative litigation involves claims that directors or officers breached fiduciary duties owed to the corporation. When these duties are breached the corporation (an entity separate and apart from the officers and directors who manage it and the shareholders who own it) is hurt and has a right to sue. But when the claim is against the directors or officers themselves, the law cannot trust the officers and directors to authorize the corporation to sue because they have an obvious conflict of interest. If the officers and directors elected to sue, they would, in effect, be electing to sue themselves.

2. THE GENERAL NATURE OF A SHAREHOLDERS' DERIVATIVE SUIT

To deal with this "governance dilemma," courts of equity many years ago developed a procedural device called the "**shareholders' derivative suit.**" This is a action in which an individual shareholder (who under normal circumstances would not have authority to authorize the corporation to sue) sues on behalf of the corporation. The cause of action belongs to the corporation and, with rare exceptions, any recovery belongs to the corporation. The shareholder merely serves as the self-appointed enforcer of a corporate right.

Conceptually, a shareholders' derivative suit is two suits in one: (*Suit One*) the shareholder sues the corporation, in equity, seeking to force the corporation to (*Suit Two*) bring suit against the directors and officers for violating their fiduciary duties. Today, both suits are consolidated into one action, but thinking in terms of the historical notion of two suits in one, makes the conceptual framework and peculiar procedures of a shareholders' derivative suits easier to understand.

Who are the necessary parties?

Obviously, the plaintiff is the shareholder attempting to vindicate a wrong done to the corporation. The directors and officers, who allegedly breached their fiduciary duties, are, of course, defendants. But the corporation must be also be a party to the case. In derivative litigation, not only is the corporation an indispensable party, it is on both sides of the case—both a plaintiff and a defendant, as follows, to wit:

Plaintiffs: Shareholder & Corporation v. ***Defendants***: Corporation & *A, B, C, D* & *E* (directors).

Often the corporation is called a **nominal** defendant and the individual directors, who allegedly breached their fiduciary duties, are called the **real** defendants.

There are two legal reasons that the corporation has to be both a plaintiff and a defendant: (1) As an entity affected by the judgement the corporation must be before the court and (2) joining the corporation ensures that the judgment will be res judicia against the corporation.

What is the difference between a derivative suit and a direct suit and why is it necessary to distinguish?

There are two types of suits shareholders can bring against their corporation—**direct suits** and **derivative suits**. As we have already pointed out **derivative suits** are suits in which the shareholder asserts a corporate cause of action and seeks recovery on behalf of the corporation. Examples are suits for breach of fiduciary duties owed to the corporation by directors, officers or control persons.

Direct suits, on the other hand, are suits in which a shareholder sues the corporation to enforce her rights as a shareholder. Recovery in a direct suit belongs to the shareholder, either individually or as representative of shareholders similarly situated. Examples include suits to protect voting rights, to compel payment of dividends, to redress fraud on shareholders by the purchase or sale of securities, to compel dissolution of the corporation, etc.

The distinction is clear in most cases, even in cases where both the corporation and the shareholders are harmed by the directors acts or omissions. For example, assume the directors are grossly negligent and as a result the business of the corporation is severely harmed. In that situation the shareholders will also probably suffer harm since the value of their shares will likely decline as a result of the directors negligence. However, courts have generally held that shareholders can not bring direct actions for decline in the value of their shares resulting from harm to the corporation.

Sometimes the distinction can get blurred. If the essence of the claim is indirect damage suffered by the shareholder resulting from director conduct that harms the corporation, the action is derivative. On the other hand, if the essence of the shareholder's claim is that the directors actions directly impacted her rights as a shareholder, the action will be classified as direct, even though conduct complained of also had an adverse impact on the corporation. This distinction can be subtle and, in part, may depend on how the shareholder pleads her case.

For example, in *Smith v. Van Gorkom*, discussed earlier, the plaintiff complained that the directors breached their duty of care by voting to accept a merger proposal under which shareholders would receive $55 per share for their stock. The suit was not about the impact of the directors' decision on the corporation's future operations or profitability. Instead, the suit focused on whether the shareholders could have received a price higher than $55 for their shares. Thus, the linchpin of the suit went to the value of the shareholders' shares and the shareholder were allowed to bring a direct suit.

Eisenberg v. Flying Tiger Line, Inc. was an even closer case. There a shareholder challenged a corporate reorganization in which shareholders in an operating company became shareholder in a holding company. The court allowed this suit to be brought as a direct action because the reorganization deprived the shareholder of any voice in the affairs of the operating company. This case contains a good judicial discussion of the basic differences between direct and derivative litigation, which is why this case is found in most casebooks.

The *Eisenberg* case also illustrates why the direct/ derivative distinction is important. Since the suit was classified as a direct action, the plaintiff did not have to post a security for costs bond. There are a number of procedural hoops that plaintiffs must jump through in derivative suits that go away if the case can be brought as a direct suit. We will discuss the main procedural requirements in derivative litigation later.

What is a class action and how does it compare with a derivative suit?

A class action is a direct suit, not a derivative suit. Derivative suits and class actions are different procedural devices used to assert different types of substantive claims. In a class action, a representative of the class is suing on his own behalf and on behalf of others with the same claim (*i.e.,* similarly situated). All members of the class are asserting personal claims; no one is asserting a claim on behalf of the corporation. Class action law suits are governed by a different set of procedural rules, which are outside the scope of the basic business course and this book. Class actions are covered in procedure courses such as complex litigation.

Class actions share one common characteristic with shareholders' derivative suits. In both, a litigant is representing someone else. This common characteristic makes them both controversial. Just as all members of the class have an interest in a class action because they all share in the recovery, all shareholders of a corporation have an interest in the outcome of a shareholders' derivative suit because whatever the corporation recovers at least in theory inures to the shareholders' benefit. The following examples illustrate what class actions and shareholders' derivative suits have in common and why both are controversial.

Class action: Suppose an item is subject to price controls. You buy that item and later find out the company overcharged you by $10. That might make you angry, but no rational person would bring a lawsuit for $10.

But if a lawyer notices that you are one of 2 million customers who were overcharged by $10, the economics change dramatically—your $10 claim becomes a potential claim for $20 million.

Shareholders' derivative suit: Exactly the same economics drive shareholders' derivative suits. *X*, who owns 200 shares of IBM sues IBM derivatively and gets a judgement for $100 million.   IBM has millions of shareholders and hundreds of millions of shares outstanding.   Thus the pro rata share of the $100M judgement which would inure to *X*'s benefit as one of several million IBM shareholders would be quite small.

<u>Why would a plaintiff take the time and trouble to sue in either case when her stake in the recovery is so small?</u>

The obvious answer is **attorney's fees**. Attorney's fees are the economic engine that drives both class actions and shareholders' derivative suits. To understand the process you need to understand the concept of **entrepreneurial litigation**. In most cases a lawyer learns of a potential derivative claim or class action and "finds" a client to serve as plaintiff.

The plaintiff's attorney acts as a combination bounty hunter and independent entrepreneur who performs the function of deterring undesirable conduct in corporate America.   The lawyer, not the client, controls the case, finances the case and (by comparison to the recovery of the actual individual client) the lawyer gets most what is recovered.   The entrepreneurial aspect of this type of litigation is very real.   The lawyer must finance the case. Usually, these cases require a tremendous investment not just in time but also in money by the lawyer. Thus, to be successful, an entrepreneurial lawyer has to know how to pick good cases and has to be good at what he does. Successful lawyers in this area are the highest paid lawyers in the world.

3. PROCEDURAL REQUIREMENTS IN SHAREHOLDERS' DERIVATIVE SUITS

a. The Demand Requirement

The demand requirement is the key derivative litigation requirement. While modern procedural rules governing the demand requirement vary in detail from state to state, the bottom line is that the plaintiff must allege that he has made a demand on the board of directors to bring suit or state with some particularity why the demand was excused. The conceptual foundation on which the demand requirement rests is the governance dilemma discussed above. It gives the board of directors which is charged with managing the corporation, an opportunity to decide whether it is in the corporation's best interest to sue.

How does the demand requirement play out?

Plaintiff must make a demand on the directors. Few, if any, states specify a specific format for the demand. Usually the plaintiff writes a letter to the board of directors demanding that they bring suit.   The letter typically alleges a wrong and the relevant facts supporting the allegation in much the same way as is done in a complaint. When the board receives plaintiff's demand letter, they have two obvious choices:

(1) Accept the demand—bring suit or

(2) Reject the demand—not sue.

If the board **accepts** the demand and decides to sue there is, of course, no need for the derivative suit. The board will hire its own lawyer and take over the suit.

If the board **rejects** the demand and can show that the rejection was "**in good faith**" and "**by an independent board**" then the derivative suit cannot go forward. The decision to reject the demand is given the presumption of propriety under the business judgement rule.   Unless plaintiff can show that there was a conflict of interest or no rational basis for rejecting the demand, the derivative suit cannot go forward.

So, if he makes a demand, plaintiff's attorney is likely to find himself in a catch 22. If the board accepts the demand, he loses control of the case (and the opportunity to earn the attorneys fee which drives these cases). If the board rejects the demand he is faced with the tough burden of overcoming the business judgement rule. He must show that the board was not independent (for example, a majority of the directors were involved in the wrongdoing) or that there was no rational basis for the decision not to sue. Thus, plaintiff often tries to get around the demand requirement by **showing excuse**.

When can the demand be excused?

The main ground for excusing demand is **futility**. The case of *Marx v. Akers* surveys the three major approaches to excusing demands. Before we discuss the New York

approach (reflected in *Marx)* we will discuss the other two
approaches discussed in the *Marx* opinion.

The Delaware approach was set out in *Aronson v.
Lewis*, a shareholders' derivative suit in which the plaintiff
sued all of the directors of Meyers Parking Systems, Inc.
The suit alleged that a 5 year employment contract with
Fink, a 75-year-old retiring director, who owned 47% of the
stock of Myers, provided excessive compensation and
sought cancellation of the contract. Plaintiff did not make
a demand on the board before filing suit. The complaint
alleged that demand would be futile because all the
directors approved the transaction, and all were chosen
and dominated by Fink.

In holding that plaintiff's complaint failed to allege
adequate facts to excuse the demand, the Delaware
Supreme Court articulated a test which has come to be
known as the "Delaware two-part test" for determining
futility:

> Demand is excused if the plaintiff can state with
> particularity, facts that create a reasonable doubt (1)
> that a majority of the directors on whom demand
> would have been made are disinterested or (2) that
> the challenged transaction was protected by the
> business judgement rule.

In other words, to prevail under the Delaware two part
test, plaintiff must point to specific facts (before discovery)
that tend to show either that (1) the board is not
disinterested or independent or (2) the underlying
transaction was improper as tested under the business

judgment rule. This is the approach taken by the majority of states today.

The Model Act approach. The model act adopts a **universal demand** approach. MBCA § 7.42 requires that a plaintiff wanting to file a shareholders' derivative suit must always first make a written demand on the board of directors (called a universal demand). The plaintiff must then wait 90 days after making the demand to bring suit, unless the board rejects the demand sooner or the wait would cause irreparable harm to the corporation.

After the 90-day waiting period expires, the shareholder can bring a derivative suit. If the board rejected the demand, plaintiff must plead particular facts that show either the board was not disinterested or that the rejection was not in good faith (similar to the *Aronson*). See MBCA § 7.44.

The New York approach was articulated in *Marx v. Akers*, a derivative suit with facts similar to *Aronson*, against IBM's board of directors. The IBM board consisted of 18 directors, 15 were outside directors and the remaining 3 were inside directors (employees of IBM). The suit was for corporate waste (violation of the duty of care resulting from payment of excessive compensation to the IBM executives). The court held that the 3 inside directors were tainted by self-interest and implicitly held that a demand on these 3 would be futile and thus excused. But the court went on to hold that the remaining 15 directors were not tainted and since they comprised a majority of the board, demand was not excused.

After surveying the Delaware and Universal Demand approaches discussed above, the *Marx* court rejected both and adopted the following approach for New York. In New York, demand is excused if any of the following is alleged with particularity in the complaint:

(1)   A majority of the board is interested in the challenged deal;

(2)   The board did not fully inform itself about the challenged deal; or

(3)   The challenged deal was so unfair on its face that it could not have been the product of sound business judgment.

b. The Special Litigation Committee

The **special litigation committee** rests on the same conceptual foundation as the demand requirement: namely, preservation, to the extent possible, of the governance role of the board in deciding whether the corporation should bring a lawsuit.

What is the special litigation committee and how does it work?

The special litigation committee rests on the application of basic principles of corporate governance. The corporate statutes in all states authorize the board to select from their members smaller groups—called committees—to deal with a specific area—*e.g.*, compensation committee, acquisition committee, etc. Based on this notion, in the 1970s clever corporate attorneys came up with a way for the "innocent" minority of directors to make the decision whether the corporation should sue the other board members. The board creates a committee consisting of some or all of the directors not implicated in the alleged wrong and delegates to that committee the power to decide if the corporation should pursue a lawsuit against the majority.

The committee composition is critical. Often, the committee is composed of people who were not directors at the time of the alleged wrongdoing. It is always composed of individuals who were in no way involved in the alleged wrongdoing. The special litigation committee typically hires counsel to investigate the facts that lead to the derivative suit. The committee commonly takes months to investigate the facts and evaluate the merits of the case, the projected costs, the potential benefits to the corporation, etc. They incorporate their findings into a report which they submit to the court along with the committee's recommendation as to whether the suit should be continued or terminated—couched in terms of the best interests of the corporation.

You can assume that the special litigation committee's recommendation is to dismiss the law suit. Studies have shown that dismissal is almost always the committee's recommendation. The attorney for the corporation then makes a motion to dismiss based on the committee's recommendation. This raises the following question:

How does the court respond to a motion to dismiss the shareholders' derivative suit, backed by a recommendation of the special litigation committee?

Obviously, you have to be a little skeptical as to whether the special litigation committee is truly unbiased and whether its recommendation is based solely on what is in the corporation's best interest. Directors are, after all, judging their fellow directors. This concern over the special litigation committee's true independence coupled with other policy concerns inherent in the special litigation committee technique has resulted in a diversity of judicial approaches to the above question. The three main approaches are as follows:

The New York approach. *Auerbach v. Bennett* states the rule followed in New York. Unless the plaintiff can prove that the special litigation committee lacked independence or failed to operate on an informed basis, the committee's recommendation is entitled to the presumption of propriety afforded by the business judgement rule. In other words, if the committee systematically follows proper procedures—*i.e.,* meets regularly, systematically reviews the facts, relies on options of independent counsel, make a detailed record, etc.—and has a rational basis for their decision—*e.g.,* the potential claim lacks merit, litigation expenses might exceed potential gains to the corporation, the suit would create bad publicity for the corporation or damage employee moral, etc.—the court will follow the committee's recommendation and dismiss the suit.

This approach, called the Auerbach Rule is the approach most favorable to the defendants. It was the majority view from the 1970s, but many courts have now retreated from this position.

The Iowa approach. A few states have followed the Iowa decision in *Miller v. Tribune Syndicate, Inc.* and adopted a simple approach favorable to the plaintiff. This approach basically states that if the board is disqualified from recommending dismissal, than any committee appointed by that board would be likewise disqualified. This is clearly a minority rule.

The Delaware approach. In 1981 in *Zapata v. Maldonado*, the Delaware Supreme Court adopted an approach between the two extremes discussed above. It has now clearly emerged as the majority rule.

The *Zapata* case was a shareholders' derivative suit against the entire board of directors of Zapata Corporation for self-dealing. Plaintiff alleged that the board moved up the expiration date of some options so that the directors could exercise the options and save taxes, thus enriching themselves at the expense of the corporation.

Four years into the suit, the board appointed directors, who were not on the board when the wrongdoing occurred, to be a special litigation committee. The committee conducted an investigation and recommended that the suit be dismissed.

Zapata established a two part test to determine whether or not a special litigation committee's recommendation to dismiss would be followed.

(1)   First, the defendants have the burden of proving the committee members' independence and the procedural completeness of their investigation; and

(2)   Second, if the special litigation committee's recommendation passes the first part of the test, the court exercises its own independent discretion in determining whether or not it is in the corporations best interest to dismiss the suit.

Under the second prong of the *Zapata* test, the court applies its own business judgment as to whether the suit should go forward, rather than giving the special litigation committee's recommendation a presumption of propriety under the business judgment rule.

Some scholars have criticized the *Zapata* decision on the ground that the case vitiates the business judgment rule as to litigation decisions. This is a more limited intrusion on the business judgment rule than would be a decision vitiating the business judgment rule as to how the business should be operated (*i.e.*, day and night baseball). But as some have pointed out governmental intrusions tend to be incremental in nature. *Zapata* was decided four years prior to *Smith v. Van Gorkom*, where the Delaware court intruded further on the business judgment rule. Some say *Zapata* was a precursor of things to come in *Van Gorkom.*

On the other hand, the *Zapata* test only applies in cases where demand has been excused. Three years after the *Zapata* decision, in *Aronson v. Lewis*, discussed above, the Delaware Supreme court significantly limited the number of situations in which demand would be excused. Thus, *Aronson* has limited the importance of the *Zapata* rule.

c. Other Procedural Requirements

Shareholders' derivative suits trigger a number of other procedural requirements. The specific requirements vary significantly from state to state. Some are found in the states' corporate statutes, while other are found in the states' rules of civil procedure. All directly or indirectly relate to the three main concerns courts have with respect to shareholders' derivative suits—the governance dilemma, strike suits and conflicts of interest. The "other procedural requirements" are rarely covered in any depth in the basic business course, except by professors who have a particular interest in procedure. They are beyond the scope of this book. We will, however, discuss the most two significant of the other procedural requirements in a cursory way.

The contemporaneous ownership rule. Most state statutes require that the plaintiff be a shareholder when the wrong occurred. This is sometimes referred to as a standing requirement. The details on what is required varies from state to state. MBCA § 7.41(1) is fairly typical. Some state statutes go further than MBCA § 7.41 and require that the plaintiff continue to be a shareholder through trial and/or final judgement.

Security for expenses. Some states require that plaintiff, as a condition to bringing a derivative suit, post security to cover the defendant corporation's litigation costs. The obvious purpose behind this requirement is to weed out strike suits. Security-for-expense statutes have been a powerful disincentive to derivative litigation because both the costs of posting a bond and the risks of having to pay defendant's expenses are high. Today, only a minority of states have security for expense statutes. Delaware has no such statute. Most of the security-for-expense statutes exempt shareholders who own more than a specified minimum of the corporation's stock (*i.e.*, 3% or 5%) from this requirement.

Bottom line: As the above discussion reflects, the procedural rules surrounding derivative litigation (*i.e.*, the demand requirement, the deference given recommendations of the special litigation committee, the security-for-expense statutes, etc.), are diverse and state specific. Consequently, the manner in which you handle these requirements will depend upon your professor's emphasis. However, whatever the emphasis in your particular class, if you understand the process underlying derivative litigation and understand what we refer to as the "governance dilemma"—the tension between the directors' authority to make corporate decisions and the shareholder's right to bring shareholders' derivative suits—you should be able to effectively work your way through any of the specific issues that might arise on your exam.

CHAPTER VIII

WHAT PROTECTION DOES THE LAW GIVE TO PERSONS WHO BUY OR SELL SECURITIES? (herein Rule 10b-5)

In the last chapter we focused on shareholders (as well as owners of interests in other business structures) as **owners**. We learned that shareholders have certain rights derived from ownership. Among those rights are protection from incompetent or disloyal directors and officers who violate certain duties, which the law has labeled fiduciary duties.

In this chapter we change focus. Rather than looking at shareholders as owners entitled to certain ongoing rights as an attribute of ownership we look at them as **investors** who make decisions to buy or sell stock. In this capacity shareholder-investors might be induced to buy or sell stock in a particular company by false or misleading statements or material omissions. We will refer to this kind of conduct as "fraud," a term we will define with more particularity later in the context of the way the term is used in this chapter.

What protection does the law afford investors against fraud in connection with the purchase or sale of securities?

The law provides investors many remedies against fraud. First, it affords remedies under the common law of fraud and deceit—tort law. Also most states have so called deceptive trade practices statutes and state securities (or

"Blue Sky") laws which provide remedies for fraudulent conduct. These remedies are outside the scope of this book. Today, the main remedy—a remedy which dwarfs all the others in importance—is a body of case law which has developed around a rule adopted by the SEC under the Securities Exchange Act of 1934 ("34 Act"). This body of jurisprudence goes by the unassuming name of **Rule 10b-5**.

A. RULE 10b-5—OVERVIEW

Rule 10b-5 must be understood. It transcends the specialized body of jurisprudence called "securities law" and is part of a more general body of jurisprudence called "general corporate law." Most corporate law is governed by state law, but questions arising under Rule 10b-5 are governed by federal law.

1. HISTORY

The 33 and 34 Acts contain a number of anti-fraud provisions aimed at "fraud" in certain specific practices (*i.e.*, the sale of securities by issuers going public, the solicitation of proxies, fraud by broker/dealers, etc.). But in 1942, when an SEC investigation revealed that the president of a publicly held company in Boston was making pessimistic statements about the company's earnings while buying the company's stock, the SEC staff realized there was a loophole in the statutes. The statutes did not contain a broad anti-fraud provision which prohibited fraud in the purchase or sale of securities by anyone.

The SEC closed the loophole by using the catchall authority of § 10(b) of the 34 Act. Section 10(b) gives the SEC authority to promulgate rules that prohibit "Manipulative or deceptive devices or contrivances . . . in connection with the purchase or sale of any security." Under the authority of § 10(b), the SEC staff proposed a new rule which prohibited "fraud" by "anyone" in connection with the purchase or sale of a security. The Commission adopted the new rule without debate. The only recorded comment was: "we are all against fraud aren't we?" The new rule was named Rule 10b-5, because it was the fifth rule adopted under the enabling authority of § 10(b).

About 4 years after its adoption, a federal district court held that violation of Rule 10b-5 gives rise to a private remedy in favor of injured investors. The rest is history. A significant body of jurisprudence has developed around the Rule in the last 50 years. Rule 10b-5 is a powerful weapon with wide application. While Rule 10b-5 has been used extensively in administrative proceedings and civil or criminal actions brought by the government, its primary impact has been in private civil actions brought by individuals.

2. APPLICATION—IN GENERAL

Rule 10b-5 is the broadest provision in the federal securities law. This rule has probably had more impact on corporate conduct during the second half of the 20th century than any other single rule of law.

The fraud may be perpetrated by anyone. It might be perpetrated by the corporation itself. Recall in Chapter V when we discussed the registration requirement imposed on corporations selling securities, we also alluded to the fact that the corporation and others were prohibited from committing fraud in connection with such sales. In Chapter VI we discussed fraud in connection with the solicitation of proxies. The same disloyal or incompetent directors we saw in the last chapter violating their fiduciary duties might also be committing various acts of fraud. The fraud could be committed by the investors themselves, as when investor *A* sells outstanding securities to investor *B* by means of fraud.

No business or transaction is too small to escape the reach of Rule 10b-5. Rule 10b-5 applies whether the securities are publicly traded or closely held and whether the transaction is subject to SEC registration or exempt. All you need to bring Rule 10b-5 into play is a purchase or sale of securities through the use of the mails or the instrumentalities of interstate commerce.

For example, assume *A* and *B* each own 50 shares of the 100 shares of stock a company whose sole asset is a lemonade stand. *B*, who operates the lemonade stand, talks *A* into selling *B* his 50 shares by lying about how much lemonade the company sold last year. *A* probably has a cause of action under Rule 10b-5.

Operative language of the rule; securities fraud defined. In considering the application of the rule we need to begin by looking at the specific language of the rule. The three operative clauses of the Rule prohibit:

(a) any device, scheme or artifice to defraud;

(b) any omission or misstatement of a material fact;

(c) any act or practice that would operate as a fraud or deceit.

In this chapter we use the word "fraud" as a shorthand reference to the acts, practices or omissions prohibited under the three operative clauses of the Rule.

Nobody, not even the Justices of the Supreme Court, know exactly what the language of the Rule means. Through interpretation, the Justices seem to make up the meaning as they go along.

The language of the rules three operative clauses is potentially broad enough to "cover the world" and the factual patterns that might give rise to an action under Rule 10b-5 are infinite. It covers all forms of fraud, manipulation and deception. It covers silence if there is an affirmative duty to speak.

The SEC wants flexibility and is content to let the courts apply the rule on a case-by-case basis. This approach results in uncertainty and a high degree of subjectivity.

Many areas of securities law and general corporate law require analysis of detailed statutory regulations. This is not the case with Rule 10b-5. When analyzing a Rule 10b-5 problem think in terms of **common law** analysis. The courts, not the SEC or Congress, have defined the scope, consequences and limitations of this rule. You will not find any detailed or arcane rules in this area. All you find is the broad and vague language of the Rule itself and a lot of case law interpreting that language in an infinite variety of fact situations. Do not think of Rule 10b-5 as merely as a legal rule but as a body of jurisprudence. As to securities transactions, Rule 10b-5 has largely superceded most of common law fraud in the second half of the 20th Century. Both at exam time and when you get out in practice, when you see a fact pattern where someone is buying or selling securities, **always consider the possible application of Rule 10b-5**.

While Rule 10b-5 has been applied in a wide variety of factual contexts, the two most common categories of Rule 10b-5 cases (the only categories covered in this book or likely to be covered in the basic business course) are (1) misrepresentation cases and (2) insider trading cases.

Misrepresentation cases. This is the most common application of Rule 10b-5. It is the label used to describe cases where somebody lies, tells half truths, puts out false financial statements, phony press releases, files false documents with the SEC, uses a prospectus or proxy statement containing false or misleading information, etc.

Insider trading cases. While not as common in terms of number of cases brought, insider trading cases is the category of cases for which 10b-5 is best known, because many of the insider trading cases have been brought against rich and famous people and have, therefore received much media attention. The insider trading case against Martha Stewart, which is currently making headlines, is an example. "Insider trading" is the label used to describe cases where someone buys or sells securities on the basis of undisclosed information available only to the "insider." The gist of insider trading cases is not misrepresentations, but rather non-disclosure.

B. MISREPRESENTATION CASES
(herein Elements of a Rule 10b-5 Case)

The gist of this application is some kind of misrepresentation—somebody lies, tells half truths, puts out false financial statements, phoney press releases, etc. Recently we have seen a lot of that—*e.g.*, Enron, Tyco, WorldCom, etc. Most of the companies and individuals involved in these situations are being or will be prosecuted criminally and/or sued civilly under Rule 10b-5.

For purposes of organization and analysis, it is convenient to break the 10b-5 cause of action down into elements. Different writers classify the elements of a 10b-5 cause of action in slightly different ways or they use slightly different labels for the elements. Any classification is nothing more than an analytical tool. The classification that works best for us in explaining the Rule's application is an eight element classification as follows:

(1) **Jurisdictional Means**
(2) **Fraud**
(3) **Materiality**
(4) **Culpability—Scienter**
(5) **In Connection with the Purchase or Sale of Securities**

1. JURISDICTIONAL MEANS

By its express terms Rule 10b-5 requires that the purchase or sale of securities be made through the use of "interstate commerce or the mails." These are called the **jurisdictional means**. While a requirement, this element is seldom an issue, because the requirement is almost always satisfied. The misstatement or omission need not be made in the phone call or letter. Any use of the mails or the telephone at any time in connection with a securities transaction will satisfy this requirement. The telephone call or letter does not have to cross state lines; nor does the actual offer to buy or sell securities have to be by mail or telephone. For example, the buyer and seller can work in the same building and the offer and sale can be in a face to face conversation in that building. But if one party calls the other to arrange the meeting or to clarify some detail or if a check or stock certificate is transmitted by mail, the requirement has been satisfied. See, *e.g.*, *Dupuy v. Dupuy*, a case in which phone calls between two brothers in the same apartment complex in New Orleans, negotiating the sale of an interest in a closely held family business, were enough to satisfy the jurisdictional requirement.

2. FRAUD

In shorthand terms we refer to the type of misconduct prohibited by Rule 10b-5 as fraud. But "fraud" like "fiduciary" is a term whose meaning depends on the context in which it is used. In the context of Rule 10b-5 "fraud" means committing any of the acts, omissions or practices specified in the three operating clauses of the rule, quoted verbatim above. Thus, the question becomes:

What specific conduct do these clauses prohibit?

Lies. Lies are obviously prohibited. But there are lies and there are lies.

Does there have to be an evil motive behind the lie?

No. In *Basic v. Levinson*, an important Supreme Court decision on several points, Basic Industries, a publicly held company was negotiating a merger. The deal was a friendly acquisition by which a larger company would acquire Basic. Negotiations were obviously being conducted in secret. If the deal got done, the shareholders of Basic will get a premium for their shares.

While these negotiations were in process, trading in Basic Industries picked up and the stock rose in price. A representative of the New York Stock Exchange asked the president of Basic, who was involved in the negotiations, if he knew why trading volume had increased and why the price was moving up. The president's answer was that he did not know. And he denied that the company was in negotiations to be acquired.

That was a lie. But the president was not lying to line his pockets. There was no evil motive behind the lie. The president was lying to protect the confidentially of sensitive merger negotiations, which if consummated (which they eventually were) would result in the shareholders getting a premium for their stock. Although the president was lying to protect the best interests of the company and its shareholder, in *Basic v. Levinson* the Supreme Court held that this lie was enough to invoke liability under Rule 10b-5.

Manipulating, misleading, or deceiving acts or statements all invoke liability under Rule 10b-5. Obviously, these terms are like "obscenity"—sometimes hard to define but lawyers need to learn to recognize them when they see them in a given fact situation. Likewise students need to learn to recognize them at exam time to spot potential Rule 10b-5 issues.

Half truths. The hornbook definition of a half truth is: A statement that is technically correct but it omits a fact that is necessary to make the statement not misleading. We had a recent ex-president who gave you more examples of half truths during his eight years in office than the authors could think up in their collective lifetimes. An example of a half truth would be:

Example: Assume in *Basic v. Levinson* the guy from the stock exchange asked the president: "Are you negotiating a merger?" The president answers, "no," because the company wasn't negotiating a "merger" in the technical legal sense. It was negotiating a "sale of assets." While technically true, since a sale of assets is the functional equivalent of a merger in the context of potential impact on stock prices, that answer is a half truth—which is prohibited under the Rule.

Opinions, predictions and other soft information. Sometimes courts must decide whether a particular statement is a statement of fact as opposed to a mere opinion or prediction. Numerous cases have characterized broad qualitative statements such as "this should be our most profitable year ever" or "this product should be our best product ever" as mere unactionable opinions or puffing. But the Supreme Court in *Virginia Bankshares, Inc. v. Sandberg* held that a statement that a price offered to shareholders in a freeze out merger was "high" could constitute an actionable false statement if the speaker knew that the statement was untrue.

Courts have struggled with these types of questions for years. A related struggle has been in the area of predictions (so called "soft information"). If a consequence of a good faith prediction that does not come true is potential liability for violation of Rule 10b-5, then forward-looking information about future earning or prospects, common in investment analysis, would in effect become an insurance policy for anyone buying a security that turns out to be a bad investment.

In recent years, not only the courts, but also the congress and the SEC have become more permissive with respect to so called soft information. The SEC, which for years opposed providing earnings projections, valuation reports and other soft information in documents filed with the commission, came to realize that such information is exactly the type of information that sophisticated investors find most useful. Today the SEC not only allows, but in some cases, requires such information. The SEC has provided protection against liability by creating "safe harbor." The Private Securities Litigation Reform Act of 1995 incorporated many of these safe harbors into the statutes. In general, the safe harbor rules now provide protection for forward looking information if the provider of the information had a reasonable basis for the opinion or prediction and the provider believed the opinion or prediction.

Silence or nondisclosure. Silence can be actionable when there is an affirmative duty to speak. We will explore the question of when there is an affirmative duty to disclose later when we discuss the application of 10b-5 to insider trading cases.

The deception requirement established by the Supreme Court in the case of *Sante Fe Industries v. Green* limited the scope and better defined the application of Rule 10b-5.

Prior to *Sante Fe,* several lower federal courts (and the Supreme Court), rendered a number of decisions which held that Rule 10b-5 afforded a federal remedy against corporate officers, directors and control shareholders for breaches of fiduciary duties, if in some remote way the breach of fiduciary duties could be connected to a purchase or sale of securities. The effect of applying Rule 10b-5 in this way would have been to federalize a large portion of the law of fiduciary duties, which had traditionally been part of state corporate law.

The best example of this expansive application of Rule 10b-5 can be found in *Superintendent of Insurance v. Bankers Life & Causalty Co.*, a case decided by the Supreme Court in 1971. In that case an insurance company owned some treasury bonds. A person named Begole acquired the insurance company from Bankers Life. After acquiring control of the insurance company, Begole had the insurance company sell the bonds. Begole then looted a significant amount of cash, including the cash received for the bonds, from the company and fled the country.

The Supreme Court held this constituted a violation of Rule 10b-5 in connection with the purchase or sale of a security (*i.e.*, the treasury bonds). The "fraud" was Begole's failure to tell the board, which authorized the sale of the bonds, that he intended to steal the proceeds. The court also found a nexus between the sale of the bonds and the looting, even though the fraud had nothing to do with the sale of the bonds, but rather had to do with Begole's looting the proceeds derived from the sale. *Bankers Life* is **not** the law today. Not after *Sante Fe v. Green*.

In *Sante Fe v. Green,* Sante Fe Industries owned 95% of the stock of Kirby Lumber Co. It sought to acquire the remaining 5% of Kirby's stock held by the minority stockholders pursuant to a "short form" merger governed by the Delaware short form merger statute. Under this procedure the minority shareholders, including Mr. Green, were cashed out at a price arrived at on the basis of an appraisal prepared by Morgan Stanley. Sante Fe complied with the Delaware short form merger statute, which does not require a vote of shareholders. After completing the merger, Sante Fe informed Kirby's minority shareholders of the merger, told them that they would be getting $150 per share for their stock and advised them of their statutory right of appraisal, the remedy provided under Delaware law, if they felt they were entitled to more.

Morgan Stanley, an investment banking firm, had appraised Kirby's assets—its land, timber, oil and gas properties, etc. The appraisal valued these assets at $125 per share and the price paid for the Kirby shares was $150 per share. Sante Fe sent the minority shareholders copies of the Morgan Stanley appraisal along with other relevant information. This information convinced one of the minority shareholders, Mr. Green, that the value of Kirby's assets was not $150 per share but rather $770 per share.

Rather than pursuing his appraisal rights in state court, Mr. Green brought an action in federal court which sought to set aside the merger because it violated Rule 10b-5. Green's complaint stated, and the theory of his case was, that the Kirby shares were worth $770 a share. He claimed that the price Sante Fe paid the minority shareholders was too low and was based on a fraudulent valuation. He alleged that this amounted to fraud prohibited by Rule 10b-5.

This case was decided on the pleadings. It is important to understand that the complaint did not allege any material misrepresentations or omissions. The premise on which this case was decided is that there was full disclosure—no lies, no material omissions, no half truths, etc. The gist of minority shareholder's complaint was simply, **we are being forced to sell our shares to the parent corporation at an unfair price**.

The Supreme Court held for the defendant. In holding that the plaintiff had failed to state a cause of action under Rule 10b-5, the *Santa Fe* Court says 10b-5 is a **disclosure rule not a fairness rule**. If there has been full disclosure there is **no violation of Rule 10b-5**, even though the underlying transaction is unfair. Please understand that the Supreme Court did not tell Mr. Green that he did not have a remedy if the price is unfair. They simply said you are in the wrong court Mr. Green. Go to state court to redress this kind of a grievance.

The basic teaching of *Sante Fe* is that **Rule 10b-5 is not a fiduciary duty rule, it is not a fairness rule—it is a disclosure rule**. *Sante Fe* draws a clear line in the sand. Cases on one side of the line are classified as "fiduciary duty or fairness cases" and go to state court. Cases on the other side of the line, which are about "deception," can go to federal court under Rule 10b-5. While *Sante Fe* defines the problem, does not solve it, because fairness and deception do not exist in water tight compartments. There is significant overlap in the two categories of cases. Some form of deception is probably present in almost every case where someone breaches his fiduciary duties. People who loot companies, self-deal or overreach do not typically disclose to others that this is what they are doing. That failure to disclose may be deception and if there is sufficient causal connection between the deception and the misconduct one might have a action under Rule 10b-5.

Sante Fe told us we **have to have deception** but it did not tell us what constitutes **deception** nor did it speak to the degree of causal connection required. Thus, the scope of the decision is subject to both interpretation and debate. The Supreme Court's opinion left the task of drawing the line created by *Santa Fe* to the lower courts. The lower federal courts are currently in the process of trying to draw that elusive line.

Bottom line. *Sante Fe* took many cases which in the 1960s and early 1970s would have been brought in the federal court out of that arena and put them back in the state court. Today no court would make the stretch the *Bankers Life* court made to bootstrap a fiduciary violation case into a 10b-5 case. But today's courts are not in agreement as to where to draw the line regarding the nexus required between the deception and the wrongdoing.

Consider the *Weinberger* case, discussed in § VII.B.3, *supra* in the context of our current discussion. *Weinberger*, decided by the Delaware supreme court six years after *Sante Fe* (and similar to *Sante Fe* on its facts) established the "entire fairness test" in Delaware. Thus, today it may be less important to get under Federal law, now that state law seems to provide an adequate remedy. On the other hand, given a choice most plaintiffs would still likely prefer to bring their cases under Rule 10b-5 rather than suing in state court because suing under Rule 10b-5 may enable plaintiffs to do an end run around many of the stringent procedural requirements that surround shareholder derivative suits such as (1) the contemporaneous ownership rule, (2) the demand requirement, (3) posting security for costs, etc.

Learning how *Weinberger* and *Sante Fe* fit together is called learning the process. While the rules may change, the process tends to remain the same. Most professors try to teach the "**process**" and at exam time they try to test the students' understanding of the process.

3. MATERIALITY

For liability under Rule 10b-5, a misstatement or omission must rise to the level of materiality. As previously stated materiality is a controlling concept under both the 33 and 34 Acts, whether we are talking about liability for false and misleading statements in a 33 Act prospectus, violation of the proxy rules or violation of Rule 10b-5. The basic test of materiality is the same in all these areas.

The test of materiality was formulated by the Supreme Court in *TSC Industries, Inc. v. Northway, Inc.*, a case brought under Rule 14a-9. That well settled test was quoted verbatim in § VI.B.4.b, *supra.* Under the *TSC Industries* test, a fact is material if there is a substantial likelihood that a reasonable investor would find the fact important in deciding whether to buy or sell a security.

On its face, when viewed in an academic setting, the *TSC Industries* test appears to be a reasonable, jury oriented, objective test. However, in a real world trial of a securities fraud case, the test favors the plaintiff. Plaintiff's lawyer will typically ask the following question with respect to the piece of information whose materiality is challenged: *"Would you have liked to have had this information when you bought the stock?"*

When the question is put that way, after the fact, the answer will almost invariably be "yes." Though the jury will be instructed to view the information as of the time of the purchase or sale, few jurors are capable of ignoring facts the materiality of which were highly questionable at the time made or omitted, but which clearly became material as a result of subsequent events.

Determining materiality in a given situation can be difficult since the factual variations relating to materiality are infinite. We will focus on two legal issues pertaining to materiality that frequently arise in cases and exams.

The probability/magnitude test. How do we determine the materiality of facts relating to the possibility of a future event occurring, when the materiality of the event would be clear, but at the time of the purchase or sale, it was not clear whether the event would occur.

A good example of this problem occurred *Basic v. Levinson*. Here a corporation denied that it was in merger negotiations when the corporation was in fact negotiating a merger which ultimately resulted in shareholders receiving a premium of about 50% on their stock over the pre-merger market price. At the time of the misstatement, however, it was not clear that the merger would be consummated. A statement disclosing the merger negotiations, had the merger failed to materialize, would just as likely have resulted in liability.

In *Basic,* the Supreme Court applied the so called **probability/magnitude test**. Under the probability/ magnitude test as of the moment of the event the jury is supposed to balance the probability that the event will occur against the magnitude of the event if it occurs. The conceptual framework is easy to understand—the lower the probability, the higher the magnitude necessary to find materiality and vice versa.

On its face, particularly in an academic setting, weighing probability and magnitude seems to make sense. But in a real life litigation situation, irrespective of the instruction that says the jury should apply the test at the time of the transaction, can the jury ignore the accomplished fact that the merger did go through and that shareholders who held their shares until the merger occurred got a 50% premium? Most practicing lawyers, as well as many scholars, doubt that they can. That having been said, probability/magnitude is still the test to use on your exam if you encounter a developing situation in which you must determine the materiality of information pertaining to an event that may or may not happen.

The bespeaks caution doctrine. Another issue that often comes up in the context of materiality involves projections or opinions followed by warnings the projections or opinions might not pan out. It is called the "**bespeaks caution doctrine**." The 34 Act has been amended to incorporate provisions of the Private Securities Litigation Reform Act of 1995 which added a safe harbor that codifies the bespeaks caution doctrine for forward looking statements.

The main issues that arise in the bespeaks caution doctrine relate to the scope of its application. The cautionary statement must be detailed and specific, there must be a reasonable basis for the statement, and the statement must be made in good faith.

4. SCIENTER

The operative language of Rule 10b-5 does not specify the level of fault required. If negligence was the standard there would be little difference in the implied liability under Rule 10b-5 and the strict liability imposed under §§ 11 and 12 of the 33 Act on companies which make materially false or misleading statements or omissions in connection with stock offerings.

Ernst & Ernst v. Hochfelder established a test for scienter in Rule 10b-5 actions.[1] *Hochfelder* was an action by defrauded customers of a stock brokerage firm, whose president and controlling shareholder was stealing money from the clients' accounts. The suit was against the firm's auditor, Ernst & Ernst. Plaintiff argued that Ernst & Ernst was negligent in the way they conducted their audit, and that their negligence was actionable under Rule 10b-5.

The Supreme Court reversed the Seventh Circuit and sustained a summary judgement granted by the trial courts in favor of Ernst & Ernst. The high court held that

---

1. Prior to that case the circuit courts around the country were divided. Some said plaintiff had to show an intentional violation to sustain a cause of action under Rule 10b-5, but the majority said that negligence was enough.

without scienter there can be no violation of Rule 10b-5.
The court concluded, based on the words of the enabling
Section 10(b) and the legislative history of the 34 Act, that
Congress did not intend to create 10b-5 liability for mere
negligence.[2]

The opinion in *Hochfelder* defines scienter as **"an intent
to deceive, manipulate or defraud."** Unfortunately, that
definition raises almost as many questions as it answers.

Does scienter require bad faith or evil motive?

Basic v. Levinson provides at least a partial answer to
that question.   Recall *Basic* was the case where the
president of the company falsely denied that the he knew
what was causing an increase in the volume of trading of
Basic shares.   He lied to protect the confidentiality of
sensitive merger negations.   There was no evil motive
behind that lie—the president was acting in a sensible
businesslike way, trying to protect the best interests of the
company and its shareholders. He was not lying to line his
own pockets.

In *Basic* the Supreme Court implicitly said none of that
matters.   Good faith, business judgement, etc. are not
defenses in the context of Rule 10b-5. **Rule 10b-5 merely
requires that the statement is false or has a propensity to**

_____

2. *Hochfelder* is one of several cases in which the Supreme Court has
limited the scope of Rule 10b-5's application on the basis of the language
in the enabling section 10(b)—"manipulative or deceptive device or
contrivance"—which, as interpreted by the court, is narrower than the
language in the Rule itself.

mislead—it does not require bad faith, evil motive, malice or evidence that someone is trying to line his pockets.

Is recklessness enough to support liability under Rule 10b-5?

In *Hochfelder,* the Supreme Court left open the question of whether making a statement in reckless disregard of the truth is sufficient to support a Rule 10b-5 action. The circuit courts, that have considered this question subsequent to *Hochfelder,* have held that reckless is enough to support a violation of Rule 10b-5. The courts are not, however, in agreement as to what "reckless" means in the context of Rule 10b-5. Most seem to be saying that reckless means: **If you speak, knowing that you do not know whether what you are saying is true or false, but you speak anyway, without qualification, that is reckless, and reckless is enough to invoke potential liability under Rule 10b-5.**

5. IN CONNECTION WITH THE PURCHASE OR SALE OF A SECURITY

Obviously Rule 10b-5 does not apply to all frauds. The fraud must occur "**in connection with the purchase or sale of securities.**" For example, if the CFO of a company embezzles $5 million, he has committed a crime and a tort and violated his fiduciary duties, but he has not violated Rule 10b-5, because no purchase or sale of securities took place in this example. Two other basic and rather obvious points flow from this requirement.

(1)   For Rule 10b-5 to apply, there must be a purchase or sale of a "security." The rule does not prohibit fraud in connection with the purchase or sale of used cars, real estate or other types of property. In this section we mainly deal with corporate stock which is obviously a security. But recall there are other types of interests which fit within the broad definition of a security. We previously discussed the definition of a "security" in § V.G.2.b.(3) in connection with our discussion of the registration requirement under the 33 Act. The definition is the same for purposes of invoking Rule 10b-5.

(2)   Rule 10b-5 applies to purchases or sales exempt from the registration requirement of the 33 Act as well as purchases or sales which require registration. Therefore the distinction between sales by the issuer of new securities and resales by investors of outstanding securities, while extremely important for 33 Act purposes, is not important under Rule 10b-5. The Rule covers both types of transactions. For example, if a sale is made by an issuer by means of a false or misleading registration statement, plaintiff would have a cause of action under Rule 10b-5 as well as under § 11 of the 33 Act. This is an example of the overlap discussed earlier. Rule 10b-5 and §11 both prohibit false or misleading statements, but there is a difference. Section 11 imposes strict liability, while Rule 10b-5 requires scienter.

In addition to its above obvious aspects, the "in connection with" requirement relates to the connection between the purchase or sale and the fraud or misconduct.

This aspect of the "in connection with" clause is similar to **proximate cause**. Remember from torts that there has to be a causal connection between the wrong and the injury. Rule 10b-5 works the same way. There has to be a causal connection (a "nexus") between the purchase or sale of securities and the misconduct.

6. STANDING—PLAINTIFF MUST HAVE BOUGHT OR SOLD SECURITIES

In *Blue Chip Stamps v. Manor Drug Store*, the Supreme Court held that, in order to have standing to bring a suit under Rule 10b-5, the plaintiff must have been a buyer or seller of securities. In a case where plaintiff's decision *not* to sell or not to buy is induced by fraud, plaintiff cannot maintain an action under Rule 10b-5.

For example, assume that in the fall of 2001 Enron Corporation put out a false and misleading press release, which grossly overstated earnings, understated debt and lied about the companies business and prospects. In reliance on that press release one group of Enron employees bought stock in the company. This group would have standing to sue under Rule 10b-5. But assume another group, who owned stock in the company prior to the false press release, decided, in reliance on the press release, not to sell their stock, which subsequently became worthless after the fraud was exposed and Enron went into bankruptcy. This group would not have standing to sue under the rule of *Blue Chip Stamps,* even though they might have been more damaged by the false press release as much as the group who bought.

Students in the basic business course, need to understand the converse of the *Blue Chip Stamps* holding: **The defendant does not have to be a purchaser or seller of securities**. Only the plaintiff has to meet the buyer or seller requirement.

Consider our earlier example of the Enron false release, which caused plaintiffs to buy stock in the open market. Enron would be potentially liable under Rule 10b-5, even though Enron did not buy or sell any stock itself, if plaintiff can show a causal connection between the Enron's misconduct (the false press release) and plaintiff's purchase or sale of securities.

7. CAUSATION/RELIANCE

Causation, an element of common law fraud, is also an element in suits under Rule 10b-5. In securities fraud cases causation encompasses two separate, but somewhat related concepts—"**loss causation**" and "**transaction causation**."

Loss causation embodies the concept that the defendant's fraud caused or at least materially contributed to the plaintiff's pecuniary loss—*i.e.,* the false statement caused the decline in the price of the stock. Assume for example, that X Airline puts out an annual report which materially overstates its earnings for the fiscal year ending June 30, 2001. During the fall of 2001, after the earnings misstatement is discovered the price of X Airline's stock declines materially. However, in the interim, the terrorist attack of September 11, 2001 occurred, which resulted in a significant decline in airline travel and massive operating losses for X Airline. This is an obvious example of what is known in torts as an intervening cause. In the world of securities litigation, it is called a lack of loss causation.

In re Apple Computer Securities Litigation involved a more sophisticated application of loss causation. The application in that case requires introduction to another concept called the "Efficient Market Hypothesis," which is a catchy name given to a theory that says that stock prices in active trading markets respond rapidly to all available information about a stock—both true information and false information. That concept underlies the "fraud on the market" presumption discussed below.

In the *Apple* case, Apple Computer put out what the trial court found to be a materially misleading press release which overstated the potential capabilities of two new products—the Lisa Computer and a compatible disk drive called Twiggy. There is a good reason that most of you have never heard of these two products introduced in the 1980s. They both turned out to be flops, which had a material adverse impact on Apple's earnings and the price of its stock.

The Ninth Circuit reversed a trial court's multimillion dollar verdict against Apple for material misstatements in the press release. The reversal was based on reasoning flowing from the Efficient Market Hypothesis. The court stated that during the same time frame as Apple put out its overly optimistic release about Lisa and Twiggy, independent analysts were putting out releases of their own which were skeptical of these products. The releases put out by the independents were not as widely disseminated as the Apple release. They were published mainly in technical journals, rather than the Wall Street Journal, but the conflicting information and opinions were publicly available and the court believed that the market professionals had absorbed all of the conflicting information. Thus, under the Efficient Market Hypothesis all of the conflicting information was reflected in the price of the stock. In other words, Apple was able to get a reversal on the theory—we lied, but the market did not believe us—and thus there was no loss causation.

Transaction causation is often termed "reliance" because the plaintiff's reliance on the false statement is the usual way in which the false statement caused plaintiff harm—*i.e.*, reliance on the false statement caused plaintiff to enter into the transaction. Thus, transaction causation, which in essence is just another way of saying plaintiff relied on the fraud, relates to the nexus between the fraud and the investment decision.

The fraud on the market theory is a means of proving transaction causation (or reliance, which we said earlier are one and the same) when there is an active trading market for a security. Rule 10b-5 applies to face-to-face transactions as well as transactions in the organized trading markets. In face to face transactions, reliance means exactly what it means at common law. Plaintiff has to show she was aware of the misstatement and was deceived by it. However, most Rule 10b-5 cases do not involve direct dealings between plaintiff and defendant. Rather they involve persons buying or selling in active trading markets such as stock exchanges.

What if the plaintiff (or some members of the class in a class action) was not aware of the specific misrepresentation?

Basic v. Levinson provides the answer to this question. Recall that in *Basic,* management issued statements which falsely denied that Basic was in merger negotiations. After the merger, in which Basic shareholders received a 50% premium over the market price of the stock before the merger, was announced, a class action law suit was filed on behalf of all persons who had sold their stock between the time of the false statements and announcement of the merger. Although the false denial of the merger negotiations was published in the Cleveland Plain Dealer and other newspapers, it was virtually certain that many of the plaintiffs in the class never read or heard of Basic's denial before selling their shares.

How can those plaintiffs satisfy the element of reliance or transaction causation?

In *Basic,* the U.S. Supreme Court told us the reliance requirement can be satisfied by a presumption known as **fraud on the market theory**, in the following words:

> The fraud on the market theory is based on the hypothesis that, in an open and developed securities market, the price of a company's stock is determined by the available information regarding the company and its business. . . . Misleading statements will therefore defraud purchasers of stock even if the purchasers do not directly rely on the misstatements. . . . The causal connection between the defendants'

fraud and the plaintiffs' purchase of stock in such a case is no less significant than in a case of direct reliance. . . ."

The fraud on the market theory does not obviate the need to prove materiality, scienter, or loss causation. All it provides is a means of proving transaction causation or reliance by a rebuttable presumption in situations where the stock in question is widely traded in an active market. The presumption applies to stocks traded over a stock exchange or in the NASDAQ, automatic quotation system. Whether it applies to other markets is still unclear. When it applies, the fraud on the market theory creates a powerful presumption that is hard to overcome.

8. DAMAGES

Private Rule 10b-5 plaintiffs have a full range of equitable and legal remedies. Section 28(a) of the 34 Act has been read to say that (1) the goal is **compensatory damages** and (2) **punitive damages** are not available under Rule 10b-5.

The most common measure is **out of pocket damages—the difference in the amount paid for the security and its actual value as of the time of the transaction**. However, courts are not limited to that measure of damages—they can and have awarded rescissory (disgorgement), restitution, and even, on occasion, benefit of the bargain (cover) measure damages.

Also, in the 1980s, Congress amended the 34 Act to allow the SEC to enforce insider trading violations, through statutory civil actions for treble damages. Today, while most Rule 10b-5 cases involving corporate misrepresentation are brought by private plaintiffs, most 10b-5 insider trading cases are brought by the SEC.

C. INSIDER TRADING

The best known application of Rule 10b-5 is the area of **insider trading**. This application is well known mainly through media coverage, since a number of insider trading cases have been brought against celebrities. Despite all the publicity, insider trading is a new area of the law, which developed in stages over the last 40 years. The practice of insider trading, except in certain face to face transactions, was not even illegal until the 1960s and the rules that currently govern in this area were laid down by the courts in the 1980s and 1990s.

1. WHAT IS INSIDER TRADING?

It is simply a short-hand description of a factual pattern where an officer or director of the company, a rank and file employee, such as a secretary or the guy in the mail room, or an associate in a law firm or an accounting firm that represents the company acquires material information about the company. That information could be good or bad news, but it is news which will likely cause the price of the stock to move up or down—*e.g.*, the company is about to be acquired at a premium, it is about to get a very large new contract, it is about to file for bankruptcy, etc.

Before that information is made public, that person (the "insider") buys or sells the stock and later makes a profit when the news is made public. Or the recipient of the information may tip someone else (a "tippee") who buys or sells the stock and profits from the inside information.

In the insider trading cases, we are not dealing with lies, misrepresentations, half truths or the like. Rather we are dealing with **complete silence**—lack of disclosure.

The rules can apply in face-to-face transactions. But most of the time the actual trades occur over a stock exchange or NASDAQ. The so called "insider" has no idea who the person on the other side of the trade is. The insider's motive is to make money, but it is not to cheat or mislead the person on the other side of the trade. Seldom does the inside trader even know who that person is.

2. WHAT LAWS OTHER THAN RULE 10b-5 APPLY TO INSIDER TRADING?

a. Insider Trading Under State Law

While Rule 10b-5 is now the principal provision used to police insider trading, through criminal and civil actions brought in Federal courts, we can get a better perspective of what is involved by first looking briefly at how state law treats insider trading. Most casebooks also take this approach and include *Goodwin v. Agassiz*, which reflects how insider trading is dealt with under state law. Because of the similarity in the facts of this case and the seminal federal case on insider trading, *Texas Gulf Sulphur*, which we will discuss later, *Goodwin* is a good vehicle that shows the contrast between state and federal law in this area.

In *Goodwin v. Agassiz*, plaintiff Goodwin sold 700 shares of Cliff Mining Co. on the Boston Stock Exchange. Defendant Agassiz, the president and a director of Cliff Mining, bought those shares on the same exchange. Agassiz had inside information—a geologist's report that indicated the property in which Cliff Mining had the mineral rights might be rich in iron ore. Goodwin and Agassiz did not know one another and had never spoken. Their respective buy and sell orders simply reached the floor of the Boston Stock Exchange at about the same time through normal brokerage channels and were matched. In holding for the defendant and refusing to impose liability, the Massachusetts Supreme Court emphasized (1) the anonymous and impersonal character of this transaction that occurred over a stock exchange and (2) that officers' and directors' fiduciary duties run only to the corporation not to the individual shareholders.

This 1933 case represents what is still the rule as to insider trading under state law. **There is no liability for insider trading under state law with one exception**.

The exception, called the "**special facts doctrine**," comes from *Strong v. Repide*, a famous early case discussed in *Goodwin* (and often discussed in the basic business course). The special facts doctrine is simply a common law doctrine which says: **An officer or director is under an affirmative duty to disclose special facts when buying shares from existing shareholders**.

The elements necessary to state a cause of action under the special facts doctrine are all captured in the sentence in bold above:

(1) Only officers and directors are subject to the doctrine.
(2) While originally the special facts doctrine only covered **purchases**, today it applies to **purchases** or **sales**.
(3) While "the special facts" doctrine originally was only triggered by facts, that were truly extraordinary, today **any material information** is likely to trigger the doctrine.
(4) Finally, and most importantly, there has to be **privity**—face to face dealings between the officer or director and the party on the other side of the transaction.

Since the **special facts doctrine** only applies to **face to face** dealings, not dealings over a stock exchange, the special facts doctrine did not apply in *Goodwin*.

b. Section 16(b) of the 34 Act

Goodwin v. Agassiz is still the law today with respect to insider trading under state law. But federal law is quite different because of Rule 10b-5 and the body of jurisprudence which has developed under that rule with respect to insider trading.

The federal law of insider trading developed in stages over the second half of the 20th century. The genesis of regulation of insider trading under Rule 10b-5 occurred in

1961. Until then the federal rule was the same as the rule under state law—no liability except under the special facts doctrine—subject only to § 16(b) of the 34 Act.

Long before 1961, Congress was aware that insider trading was a problem. The hearings which preceded passage of the 34 Act revealed flagrant insider trading abuses. While Congress knew that insider trading was a problem which undermined the integrity of the securities markets, they did not know how to deal with the problem.

Congress's only attempt to deal with the problem was § 16(b) of the 34 Act, which the legislative history describes as a "crude rule of thumb." Section 16(b) is still used as crude but potent remedy for capturing profits made as the result of short term trading by certain high level people. You could not find two provisions more different in concept or application than §16(b) and Rule 10b-5.

Section 16(b) imposes strict liability on any director, officer or 10% shareholder of a company, subject to § 16(b), who makes a profit (as defined for purposes of § 16(b)) within a six month period from the purchase or sale or the sale and purchase of equity securities of her company. No fraudulent intent is required. If a person subject to § 16(b) waits six months and one day between trades she can engage in the worlds worst fraud without liability under § 16(b). On the other hand, if the purchase and sale occur within six months of one another and there is a profit, then there is liability regardless of how well intended or reasonable the transactions might have been.

The legislative history clearly reveals the philosophy behind § 16(b) was to impose **strict liability** so as is to remove all temptation on the part of high-level insiders to trade short term in the stock of their corporations. The remedy requires the § 16(b) insider who profits from trades within six months of one another to turn all profits over to the corporation. The enforcement mechanism for enforcing § 16(b) is a statutory shareholders' derivative suit and the economic engine which drives this type of lawsuit is the liberal attorney's fees authorized by the statute.

Section 16(b) liability is computed by matching the price received in any purchase or sale, regardless of order, during any six-month period in which the sales price is higher than the purchase price and there is no offset for losses. This is called the lowest-in, highest-out formula. It is designed to squeeze out all possible damages resulting from violations.

The rules which govern the application of § 16(b) are arcane and, for the most part, counterintuitive. They are devoid of logic and recognize no equitable exceptions. The bad news is that this makes §16(b), which on its face seems simple, one of the most complex provisions of the Federal Securities Laws. But the good news is that details pertaining to § 16(b)'s application are beyond anything usually covered in the basic business course. Unless you happen to have a professor that emphasizes § 16(b), the rule to remember is that: **Persons subject to § 16(b) should always wait at least six months between trades**.

3. HOW DOES RULE 10b-5 DEAL WITH INSIDER TRADING?

a. Comparison of § 16(b) and Rule 10b-5

In addition to the rule set forth in bold above, you should be aware of the fundamental differences between § 16(b) and Rule 10b-5: (1) Section 16(b) only applies to companies registered under the 34 Act (*i.e.,* the same subset of companies subject to the proxy rules are subject to § 16(b)). (2) The so called "insiders" subject to the § 16(b) prohibition are limited to directors, officers and 10% shareholders of companies subject to § 16(b). As you will see, this is much narrower than the class of persons subject to Rule 10b-5 liability. (3) While § 16(b) imposes automatic strict liability regardless of any wrong doing or intent, Rule 10b-5 requires trading based on material, non public information, a fiduciary duty of confidentiality and scienter. Today, the number of actions brought under § 16(b) is only a small fraction of the actions brought under Rule 10b-5.

b. The Disclose or Abstain Rule and *Texas Gulf Sulphur*

A famous professor of corporate and securities law at the Columbia law school, William L. Cary, had developed the notion that insider trading ought to be illegal even if trading took place in the anonymous, impersonal world of a stock exchange. Professor Cary had written law review articles explaining his view. But, no one outside of academia paid much attention. In 1961, President Kennedy appointed Professor Cary Chairman of the SEC. That put the professor in a position where he could make his view the SEC's view, which is what he did. This did get the people's attention.

The vehicle through which Professor Cary's view (*nee* the SEC's view*)* was first articulated was *In re Cady Roberts*, an administrative proceeding by the SEC against a broker/dealer, Cady Roberts & Co., for violating the securities laws. Cowden, a partner in Cady Roberts, was on the board of Curtiss Wright Corp. He attended a board meeting at which the Curtiss Wright board voted to cut the dividend. At a morning recess of the board meeting Cowden called one of his partners at Cady Roberts, Gintel, and told him that Curtiss Wright was going to announce a dividend cut later in the day. Gintel sold Curtiss Wright stock in his own account and the accounts of several Cady Roberts customers, before the dividend cut was announced.

The SEC held that Cady Roberts had violated Rule 10b-5. The opinion, written by Chairman Cary, stated that Gintel had an affirmative duty to either disclose the material facts he knew or refrain from trading until those facts became public. This has come to be known as the **disclose or abstain rule**.

The rationale for the SEC's decision in *Cady Roberts* was simply that it is **unfair** for "anyone" who acquires inside information to exploit that information when the typical shareholder does not have access to the same information. This came to be known as the **equal access rule**. As we shall see, the rationale for the disclose or abstain rule is no longer fairness and equal access. And the prohibition no longer applies to "anyone."

Cady Roberts is an example of a practice often employed by the SEC, when they want to change or clarify the law. The SEC brings an administrative proceeding, decides the case and writes an opinion announcing their position. In broker/dealer proceedings such as *Cady Roberts*, the SEC staff is the prosecutor and the commission is the judge. You cannot find a friendlier forum than that. Since *Cady Roberts* was just an SEC administrative proceeding, the SEC knew that for its position to carry any weight, it would have to stand up in court.

The case in which the SEC tested its new position on insider trading was the seminal case of *SEC v. Texas Gulf Sulphur*. In November, 1963, Texas Gulf Sulphur Co. ("TGS") was exploring for minerals near Timmons, Ontario in Northeastern Canada. They drilled a hole and took a core sampling, the now famous K-55-1 core sample, which on visual inspection suggested the land might contain exceptionally high deposits of silver, copper, zinc and other hard minerals. Shortly after the K-55-1 core sample was taken, since it was November, it was time to shut down operations for the winter. TGS moved the rig, sent the core sample to Utah to be assayed and began quietly buying up mineral rights from landowners in the area. Only a few select people in the company, who needed to know, were told of the K-55-1 core sample and those people were instructed to maintain absolute silence. The news did, however, get up the corporate ladder to a few people in TGS, including its president.

During the period between November 12, 1963, when the core sample was first examined in the field and April 16, 1964, after operations resumed and rumors of a large mineral discovery started to surface, several TGS employees from the field geologist to the president, who had knowledge of K-55-1, bought TGS stock or options. Some of those people also told friends—golfing buddies, relatives, girlfriends, etc.—about core sample and those people (designated "tippees" by the court) also bought TGS stock or options.

The SEC brought an action under Rule 10b-5 against, inter alia, the TGS employees (and their tippees) who bought TGS stock or options with knowledge of the K-55-1 core sample, before the news was made public. The Second Circuit held that the defendants had violated Rule 10b-5, stating:

Anyone in possession of material non public information has a duty to disclose that information before trading in the stock" and "Rule 10b-5 is based in policy on the justifiable expectation of the securities marketplace that all investors trading on impersonal exchanges have relatively equal access to material information. . . .

Notice that the rationale of *Texas Gulf Sulpher* was exactly the same as the rationale of *Cady Roberts*— **fairness** and **equal access to information**.

After *Texas Gulf Sulphur* lawyers and their clients faced a serious line drawing problem. Obviously, a corporate officer who buys or sells stock in his company, knows more about the business and prospects of the company than a shareholder in the boondocks, who happens to be on the other side of the transaction. No knowledgeable investor, who bought or sold stock, could say for sure that liability might not in some way attach on the basis that he knew more about the security than the person on the other side of the transaction.

There was also an outpouring of scholarly articles on insider trading in the law reviews and a backlash began to develop as many scholars questioned the assumptions underlying the prohibition against insider trading. Most scholars agreed with the concept, but many argued that a law based simply on the broad and undefinable concept of fairness (which is the linchpin of the equal access rule) was too open-ended, too unpredictable and not in touch with the reality of the market place, which always was and always will be information driven. Fairness is often the goal of the law, but rarely is it the defining legal standard. It is simply too amorphous a concept—like beauty, it can only be defined through the eyes of the beholder.

While these issues were being debated both in academia and the board rooms of corporate America, a new character came on the scene. He would be the catalyst for the next change in the rules governing insider trading. His name was Vincent Chiarella.

c. Finding the "Fiduciary Nexus"—*Chiarella v. United States*

The facts of the *Chiarella* case are simple, and the opinion is the cornerstone of the rules that govern insider trading today. Mr. Chiarella was an employee of Pandick Press, a printer of prospectuses, proxy statements, tender offer documents, etc. The takeover boom of the 1980s had begun and Pandick was one of the companies that "bidder companies" hired to print the offering material which the securities laws required them to used in connection with tender offers to acquire so-called "target companies."

As a security measure, the names of both the "bidder" and "target" companies were not revealed until the final printing, which occurred the night before the tender offer was announced. In preliminary drafts the names of the "bidder" and "target" companies were left blank. Mr. Chiarella was able to figure out the identity of the target companies in five different cases over a 14-month period. He bought stock of the target companies before the tender offer was announced and sold the stock at a profit following the announcement. He made about $30,000 in profit before an SEC investigation uncovered his trading.

After Chiarella had settled a civil action brought by the SEC by repaying all of his illicit profits plus penalties, he was indicted criminally for violating Rule 10b-5. Chiarella was convicted at trial and the Second Circuit upheld his conviction. The Supreme Court reversed the conviction and in so doing, changed the rule governing insider trading. This decision by a divided court, while approving the basic disclose or abstain rule of *Texas Gulf Sulphur*, **completely changed the analytical framework for resolving insider trading cases**. The case also provided the foundation for additional changes which were yet to come. Thus, we will focus not only on the majority opinion but also on Justice Burger's dissent.

The majority opinion. While approving the result of *Texas Gulf Sulphur* and the basic disclose or abstain rule, the Supreme Court nevertheless overturned Chiarella's conviction and in so doing limited the persons subject to the disclose or abstain rule from anyone to persons in a fiduciary relationship. Recall in *Texas Gulf Sulphur*, the rationale behind the disclose or abstain rule was **equal access to information**. Under the holding of that case the mere possession by anyone of material information not available to other traders was sufficient to trigger the duty to disclose or abstain. In *Chiarella,* the majority said that rule is too broad. In the words of the majority, when "fraud" is based on nondisclosure (as it always is in insider trading cases): "there can be no fraud absent a duty to speak." In other words, the Court held **there is no equal access rule**.

If mere possession of material information, which is not available to other traders does not create a duty to disclose before trading, what does create such a duty?

Chiarella completely changed the framework of analysis in insider trading cases. After *Chiarella, we* must find a **fiduciary nexus** (*i.e.,* a duty of confidentiality) between the person with the inside information (*i.e.,* the "insider") and the other party to the transaction. This fiduciary nexus is the foundation on which the duty to disclose or abstain rests, according to *Chiarella.* Today this is called the **"fiduciary nexus theory"** or the **"classical theory"** of insider trading.[3]

---

3. To distinguish it from an alternative theory for imposing liability, called the "misappropriation theory," which we will discuss later.

Applying the fiduciary nexus theory, the Supreme Court reversed Chiarella's conviction because the jury instruction (based on the equal access rule), which prohibited anyone with inside information from trading, was too broad.

How do you find a fiduciary nexus between the buyer and seller of the securities?

When an employee is trading in the stock of her own company, finding the fiduciary nexus is not a problem. *Chiarella* would not have changed the result of *Texas Gulf Sulphur*, where all the buyers were employees of TGS or tippees of such employees. The sellers by definition were shareholders of TGS. There is "a relationship of trust and confidence" (*i.e.*, a fiduciary relationship) between shareholders and the insiders who obtained confidential information by reason of their position with that corporation.

employee ➜ corporation ⬅ shareholder

All employees of the company whose stock is being bought or sold are covered—the **CEO** to the **mail room clerk**. If you are an employee of a company and have material undisclosed information about your company, you are subject to the disclose or abstain rule and may be liable civilly or criminally if you violate that rule. The notion that triggers application of Rule 10b-5 is that all employees have a duty of confidentiality to the company for which they work.

The duty of confidentiality and resulting duty to disclose or abstain also extends to attorneys, accountants, public relations firms and investment bankers (and all employees of such firms) engaged to do work for the company in whose stock they trade. These people are sometimes called "constructive fiduciaries" or "temporary insiders." The notion that triggers their duty is the same as that which triggers the duty of employees. By virtue of their engagement, these temporary insiders have a duty of confidentiality that runs to the company.

As this test plays out Mr. Chiarella was not be covered. Chiarella was buying stock of the target company. While Rule 10b-5 would have applied to any purchases by Mr. Chiarella of the bidder company's stock, neither Chiarella, his employer Pandick or Pandick's client (the bidder company) owed a fiduciary duty to the target company, the company whose stock Mr. Chiarello was buying. Thus, the fiduciary nexus was broken and Mr. Chiarella was not prohibited from trading in the target company's stock.

Fiduciary Nexus Test under Chiarella
      Attorney ↘
      Employee → Bidder Company → Shareholder

Test not met in Chiarella case
      Chiarella(buyer) → Pandick → Bidder Company
                  (break in fiduciary nexus)
      Target Company ← Shareholder (seller)

Chiarella is the law today and most insider trading cases are brought under the classical or fiduciary nexus theory established in that case. *Chiarella* was a major step in the development of the law of insider trading. But the

Chiarella case is not the end of the story. If the Chiarella case had come up today, Mr. Chiarella would have gone to jail. He would be convicted today, not under the fiduciary nexus theory, but under an alternative theory of liability called the "**misappropriation theory**," which was established by the U.S. Supreme Court in *United States v. O'Hagan*, the next case considered. While *O'Hagan* was not decided until, 17 years after *Chiarella,* that theory had its genesis in Justice Burger's dissent in *Chiarella*.

The Burger dissent. In their briefs to the Supreme Court, the government attorneys, probably suspecting that a majority of the justices might not buy the equal access rule, presented the court with an alternative theory for upholding Chiarella's conviction. It has come to be called the **misappropriation theory**. It probably got its name from language in Justice Burger's dissenting opinion in which the Chief Justice said he would have upheld Chiarella's conviction based on the alternative theory, which Burger characterized as follows: [Chiarella] "misappropriated—stole to put it bluntly—valuable nonpublic information entrusted to him in utmost confidence." The majority, however, refused to consider this theory because it had not been presented at trial.

In the 17 years between *Chiarella* and *O'Hagan,* although it had opportunities to do so, an apparently divided Supreme Court refused to consider the misappropriation theory. During this time, 5 of the circuit courts upheld the misappropriation theory, but 2 of the circuits rejected the theory. This split of authority in the circuit courts set the stage for the Supreme Court to rule on the validity of the misappropriation theory in *United States v. O'Hagan*.

d.   The Misappropriation Theory—*United States v. O'Hagan*

The *O'Hagan* case involves the sad story of a crooked lawyer. The facts closely resemble those in *Chiarella*. O'Hagan was a partner in the large Minneapolis law firm of Dorsey & Whitney ("D & W"). D & W represented Grand Met, an English company planning a tender offer for control of Pillsbury Corporation.   O'Hagan apparently learned of the transaction from his partners at D & W. O'Hagan had lost a lot of money in the stock market and had embezzled money from clients of D & W. Hoping to make enough money to cover the shortfall in his clients' accounts, O'Hagan bought Pillsbury stock and options, which he later sold after news of the Grand Met tender offer was announced. He made a profit of $4.3 million, but his windfall was short lived.

The federal prosecutors came after him with a 57-count criminal indictment, which included violation of Rule 10b-5 grounded on the misappropriation theory (the only aspect of the case we discuss). He was convicted in the trial court on all counts, but the Eighth Circuit reversed the conviction. The Supreme Court reinstated the conviction and in a well-reasoned opinion, held that Rule 10b-5 liability may be predicated on the "misappropriation theory." The opinion explains the difference between the "**fiduciary nexus theory**," which the court refers to as the "**classical   theory**"   of   insider   trading   and   the "**misappropriation theory**," which some people refer to as "**outsider trading**."

The classical theory is based on fraud on the other party to the transaction, while the misappropriation theory is based upon fraud on the source of the information. We can illustrate the application of the misappropriation theory by an example, using the parties involved in the *O'Hagan* case. The bidder company (source) **entrusts** the D & W law firm (recipient) with material confidential information. An agent of the recipient (O'Hagan) misuses the information by buying stock in the target company in violation of a duty of confidentiality owed by the recipient of the information to the source of the information.

Violation of this duty of confidence (the act of misappropriation) triggers the duty to disclose or abstain. So when O'Hagan traded in the stock of the target company, he violated the disclose or abstain rule. This trade which violated Rule 10b-5, even though no fiduciary nexus could be established between Mr. O'Hagan and the party on the other side of the trade.

Under the misappropriation theory, you are not looking for a fiduciary nexus, as you are in the classical theory. Instead, you are looking for an act of misappropriation that violates a duty of confidentiality owed by the recipient of the information to the source of the information.

When and how does a duty of trust and confidence between the source and the recipient of information arise?

To trigger the duty to disclose or abstain under the misappropriation theory, there has to be a relationship of trust and confidence between the recipient and the source of the information. Clearly there was in the *O'Hagan* and *Chiarella* cases. But in some cases questions arise as to whether such a relationship exists.

The courts have not yet given us a test for determining whether or not such a relationship exists, particularly in nonbusiness settings. But in October 2000 the SEC gave us guidance in the form of a new rule, Rule 10b5-2, which sets forth three nonexclusive bases for determining that a relationship of trust and confidence exists:

(1)   When the person receiving the information agreed to keep the information confidential;
(2)   When the persons involved in the communication had a history or pattern of sharing confidences; and
(3)   When the person who provided the information was a spouse, parent, child, or sibling of the person who received the information, unless it is shown that there was no reasonable expectation of confidentiality.

e. Tippers and Tippees—*Dirks v. SEC*

Chiarella and *O'Hagan* established the rules that apply today to determine the scope of the duty to **disclose or abstain** imposed on the **original recipients** of "inside information." But, *Texas Gulf Sulphur,* the fountainhead case on insider trading, prohibited such trading not only by the original recipients of the inside information, but also by others to whom the information was passed. The *Texas Gulf Sulphur* court labeled these persons "**tippees**."

In this section we will explore the scope of liability of tippees—*i.e.*, the brother-in-law, the golfing buddy or the girlfriend. We will also explore the scope of liability of the persons who passed on the information on to the tippee, labeled "**tippers**" by the *Texas Gulf Sulphur* court.

The case which established the rules that govern in the area of tipper/tippee liability is *Dirks v. SEC*. The company in that case, Equity Funding Co., was more or less the Enron of the 1970s. It was in the business of selling insurance, variable annuities and related financial products. Its stock, which was listed in the New York Stock Exchange, had risen dramatically.

Raymond Dirks, the defendant in the case, was a well known investment analyst and a principal in a New York brokerage firm. Dirks' specialty was analyzing stocks of insurance companies. He had, in the years preceding the case, put many of his clients into Equity Funding and they, as well as Mr. Dirks, personally, had made a lot of money from appreciation in the stock. However, at the time the case arose Dirks himself no longer owned any Equity Funding stock.

Secrist, a former officer of Equity Funding, met with Dirks and told him that Equity Funding was grossly over valued and was engaged in a massive fraud on the investing public. Secrist also told Dirks that he had tried to get the SEC to investigate, but that it did not do so.

Dirks decided to go to the Equity Funding headquarters in Los Angeles and investigate. From his investigation he concluded that Equity Funding was indeed overvalued and had indeed engaged in fraudulent business practices.

On reaching that conclusion, Dirks did two things: (1) he went to the Wall Street Journal, gave it the information, and eventually convinced it to write a series of articles exposing the Equity Funding scam; and (2) while he was investigating and convincing the Wall Street Journal to write the story, but before the story came out, Dirks discussed the Equity Funding situation with several of his clients and advised them to sell. Several of Dirks' clients sold Equity Funding holdings before the Wall Street Journal story was published. After the story was published, the price of Equity Funding's stock dropped dramatically.

The SEC then brought an administrative proceeding against Mr. Dirks for violating Rule 10b-5 by tipping his clients. In the administrative proceeding, the SEC alleged that Dirks violated Rule 10b-5, as a tippee. But the SEC went on to say in its complaint, that while he should not have tipped his clients, because of the good work Mr. Dirks had done in exposing the fraud at Equity Funding, his penalty should be a mere censure (a slap on the wrist) rather than a fine or suspension.

Mr. Dirks, obviously a proud man, was not grateful for the SEC's leniency or appreciative of its compliments. He apparently felt his good reputation had been impugned and appealed the SEC's ruling all the way to the Supreme Court.

The Supreme Court reversed, holding in favor of Dirks, and in so doing gave us the rules on tipper/tippee liability that apply today. The opinion states that to impose liability on a tippee, you have to show two things: (1) that the tipper (Secrist—in this case) breached a fiduciary duty and (2) that the tipper tipped for the purpose of obtaining some sort of personal benefit. This has come to be known as the **personal benefit test**.

The SEC's case failed to satisfy either prongs of the test. Secrist was an ex-employee of Equity Funding and thus no longer in a fiduciary relationship with Equity Funding. Obviously he did not misappropriate anything from the source of the information. And he was not tipping for personal benefit. He asked nothing in return and was merely "blowing the whistle" to expose a fraud. Therefore, Dirks received the information legally and could do with it what he wanted. He was not liable as a tippee. Also, while the issue was not before the court, clients to whom Dirks passed on the information were not liable as sub-tippees. Nor was Secrist liable as a tipper. As we will learn later, if you can establish tippee liability—both the tipper and the tippee, as well as any sub-tippees, will be liable. We will get back to that point later. First, consider the following question:

Can we change the facts of the Dirks case and establish tipper/tippee liability?

Yes. If we change the facts by (1) making Secrist a current employee of Equity Funding, when he told his story to Dirks and (2) having Secrist ask for something in return such as immunity from prosecution in exchange for the information.

In the revised facts since Secrist is a employee we can establish a **fiduciary nexus** between him and the party on the other side of the trade. And by cutting a deal in exchange for the information he would meet the **personal benefit test**.

The rules as to the liability of tippers and tippees play out the same whether the tipper's duty to disclose or abstain arises under the fiduciary nexus (or classical) theory or under the misappropriation theory. If the tipper (1) violates a duty of trust and confidence imposed under either theory by tipping and (2) the personal benefit test is met and (3) the tippee trades, both tipper and tippee may be held liable, either criminally or civilly.

How is the "personal benefit" test met?

There are several ways of meeting the "personal benefit" test. The three main ways the test has been met are: (1) selling the information, (2) giving the information to enhance one's reputation or standing or with the expectation of receiving a reciprocal benefit and (3) giving the information to someone with whom the tipper has a personal relationship. The personal benefits test is applied in a common sense, but somewhat subjective way and generally has been relatively easy to satisfy.

Are eavesdroppers who trade on the basis of inside information they overhear subject to insider trading liability?

No. A person who overhears a conversation between two insiders in a restaurant or an elevator is not liable for insider trading. The classic example is found in *SEC v. Switzer*, where the famous coach overheard a CEO and his wife talking about a transaction which would likely cause price of the stock of the CEO's company to rise, while sunbathing in the stands at a track meet in Norman, Oklahoma. The most interesting aspect of that case was the evidence, introduced by the SEC, which the jury chose to ignore (*i.e.,* telephone calls between the coach and the CEO the night before the track meet and the upgrading of the CEO's season tickets at OU football games from 10 yard line to 50 yard line seats). But according to Coach Switzer's version of the facts, which the jury believed, the coach just got lucky and escaped liability under the eavesdropper rule.

Remote tippees—How far down the line does liability extend?

All the way down the chain. Often there are chains of tipping—*i.e.,* tippee #1 becomes a tipper by passing the inside information on to tippee #2, etc. A case in point is *SEC v. Musella*. There the manager of the steno pool at a major New York law firm which was working on a lot of takeovers, like Mr. Chiarella, figured out the identity of the target companies. He followed the usual pattern of buying shares in the target prior to the announcement and selling at a profit following announcement of the takeover bid.

In this case, he also told his friend the cab driver, who told his friend, the policeman, who told his brother, the president of an investment club in a New York suburb.

The court found all of the tippers and tippees in the chain, including the members of the investment club, liable. The government overcame a defense by the investment club members that they had no idea where the information came from, by convincing the court that conscious indifference, when there was reason for suspicion, was enough to support insider trading liability.

4. SUMMARY OF THE RULES GOVERNING INSIDER TRADING LIABILITY UNDER RULE 10b-5

As reflected in the above discussion, the law of insider trading developed in stages. In the 1960s, the SEC and the federal courts through *Texas Gulf Sulphur,* constructed a disclose or abstain rule which subjected anyone who traded on the basis of material nonpublic information to possible insider trading liability. In the 1980s and 1990s under decisions of the Supreme Court, mainly *Chiarella, O'Hagan* and *Dirks,* the scope of the ban on insider trading was narrowed and more clearly defined.

The linchpin of insider trading liability under Rule 10b-5 is the misuse of material, nonpublic information by persons with a fiduciary duty of confidentiality. Today, there are two theories under which a person can violate a duty which triggers the disclose or abstain rule and thereby incur insider trading liability under Rule 10b-5: (1) when a **fiduciary nexus** is established between the inside trader and the other party to the transaction and (2) when the trader violates a **fiduciary duty owed to the source of the information**. Today the persons prohibited from trading or tipping are fairly clearly defined as follows:

a. Employees of the company in whose shares they trade, from the CEO to the clerk in the mail room. What bars them from trading on the basis of inside information is the fiduciary nexus that runs between the employees and the other parties to the trade, who by definition are shareholders of the company.

b.   Temporary or **Constructive Insiders** are nonemployees of the company, who by virtue of the nature of their work for the company, have access to confidential corporate information. Such persons include employees of law firms, accounting firms, public relations firms, investment bankers and the like.

c. Persons Who Misappropriate Information entrusted to them by the source of the information. The classic example is the wayward attorney O'Hagan, a partner in the law firm representing the bidder company in a tender offer, who bought stock and options of the target company. While O'Hagan owed no fiduciary duty to the other party to the transaction (shareholders of the target company), the act of misappropriating confidential information from the source of the information triggered the duty to disclose or abstain and resulting liability under Rule 10b-5.

d. Tippers and Tippees. The disclose or abstain rule not only prohibits trading, but also tipping persons who trade, on the basis of confidential nonpublic information. Under the *Dirks* test, if the tipper acquired the inside information in violation of a fiduciary duty and passes the information on to someone else to obtain a personal benefit, both the original tipper and tippee as well as any subsequent tippers and tippees in the chain may be subject to insider trading liability.

e. Other Persons Not Covered. Persons who have no fiduciary relationship to the corporation whose shares are traded or the source of the confidential information are not subject to the disclose or abstain rule and can thus trade without Rule 10b-5 liability. Such persons include the eavesdropping coach, the securities analysts who digs up information and a host of others, who through hard work, persistence, skill, or luck posses better information about the value of the stock they buy or sell than the party on the other side of the trade.

CHAPTER IX

HOW DO THE OWNERS OF A BUSINESS MAKE MONEY?

Generally, the owners of a business, regardless of the form of business structure, can make money by (1) being paid a salary by the business, (2) receiving distributions of all or part of the profits from the business or (3) selling all or part of their interest in the business at a profit.

Many of the answers to the issues discussed in this chapter are governed by areas of the law other than the law of business structures—*i.e.*, contract law, tax law, etc. However, the type of business structure and the governing statutes often have an impact on how the owners of the business make money. Since many of the legal issues discussed in this chapter are also discussed in other parts of the book, this chapter contains a number of cross references to avoid repetition.

A. PARTNERSHIPS

How do the owners of a partnership (i.e., the partners) make money?

1. SALARY

Partners' salaries are usually governed by the partnership agreement. If the partnership agreement does not contain a provision that governs a particular issue, certain default provisions in the governing partnership statute may come into play.

Examples:

a. Assume *A, B* and *C* are partners in the ABC Taco Stand, a partnership, governed by RUPA. *A* works at the partnership full time. *B* and *C* are investors and do not work at the partnership. In the absence of agreement is *A* entitled to receive a salary?

No. RUPA (§ 401(h)) provides that a partner is not entitled to remuneration for services performed for the partnership.[1] As we learned earlier, this is merely the default rule which the parties can alter by agreement. See, *e.g.*, RUPA § 103(a). For *A* to receive a salary, a majority of the partners must agree to pay him a salary. RUPA § 401(h).

b. Assume the partnership agreement provides that *A* will receive an annual salary of $50,000. After a year *A* feels he is entitled to a raise to $60,000. Who is required to authorize the increase?

Since the increase in salary would effect a change in the partnership agreement, all of the partners must agree to the raise. RUPA § 401(j).

c. Can the partnership pay *C* a salary even though she does not do any work for the partnership?

---

1. Except reasonable compensation for services in winding up the business of the partnership.

Yes. If the partners agree the partnership can pay her a salary. However, the salary paid to *C* would reduce the distributions the other two partners could receive.

The main points to get from the above examples are: (1) the partnership agreement usually controls, (2) if a partner is to receive a salary the partnership agreement must so provide and (3) persons drafting partnership agreements must be aware of the default provisions in the governing statute so that they can draft around those default provisions that do reflect their needs or desires.

2. DISTRIBUTIONS AND PROFITS

"Profits" and "distributions" are not synonyms. There can be profits without distributions and distributions without profits. Profits are determined by accounting principles and distributions by vote of the partners. Partners' rights to profits and distributions, like partners' salaries are usually governed by the partnership agreement. But, again, default provisions of the governing statute may control, if the parties do not contract around such provisions.

Examples:

a. Assume *A*, *B* and *C* are partners in the ABC Taco Stand, a partnership governed by RUPA. *C* invests $75,000 in the partnership, *B* invests $25,000. *C* does not invest any money in the partnership but works full time for the partnership and draws a salary. The partnership makes a profit of $99,000 in 2002. How will the profits be shared among *A*, *B* and *C*?

Each partner will get $33,000. Absent an agreement to the contrary each partner is entitled to an equal share of the profits. RUPA § 401(b).

b. Assume the partnership makes a profit of $99,000 in 2002 and the profits are allocated equally to each partner. *A* wants a distribution of substantially all of his share of the partnership's profits, but *B* and *C* believe that the partnership should make no distributions to partners, but rather should use the $99,000 for capital improvements and advertising. Who decides what distributions the partners will receive?

Assuming there is no provision in the partnership agreement which controls, the decision as to distributions would be made by a majority of the partners (here *B* and *C* could out vote *A*). See RUPA § 4.01(j).

RUPA § 4.01(a) should also be considered. This provision requires that each partner have a capital account and defines the "**partner's capital account**" as an amount that equals the partner's capital contributions *plus* allocations of profit to the partner *minus* distributions to the partner and allocations of losses to the partner.

The capital accounts of the various partners govern how the assets of the partnership will be distributed upon liquidation of the partnership, a matter you will learn about in the next chapter.

3. SALES OF PARTNERSHIP INTERESTS AND DISTRIBUTIONS UPON WITHDRAWAL OF A PARTNER

You will learn about these matters in the next chapter in connection with our discussion of the dissolution of partnerships. For now you should focus on the fundamental fact that partnerships are readily terminable. And that upon termination (discussed in the next chapter) the withdrawing partner is generally entitled to receive fair market value for her interest in the partnership. This differs significantly from corporate law where termination is usually not an option. This distinguishing attribute between partnership law and corporate law is often referred to as the "exit rules," which were discussed in Chapter II and will be further discussed in Chapter X.

How much of the money made by the partnership does the IRS get?

Under Subchapter K, partnerships and associations taxable as partnerships are not separate taxable entities, but rather are treated as conduits through which the tax consequences of their activities are passed through to their owners. As previously noted this tax scheme is generally referred to as "pass through taxation." The partnership prepares an informational tax return, but it pays no tax. Rather the tax is allocated to the partners, who receive Form K-1's and include their share of the income or loss generated by the partnership on their individual returns. The result is that taxable income is only taxed once—at the individual level. However, since the tax is on "profits" at the partnership level rather than on"distributions" to the partners, the partners may be required to pay taxes on income which they do not receive.

Under "check the box," an elective scheme of taxation adopted in 1997, except for publicly traded partnerships, the vast majority of partnerships (and other unincorporated business structures) can choose to be taxed either as partnerships or corporations on an elective basis simply by checking the appropriate box, the first time they file a tax return. As previously noted in Chapter II, generally partners get to keep a greater share of the money made by the business by electing to be taxed as partnerships and almost all partnerships so elect.

B. CORPORATIONS

How do the owners of a corporation (i.e., the shareholders) make money?

First, the way owners of a corporation (*i.e.*, "shareholders") make money will depend on whether they are shareholders of a **close corporation** or shareholders of a **public corporation**, a distinction that arises in many areas of corporate law. Recall you previously learned that the most important difference is the presence of a market for shares of a public corporation compared to the absence of a market for shares of a close corporation. This obviously has an impact on how shareholders make money.

The typical shareholder of a public corporation hopes to make money from her investment either by receiving part of the corporation's profits through distributions called "dividends" or by selling her shares for more than she paid for them, called "capital gains" or a combination of the two called "total return." She faces business issues (*i.e.,* picking stocks that go up in value rather than down), deciding when to buy and when to sell (*i.e.,* buying low and selling high) and tax issues (*i.e.,* long term capital gains are taxed at 20% as opposed to the maximum marginal tax rate of 35% on ordinary income which includes dividend income). But unless she finds herself a plaintiff in a shareholders derivative suit or a class action for violations of fiduciary duties or rule 10b-5, matters discussed earlier in Chapters VII and VIII, the ordinary shareholder will rarely face legal issues.

By contrast, shareholders of close corporations may face many legal issues which pertain to the ways in which they make money from the business. Basically shareholders of a corporation make money in the same way as partners in a partnership:

(1) profit from the sale of their interest in the business,
(2) distributions from the earnings of the business (*i.e.,* "dividends") and
(3) salary.

However, both the underlying business considerations and the legal issues differ in a corporate as opposed to a partnership environment.

1. PROFITS FROM THE SALE OF THE BUSINESS

You will learn about selling the business in Chapter X. You learned about "going public" (which is the functional equivalent to selling a part of the business) in Chapter V. For now, reconsider the problem of the minority shareholder, discussed in § VII.B.3.c, *supra*. His minority interest is likely unsalable due to the absence of a market and he does not have the ability to "exit" by forcing a dissolution like a partner in a partnership can do.

2. DIVIDENDS

a. Definitions and Concepts Related to Dividends

What is a dividend?

A "dividend" is a payment to shareholders out of current or retained earnings made to shareholders in proportion to the number of shares they own. Dividends are usually paid, at the discretion of directors, periodically to shareholders in relation to their share ownership.

Payments by a corporation to its shareholders other than those out of past or current earnings are called "capital distributions," "return of capital" or simply "distributions." Notice the definition of a dividend is based on an accounting concept—retained earnings. This is another example of a point made earlier that some knowledge of accounting is helpful in many areas of the law of business structures.

The tax laws recognize this distinction. Dividends are taxable to the shareholders as ordinary income, while returns of capital are not taxed.

What is the effect of paying dividends?

The effect of a dividend payment or for that matter any corporate distribution is to transfer assets from the corporation to its shareholders.

Who might be harmed by the payment of dividends?

Creditors. Creditors might be counting on the assets paid out as dividends to satisfy their claims against the corporation.   The creditors are concerned that the shareholders might exhaust the corporation's assets by paying dividends to themselves. For this reason, creditors often limit the amount of dividends a corporation may pay through contractual restrictions in loan agreements.

Minority shareholders. In close corporations dividend policy may be used to skew the rewards of ownership in favor of majority shareholders at the expense of minority shareholders or to "freeze out" minority shareholders. The board of directors of closely held corporations are almost always the majority shareholders and/or persons under their control. As managers of the corporation the majority shareholders typically receive money from the corporation in the form of salary and benefits rather than dividends.

On the other hand, minority shareholders' (who are not employed by the corporation) main means of receiving money from the corporation is through dividends. Unlike partners, it is difficult for minority shareholders in a close corporation to force a dissolution in which they can cash out their interest in the business at fair market value. It is important for minority shareholders to establish an exit strategy contractually through some sort of a buy/sell agreement, as discussed earlier.

Tax consideration: dividends compared to salaries.

As previously noted, except in Subchapter S corporations, dividends are subject to double taxation (the corporation is taxed on its profits and shareholders are taxed on the portion of such profits distributed to them by way of dividends). On the other hand salaries are deductible at the corporate level as an ordinary and necessary business expense.

Who decides when and in what amount dividends are to be paid?

Decisions on the payment of dividends are within the **discretion of the board of directors** and the board's discretion is protected under the business judgement rule. Some companies have a policy of paying no dividends or low dividends, while others have a policy of paying high dividends. While the board's discretion in paying dividends is extremely broad it may be limited in three ways:

1. Contractual Limitations. Provisions in loan agreements, indentures or other contracts may limit the payment of dividends, usually to protect creditors.

2. Statutory Limitations. In some states provisions in the state corporate statute limit the payment of dividends by designating the sources out of which dividends can be paid.

3. Judicial Limitations. The courts require that the board does not abuse its discretion in paying dividends.

The first of the above limitations is governed by contract law and needs no further discussion. We will discuss the second and third limitations in the next two subsections.

b. When *Can* a Dividend be Paid? ("Permissive Dividends")

The statutes of every state establish tests for determining when dividends can be paid—permissive dividends. The state corporate statutes generally impose two tests: (1) a solvency test and (2) some version of what is generally referred to as a "balance sheet" test. The balance sheet test varies widely from state to state.

Consider, for example, MBCA § 6.40, which imposes the following requirements for payment of distributions, including permissive dividends:

1. Solvency Test. If, after giving effect to the distribution, the corporation is able to pay its debts as they come due in the ordinary course of business, it may pay dividends.

2. Balance Sheet Test. If, after giving effect to the distribution, the corporation's total assets are greater than the sum of its total liabilities and the amount necessary to satisfy any preferential liquidation rights, it may pay dividends.

The MBCA merely requires that you look at the total assets (things the corporation owns, as reflected on the left side of the balance sheet) and total liabilities (what the corporation owes, as reflected on the right hand side of the balance sheet). And if the assets exceed the liabilities, dividends can be paid from any source available to the corporation, provided the solvency test is also met. This is tantamount to saying as long as paying a dividend does not render the corporation insolvent or unable to satisfy preferential rights, dividends may be paid.

Traditional approach. While some states have adopted the approach of MBCA § 6.40, most states still follow the so-called "traditional" approach which is more restrictive than MBCA § 6.40. In addition to a solvency requirement,[2] a corporate statute based on the traditional approach also contains restrictions based upon the amount reflected in accounts shown on the balance sheet. The restrictions, which vary from state to state, are phrased in accounting terms applicable to the three accounts which comprise the "shareholders equity" section on the right hand side of the balance sheet.

One such account is called "**retained earnings**" or "**earned surplus**," synonyms used to describe the total cumulative earnings of the corporation since its inception less the amount paid out as dividends or other distributions. In other words **retained earnings** (or **earned surplus**), consist of value generated by the business and retained in the business (*i.e.*, net profits over the years less distributions over the years). All states permit dividends to be paid out of retained earnings and some states limited

---

2. The definition of insolvency varies in the state statutes.

dividend payments to the amount shown in the retained earnings account.

The other two components of the shareholders equity section of the balance sheet relate to capital raised by the corporation from the sale of its stock.[3]

Stated capital (which also goes by several other names including simply "common stock" or "capital stock") is the number of shares outstanding times the par value per share (or the amount allocated to stated capital by the board of directors in the case of "no par" stock).

Capital surplus (sometimes called "paid in capital") is the dollar amount over par value (or the amount designated as capital in the case of no par stock) paid for shares of the corporation at the time of the original issuance of such shares.

Some states allow dividends to be paid out of capital surplus as well as retained earnings, but not from stated capital.

Restrictions on dividend payments under the traditional approach were designed in theory to provide a cushion for the benefit of creditors by generally requiring that the bulk of dividends be paid out of current or past earnings, rather than from monies received from the sale of stock. This goal was probably never achieved because of the discretion

---

3. Rather than the sale of its products and services.

retained by the board in determining the amount of stated capital by setting par value at any amount they choose.

The traditional approach requires that you understand the three accounts discussed above and how the various state statutes define the restrictions based on the numbers reflected in such accounts. Under the simplified modern approach, as typified by the MBCA, this becomes irrelevant. The modern approach reflects the decline in importance of the concept of par value. The extent of knowledge of this area required in the basic business course will depend upon how much emphasis your professor gives to this area.

c. When Must Dividends be Paid? (Mandatory Dividends)

Recall earlier we noted that, assuming a corporation has funds available for the payment of dividends under statutory tests discussed in the preceding subsection, the board has broad discretion as to whether or not dividends will be paid. Since the directors' discretion as to payment of dividends is protected by the business judgement rule a plaintiff must show bad faith or a conflict of interest in order to compel the payment of dividends.

Suits to compel payment of dividends usually occur in close corporations and involve suits by minority shareholders against majority shareholders, who control the board (and thus the dividend policy). *Zidell v. Zidell*, a case found in many casebooks, involves a closely held corporation owned by various members of a single family.

Arnold, the plaintiff, owned ⅜ of the outstanding shares; his brother Emery owned ⅜ of the outstanding shares and Emery's son Jay owned the remaining ¼ of the outstanding shares. Until 1973 all three worked for the corporation and drew salaries. During the years prior to 1973 the corporation paid little or no dividends. In 1973 Arnold demanded a raise in salary from $30,000 to $50,000 per year and when the raise was refused, Arnold resigned.

In a suit to compel the payment of dividends, Arnold presented evidence showing that the corporation had sufficient retained earnings to pay greater dividends, that defendants were receiving substantial (though not excessive) compensation by way of salary and benefits and that there was hostility between Arnold and the other shareholders. Defendants' evidence, introduced to explain the board's conservative business policies, included tax considerations, plans for future possible expansion, needs to make future physical improvements, seasonal needs for cash to finance the purchase of inventory, etc.

The trial court ordered the corporation to pay larger dividends. It did not hold that Emery and Jay had acted in bad faith, but based its decision on grounds that larger dividends were necessary to give Arnold a reasonable return on his equity in the corporation.

The Oregon Supreme Court reversed the trial court and held that to compel the payment of dividends plaintiff had to show "**bad faith**" on the part of the defendants. The fact that Arnold resigned his employment, rather than being fired, obviously hurt his case. This case effectively illustrates that a plaintiff seeking to compel the payment of dividends faces an uphill battle.

Occasionally, however, courts do order the board to pay dividends. The Supreme Court of Michigan so ruled in what is one of the most famous and most studied cases in corporate law, *Dodge v. Ford Motor Co.*

At the time this case arose, the Ford Motor Company ("Ford") was a closely held corporation (an extremely successful closely held corporation). Ford had paid large dividends in prior years. At the time of suit, Ford had $112 million in surplus. Profits for the then current year were expected to exceed $60 million and cash on hand exceeded $54 million. These were all very large amounts in 1916.

The early investors in Ford (minority shareholders) had made a very good investment. Two of these early shareholders, the Dodge brothers, had used a good bit of the money they had received from Ford in dividends to start their own car company. This probably did not please Henry Ford, the controlling shareholder and CEO of Ford, who announced Ford was canceling dividends.

The Dodge brothers brought suit to compel the payment of dividends. Henry Ford probably sealed his own fate at the trial. Rather than speaking vaguely about future contingencies, the large capital needs of an automobile manufacturer, the need to expand for purposes of increasing profits, etc., he was straight forward on the witness stand about his motives and intentions. Henry Ford said he wanted to build a new plant and increase production so that he could build more cars, less expensively, and drive down the price of cars.

Henry Ford testified that he wanted to make as many cars as possible, as cheap as possible so that in Mr. Ford's words "any American with a decent job could afford one." Most people thought that was dumb. Why not charge more for the cars? But Ford turned out to be right. He understood that in the long run the company could make far more money by making cars cheeper and selling more of them. Ford also paid its workers substantially more than the going wage. Most people thought that was also dumb, but it turned out to be smart. It gave Ford a stable work force in pre-union days. Once a worker got a job with Ford he was not about to give up that job. Today it is clear that Henry Ford's policies contributed greatly to the success of the Ford Motor Company. These policies are part of what students learn from this case in the business schools.

In law school, the case teaches us that if Henry Ford had testified that he wanted to produce cars less expensively so he could increase Ford's profits, it is unlikely that the court would have overruled his decision to discontinue dividends and plow the money back into the business. But the Michigan Supreme Court found that Henry Ford's stated reasons were imprudent. That, coupled with the large cash surpluses and Ford's history of paying dividends, caused the court to order Ford to pay dividends.

Courts are reluctant to compel payment of dividends. The *Ford* case is an anomaly. It is one of few cases, other than obvious attempts by the majority to freeze out the minority, where a company was ordered to pay dividends.

The reason is the business judgement rule. Judges are usually reluctant to substitute their business judgement for that of the board of directors. This case seems to support the wisdom of the business judgement rule. In hindsight, it seems clear that Henry Ford's business judgement proved to be better than the court's. This unique case does not alter the general rule, that in the absence of clear evidence of **bad faith** or **conflict of interest**, the courts will rarely second guess the business judgement of the board on questions concerning the payment of dividends.

3. SALARY

The issues likely to arise with respect to the payment by a corporation of salary and other benefits differ in publicly held and closely held corporations.

a. Publicly Held Corporations

In publicly held corporations, where ownership is separate from management, the board typically sets the compensation of the CEO and other senior executives by resolutions, usually adopted on an annual basis. The "compensation package" often consists of (1) salary, (2) bonuses, (3) deferred compensation, (4) stock options and (5) other benefits and perks.

Obviously, the executives want to obtain the most generous compensation package they can and the board of directors has wide discretion in fixing executive compensation. Often senior corporate executives are also members of the board. And many senior executives have considerable influence over members of the board, which is charged with fixing their compensation. This brings into play issues discussed earlier in conflict of interest situations and possible suits for violation of fiduciary duties. See § VII.A.3, *supra*.

Today, most publicly held companies have compensation committees, composed of outside directors (directors who are not employees of the company), which set the compensation of the corporation's top executives. Additionally public corporations usually get shareholder approval of compensation plans through the proxy solicitation process.

The law does impose a standard of **reasonableness** on compensation and in cases where shareholders attack an executive's compensation as unreasonable, the courts may review the fairness of an executive's compensation. However, even in this Enron era, full fledged judicial fairness review of executive compensation is relatively rare.

Courts are reluctant to review the fairness of executive salaries and have developed a rule for limited judicial review. When a majority of informed disinterested directors or shareholders approve the compensation of a senior executive, the compensation package will **not** be treated as a form of self dealing and will not be subject to **fairness review** by the courts.

Stated another way, if disinterested approval is obtained the courts will give decisions concerning executive compensation the same degree of deference under the business judgement as they give to other types of operating decisions, such as whether to play day or night baseball. A plaintiff has to show that the executive's compensation had no relationship to the value of the services performed—a **waste** standard.   On the other hand if disinterested approval is not obtained, courts will review the compensation package under a **fairness** standard.

In addition, the Internal Revenue Code contains rules that limit the deductibility of compensation over a certain level as an ordinary and necessary business expense at the corporate level. And the SEC's proxy rules require full and detailed disclosure regarding executive compensation. See § VI.B.4.b, *supra.*

b. Close Corporations

In the typical closely held corporation, most if not all of the shareholders are likely to be employees of the corporation.   Often such employment and the accompanying salary is the shareholder's principal reason for becoming a shareholder. When this is the case several potential legal issues might arise.

Reasonable salaries.   Salaries are often utilized to counteract the impact of double taxation which is imposed under Subchapter C of the IRC. Recall the tax rule is that while reasonable salaries are deductible by the corporation as an ordinary and necessary business expenses, the same monies paid in the form of dividends are not deductible by

the corporation.   Thus, in closely held corporations
(particularly where all of the shareholders are employed by
the corporation) there is a strong incentive to set salaries
as high as possible to avoid taxes at the corporate level.
The IRS routinely reviews the reasonableness of salaries
and often disallows the deduction for part of the salary,
which they view as a dividend in disguise.

Protecting future salary; exit strategy.   Even larger
issues relating to salary might arise in close corporations
where some, but not all of the shareholders, are employed
by the corporation. For example, assume that *A, B* and *C*
are the founders and each owns ⅓ of the outstanding
shares of ABC Tacos, Inc., a corporation. Each originally
invested $25,000 in the business, each is employed full time
in the business, and each depends on the business as the
primary source of his livelihood. As is typical of close
corporations, ABC Tacos, Inc. pays no dividends, but most
of the company's current earnings are distributed to the
owners through payment of salaries and benefits.
Following several successful years of operation, there is a
disagreement. *A* and *B* remove *C* from the board and then
fire *C* as an employee. Following *C*s termination of
employment, *A* and *B* continue their policy of paying no
dividends and distributing most of the company's earning
to themselves through salaries and benefits.

These were essentially the facts of *Wilkes v. Springside
Nursing Home, Inc.*, discussed in § VII.D, *supra*, in
connection with our discussion of the stricter fiduciary
duties that some, but not all, states impose on control
shareholders of close corporations. Here we revisit those
facts to discuss ways in which the problem could have been

avoided. This is important because lawyers who represent businesses work as "counselors" (planners to avoid litigation) as much, if not more, than they work as litigators resolving disputes. Much of the material in the basic business course is about planning and many professors like to test students' ability to see planning issues.

How would you handle an exam question that requires you to focus on planning issues raised by the above example?

First, you look at the probable expectations of the parties to the deal. Continued employment by and salary from the business were probably a big part of C's reason for doing the deal. While C's shares in the corporation are, in theory freely transferable, seldom does anyone want to buy a minority interest in a close corporation. Further, a minority shareholder in a corporation, unlike a partner in a partnership, can not easily compel a dissolution in which his interest is bought out. Controlling shareholders have some incentive to buy out minority shareholders, if the price is right, because disgruntled minority shareholders can be a nuisance. They can file suits claiming the directors abused their discretion in failing to pay dividends, that the controlling shareholders violated their fiduciary duties, etc. But the price they are willing to offer is often inadequate.

Second, once you recognize the underlying economics, the solution should become relatively clear. The minority shareholder (C in our example) should realize the importance of an exit strategy going into the deal and provide for a potential exit. In earlier sections of the book we have discussed various devices through which *C*s exit could be achieved, such as buy-sell agreements and employment contracts. Material covered earlier also raises the question of whether the corporate form of business structure is the best alternative for the ABC Tacos, Inc.

How much of the money made by a corporation does the IRS get?

Subchapter C of the IRC provides that a corporation is a separate taxable entity, independent of its shareholders. As a result, corporations file tax returns and pay tax on whatever taxable income the corporation earns. If the corporation then distributes the income to shareholders, as dividends, the shareholders pay tax on the dividends they receive.

This is referred to as double taxation because the earnings of a C corporation are subject to federal income taxation at two different levels—first at the corporate level and second at the shareholder level, if the shareholder receives dividends from the corporation. The impact of double taxation may significantly reduce the amount of the company's earnings that the owners get to keep. For example, assume a situation in which the marginal tax rate is 35% for both the corporation and a shareholder. In that case every $100 of the corporation's pre-tax earnings becomes $42.25 when it is distributed as dividends, following taxation at both the corporate and personal levels [*i.e.,* $100 x (1 - 0.35) x (1 - 0.35) = $42.25].

In closely held corporations double taxation does not necessarily mean that the corporation and its shareholders will wind up paying more taxes. The disadvantage of double taxation can sometimes be mitigated through a technique known as "**zeroing out income**" at the corporate level. Essentially this entails **not paying dividends**, but rather **accumulating cash** at the corporate level or paying out profits in the form of **salaries** or **benefits** to shareholders. Salaries can only be paid to persons actually employed by the corporation, the salaries must be reasonable, and as a practical matter, "zeroing" can only be done when there is significant identity of interest among the shareholders of the corporation. Unless you have a professor who emphasizes tax considerations, the ability to zero out income is not likely to be tested in the basic business course.

Subchapter S permits closely held corporations that meet certain specified requirements to elect to be taxed in a way that avoids double taxation. Subchapter S taxation is generally similar to the way in which partnerships and associations taxed as partnerships are taxed under Subchapter K, discussed earlier. A Subchapter S corporation is a true corporation. Filing the election does not change any of the basic corporate attributes, except the way the corporation is taxed.

To be eligible for Subchapter S tax treatment, a corporation must meet the following requirements on the date of the election: (1) It must be a domestic corporation; (2) with no more than 75 shareholders; (3) each shareholder must be an individual, a decedent's estate or a certain type of trusts; (4) no shareholder may be a nonresident alien; and (5) the corporation may have only one class of stock outstanding. In general the tax treatment under Subchapter S and Subchapter K are similar in that both provide **pass through taxation**, and thus eliminate the problem of double taxation under Subchapter C. The details vary, in ways beyond your needs in the basic business course and our ability to explain in this book.

C. LIMITED LIABILITY COMPANIES

How do the owners of an LLC (i.e., the "members") make money?

The owners ("members") of a Limited Liability Company ("LLC") make money the same way as partners of a partnership or shareholders of a close corporation: by sharing in the earnings of the business, and by selling their ownership interests for more than they paid for them. Also members employed by the LLC may receive salaries.

Most issues relating to an LLC's payments to its members are governed by the operating agreement. Recall most LLC statutes have adopted a policy of giving maximum effect to freedom of contract and the provisions of the operating agreement. See, *e.g.*, Del. LLCA § 18-1101(b).

The governing statutes do contain default rules which govern if but only if, an issue is not covered in the operating agreement. Thus, the main point to keep in mind with respect to LLCs is a drafting point—anticipate the expectations and desires of the parties to the deal and draft an operating agreement that abrogates any default provisions in the governing statute which does not reflect those expectations and desires. Many professors emphasize drafting with respect to LLCs because the statutes are diverse and the LLC is so new that there is not yet much case law.

How much of the money made by the LLC does the IRS get?

Today, under the "check the box" regulations, almost all LLCs are taxed like partnerships under Subchapter K of IRC. See § IX.A, *supra*.

Until January 1, 1997, the I RS had a set of regulations, the "Kintner Rules," under which the IRS determined which unincorporated limited liability entities would be taxed as corporations under Subchapter C and which would be taxed as partnerships under Subchapter K. The basic test under the Kintner Rules was whether a particular business structure had more corporate attributes (*i.e.,* limited liability, continuity of life, centralized management and free transferability of interests) or more noncorporate attributes. If the business entity had more than two of the corporate attributes listed above, it would be taxed as a corporation under Subchapter C. Consequently, many first generation LLC statutes had provisions intended to negate transferability and continuity of existence to facilitate pass through tax treatment. These were called "bullet proof" LLC statutes.

Since the Kintner Regulations were repealed, effective January 1, 1997, and the current "check the box" rules were adopted in lieu thereof, provisions in these so-called bullet proof statutes, like Del. LLCA § 18-702, are no longer necessary. Many states have amended their LLC statutes to reflect this change in the tax laws.

With the elimination of the uncertainty as to their tax status under the arcane Kintner rules, the LLC has emerged as the business structure of choice for thousands of closely-held businesses throughout the United States. For example, reconsider the example of ABC Tacos, Inc. in § IX.B, above. All things considered, an LLC would probably be a better form of business structure for that business than a corporation.

CHAPTER X

HOW DO BUSINESS STRUCTURES END?

Like human beings, business structures have a life cycle. At some point in time the business structure will end. Some end very quickly; others last a very long time. Happy endings; sad endings; endings that are happy for some and sad for others.

You need to be able to answer three questions about ending a business structure:

(1) Who makes the decision to end the "life" of the business structure"?

(2) Who gets what when a business structure ends?

(3) Who owes what when a business structure ends?

The answers to these questions depend on (1) the form of the business structure, (2) relevant state law and (3) the agreements of the owners of the business.

A. PARTNERSHIPS

Remember that some state partnership laws are based on the Uniform Partnership Act. Others are based on the Revised Uniform Partnership Act.

1. DISSOLUTION UNDER UPA COMPARED WITH RUPA DISSOCIATION AND DISSOLUTION

a. UPA Dissolution

Dissolution is a key UPA end game concept, which is defined in UPA § 29.

Under §§ 29–32 of the UPA, "dissolution" of the partnership occurs every time a partner files for bankruptcy, dies or otherwise withdraws from the partnership. This is consistent with the UPA's view of a partnership as an aggregate of its members. Under UPA, when a partner departs, the aggregate changes and so the prior partnership is dissolved.

And under the UPA, a partner always has the power to withdraw and thus dissolve the partnership—regardless of what the partnership agreement might otherwise provide. If, for example, the partnership agreement provides for a ten year term and each partner covenants that she will not withdraw from the partnership until the expiration of that term, a partner still has the legal power (albeit not the legal right) to withdraw and cause the dissolution of the partnership.

Dissolution under the UPA does not necessarily mean that the business is liquidated. Under certain circumstances, the partners can decide to continue the business after dissolution but it is a new partnership that is continuing the business.

Under UPA, the circumstances for continuing the business of a partnership after dissolution depend on (1) the partnership agreement's provisions on continuing the business after dissolution and (2) if there are no such provisions, the "default rules" of UPA. In the "real world," partnerships that are large enough to warrant hiring lawyers to deal with dissolution usually have written partnership agreements with provisions on continuing the business after dissolution. In law school classes, professors usually teach and test the UPA or RUPA default rules.

Under the UPA default rules, if there is no term specified in the partnership agreement or if the term specified has expired, then the partnership business can be continued by the other partners only if all of the partners, including the partner who dissolved the partnership, agree that the business can be continued. If they agree to continue to the business, then the withdrawing partner is paid the value of her interest in the business as determined by § 42 of UPA.

If a partner leaves a partnership before the end of the term specified in the partnership agreement, then the business of the partnership can be continued if all of the partners other than the one who wrongfully dissolved the partnership so agree. If they decide to continue the business, the departing partner is again paid for the value of her interest. Again, look to § 42 of UPA to value that interest except (i) "goodwill" is not included in valuing the business and (ii) the payment to the departing partner is reduced by any damages caused by the premature dissolution.

If the partners do not decide to continue the business after UPA dissolution, the business is liquidated under UPA § 37 and § 40. The partnership is "wound up" under UPA § 37; the assets are sold and distributed to creditors and then to partners (including the departing partner) pursuant to UPA § 40. Regardless of whether the partnership business continues or is liquidated, dissolution raises creditors' rights issues. UPA §§ 33–36 governs the liability of partners on dissolution for partnership debts.

Think about the law school exam possibilities of UPA dissolution. Under UPA, dissolution can always be triggered by the withdrawal of any one partner. And under UPA, unless the partnership agreement otherwise provides, dissolution in essence triggers a liquidation right in each partner. If, for example, *A*, *B*, *C*, *D* and *E* are partners, and *E* withdraws, then *A* can prevent the continuation of the partnership business even though *B*, *C* and *D* favor continuation.

b. Dissociation Under RUPA

RUPA's end game default rules are significantly different from the UPA rules considered above. RUPA adds the new concept of "dissociation."

Dissociation is about a partner's withdrawal from the partnership. Under RUPA and under UPA, a partner always has the legal power to withdraw from a partnership, regardless of what the partnership agreement provides. RUPA, however, terms such withdrawal "dissociation."

More important, under RUPA dissociation does not always result in dissolution. First, RUPA § 103 provides that a partnership agreement can provide that dissociation does not trigger dissolution. Second, RUPA § 801 provides that a partner's dissociation during a term partnership triggers dissolution only if at least half of the remaining partners so agree. Third, RUPA § 802 provides that partners can waive dissolution.

Again, think about the law school exam possibilities. *A*, *B*, *C*, *D*, *E* and *F* are partners, and their partnership agreement has a seven year term. After a year, *A* wants to withdraw. While she has the power to dissociate, her wrongful dissociation will not trigger dissolution of a RUPA partnership unless a majority of the partners so agree. If, however, their partnership agreement was at will, then *A*'s RUPA dissociation will result in RUPA dissolution unless, under § 802, all of the partners including the dissociating partner, waive the dissolution.

If a partner's dissociation is not followed by the partnership's dissolution, then the dissociating partner's interest in the partnership must be purchased pursuant to the buy out rules in Article 7 of RUPA. In statute talk, an Article 6 dissociation will always trigger either an Article 7 buy out or an Article 8 dissolution.

RUPA differs from UPA not only in its introduction of the concept of "dissociation" but also in its use of the concept of "dissolution." Under RUPA, unlike UPA, "dissolution" always results in termination of the partnership business and liquidation of the partnership assets.

Recall that under UPA, partners can agree to continue the business after dissolution. Under RUPA, partners can agree to waive the dissolution but absent a RUPA § 802 waiver, dissolution under RUPA always results in winding up the partnership.

2. WINDING UP

The partnership does not end with dissolution. UPA § 30 and RUPA § 802 provide that dissolution does not terminate the partnership; instead the partnership continues until the winding up process is complete. Winding up involves selling the partnership's assets and using the sale proceeds to pay the partnership's debts and settle partnership accounts.

UPA § 37 and RUPA § 803 answer the question of which partners have wind up rights and responsibilities. Law professor more commonly ask questions about winding up payments.

Under UPA § 40, "outside" debts, *i.e.*, debts owed to persons other than partners, are paid before "inside" debts, *i.e.*, debts owed to partners. RUPA § 807 eliminates this distinction. Under both UPA and RUPA, the partners have a contribution obligation. If the proceeds from the liquidation of partnership assets are not sufficient to pay creditors, the partners must contribute toward payment of the debt in the same proportion in which they share losses.

"Dissolution," "termination" and "winding up" are not only interrelated concepts that need to be understood. They are also "words of art" defined in the partnership statutes in a way that is different from the way people ordinarily use these words.

Dissolution is the point in time when the partners cease to carry on business together. **Termination** is the point in time when all the partnership's affairs have been wound up. **Winding up** is the period between dissolution and termination.

A simple time line and example will illustrate the process.

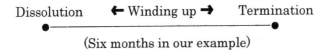

(Six months in our example)

Example: Assume that *A* and *B* form a partnership to operate a shoe store, which they call the AB Shoe Store Partnership. *A* is the financial partner who will supply the money. *B* is the "talent" who will run the shoe store. The partnership is governed by UPA. Since no term is specified for the partnership, the AB Shoe Store Partnership is terminable at will.

A and *B* begin business. They take a three year lease on a building, buy equipment and inventory and run a successful business for two and a half years. At that point *B*, the talent, who has managed to save over $20,000 from his share of the earnings of the shoe store decides he wants to go to law school. Six months before the lease expires, *B* notifies *A* that he wants to dissolve the partnership. *A*, the money, cannot find anyone else to run the shoe store so she agrees to dissolve and liquidate. At that point the **dissolution occurs** and the process of **winding up** begins.

During the wind up period the AB Shoe Store Partnership must continue to comply with all its contractual obligations, which include the lease on the building, contracts with suppliers and contracts between the partners—*i.e.,* the partnership agreement. It will doubtless quit buying inventory and try to liquidate the inventory it has on hand, probably through some sort of sale. It will reduce the assets of the partnership to cash, pay off the debts, and divide up what is left over. This is the **termination**.

3. PARTNERSHIP ACCOUNTS

Dissolution can trigger not only an obligation on the part of partners to share in operating losses by contributing to pay partnership debts, but also an obligation to share in investment losses by contributing to the settlement of partnership accounts.

A partnership account is a bookkeeping device to keep track of how much a partner has invested in the partnership. Separate partnership accounts are kept for each partner.

When a partnership is dissolved, the partnership is obligated to pay each partner an amount measured by the balance in her partnership account. Both UPA § 40 and RUPA § 807 set out this default rule, obligating the partnership to repay partners' their capital contributions, after the partnership has paid its creditors. And, under both UPA § 40 and RUPA § 807, if, at dissolution, the sum of the balances of each the individual partner's partnership accounts exceeds the liquidation proceeds remaining after payment of creditors, then the partners will have to contribute additional funds to the partnership so that the losses from investments are shared appropriately.

Assume, for example, that A, B and C are partners. A made a $100,000 investment in the partnership. Although only A invested in the partnership, A, B and C agreed to share profits and losses equally. On dissolution, the liquidation proceeds are inadequate to pay creditors. Partnership debts exceed liquidation proceeds by $20,000. A's partnership account has a $100,000 balance. The other partnership accounts have a zero (0) balance.

Obviously A, B and C are jointly and severally liable for the payment of the $20,000 to creditors. It should be equally obvious that the partnership also owes A $100,000 and this too becomes a liability of B and C. Remember A, B and C agree to share losses equally. Losses total $120,000 ($20,000 in operating losses plus 100,000 in investment losses). Under these facts, each of the three partners should bear $40,000 of the losses. If A and B both pay $40,000 to the partnership and the partnership pays $20,000 to the creditors and the other $60,000 to A, then each partner will lose $40,000.

In theory (and in some law school hypotheticals), the proceeds from dissolution of a partnership can exceed the partnerships obligations to creditors. If so, that excess goes first to satisfy partnership accounts. Again, to illustrate, A, B and C are partners. A made a $100,000 investment.

Although only *A* invested in the partnership, they agreed to share profits equally. On dissolution, the liquidation proceeds exceed the debts owed to creditors by $160,000. And *A*'s partnership account has a $100,000 balance. The other partnership accounts have a zero (0) balance. Under these facts, the first $100,000 of the surplus would go to *A* to pay the partnership account balance. *A*, *B* and *C* would then share equally in the remaining $60,000 – $20,000 each.

B. CORPORATIONS

1. DISSOLUTION

A possible "end game" for the corporation as a business structure is dissolution. State corporation statutes generally provide for judicial dissolution in a proceeding brought by a shareholder who establishes that "those in control of the corporation have acted . . . in a manner that is illegal, oppressive, or fraudulent." Cf. MBCA § 14.30(2). Judicial dissolutions are also called "involuntary dissolutions." We previously discussed involuntary dissolutions in § VI.B.3.d.(2), *supra*.

State corporation statutes also generally provide for "voluntary dissolutions." Corporation statutes generally require that "voluntary dissolution" of the corporation be recommended by a majority of the directors and then be approved by ⅔ of the shares entitled to vote. Cf. MBCA § 14.02.

In both involuntary dissolution and voluntary dissolution of a corporation, it is important to remember that (1) the corporation continues after dissolution for the limited purpose of "winding up," (2) the creditors must be paid in full before the shareholders get anything from the dissolution and (3) the shareholders are not personally liable for the corporation's debts even if the corporation's creditors are not paid in full from the dissolution.

2. FRIENDLY ACQUISITIONS

a. Merger

Merger is another possible end game for a corporation as a business structure. In a merger, two or more business entities combine into one business entity—for example, assume Bubba's Burritos, Inc., a chain of Mexican restaurants, merges into McDonald's Corporation.

In this example, McDonald's would be referred to as the "surviving corporation" and Bubba's Burrtios would be referred to as the "disappearing corporation" because it would in fact and in law disappear. MBCA § 11.06 is typical of corporate codes in providing that, "When a merger takes effect . . . the separate existence of every corporation except the surviving corporation ceases."

(1) Effects of a Merger

The merger agreement governs the effects of a merger on the shareholders of the disappearing corporation. The merger agreement can provide for the issuance of stock of the surviving corporation to the shareholders of the disappearing corporation. Alternatively, the merger agreement can "cash out" the shareholders of the disappearing corporation; this is called a "cash out merger" or "cash merger."

State corporate law codes govern the effects of a merger on the creditors of the disappearing corporation. Typically, the surviving corporation gets both the assets and the liabilities of the disappearing corporation. In other words, creditors of the disappearing corporation become creditors of the surviving corporation.

Now think about the possible effects of a merger on the surviving corporation and its shareholders. New assets, new liabilities, possibly new shareholders. To control the effects of the merger on the surviving corporation, deals are sometimes structured as triangular mergers. The surviving corporation creates an acquisition subsidiary and obtains all of the stock of this subsidiary in exchange for its stock (or cash if the merger is a cash out merger). The disappearing corporation is then merged into this new wholly owned subsidiary and the shareholders of the disappearing corporation receive stock of the parent of the acquiring entity or cash.

(2) Shareholder Protection

Because of the effect of a merger on shareholders of both the surviving and the disappearing corporations, shareholders of both corporations, by case law and by statute, have three different forms of legal protection: (1) sue the directors who approved the merger alleging breach of common law or statutory duty of care or duty of loyalty,

(2) vote against the merger and (3) assert dissenting shareholder's right of appraisal.

(a) Sue the Directors Who Approved the Merger for Breach of Duty of Care or Breach of Duty of Loyalty[1]

The MBCA and other corporation codes, contemplate that the board of directors of each of the merging corporations will agree on a plan of merger. See MBCA § 11.01(a).

As we have seen from our earlier consideration of cases such as *Smith v. Van Gorkum*, discussed in § VII.A.2, *supra*, shareholders who are dissatisfied with what they receive from a merger sometimes sue the directors, who approved the merger, alleging breach of duty of care in approving the merger.

Shareholders may also sue directors for breach of the duty of loyalty when a director engages in self-dealing or is on both sides of the deal. We have previously considered *Weinberger v. UOP, Inc.*, discussed *in* § VII.B.3, *supra*. Recall that case involved a cash out merger of UOP into its parent corporation Signal—the non-Signal shareholders of UOP gots cash and Signal, which prior to the merger owned 50.5% of the outstanding stock of UOP, became the sole owner of UOP as a result of the merger. The

---

1. Shareholders may also be able to bring suit under Rule 10b-5 under the 34 Act, if they can show deception in connection with the merger. See § VIII.B.2.—The Deception Requirement, *supra*. However, such actions were significantly limited in the case of *Sante Fe v. Green* discussed in that subsection.

Weinberger case established the so called "intrinsic fairness" test which requires both "fair dealing" and "fair price" in cash out mergers and held that Signal failed to meet the test in this transaction. A footnote to the *Weinberger* opinion pointed out that the result might have been different if UOP had appointed a committee of independent directors, not connected with Signal, to negotiate the merger of the subsidiary UOP into its parent Signal.

(b) Vote Against the Merger

Subject to limited exceptions, a merger requires not only approval by the board of directors of each of the merging companies, but also the approval of the shareholders. State corporation statutes vary as to what level of approval is required and what the exceptions for shareholder approval are.

(c) Assert Dissenting Shareholders' Right of Appraisal

A single shareholder's vote against a merger will not prevent the merger from happening. While state corporation statutes vary as to what level of approval is required, no state still requires unanimous approval of the shareholders for a merger. Instead of providing a veto to shareholders who oppose the merger, state corporations statutes today provide "appraisal rights" to such shareholders. See, *e.g.*, Del. § 262.

The phrase "appraisal rights" is somewhat incomplete if not misleading. A shareholder who opposes a merger and complies with the detailed statutory requirements in Del.

§ 262 (or MBCA chapter 13 or the relevant state corporation statute) has more than the right to have her shares "appraised" or valued. Rather, a shareholder who properly asserts her dissenting shareholder's right of appraisal can compel the corporation to pay her in cash the "fair value" of her shares as determined by a judicial appraisal process.

To illustrate, *S* is a 10% shareholder of T Co. which merges into A, Inc. No more T Co.; no more T Co. shares. The merger agreement values T Co. at $3 million and provides that T Co. shareholders will receive consideration that has a value of $3 million. This consideration can be A, Inc. stock, or other stock, or other property or cash. Cf. MBCA § 11.01. As a 10% shareholder, *S* would get consideration with a value of $300,000. *S* instead "complies with the detailed statutory requirements" and properly asserts her dissenting shareholder's right of appraisal. What if the court decides that the "fair value" of T Co. was $5 million, not $3 million? Even though T Co. only received consideration with a value of $3 million, *S*, as a dissenting shareholder who "complies with the detailed statutory requirements" has a right to be paid $500,000 in cash from T Co. This will mean not only more for *S* but less for T Co.'s other shareholders. T Co. will only have consideration with a value of $2,500,0000 (not $2,700,000) to distribute to the other shareholders.

Note the limiting phrase in the preceding paragraph: "Complies with the detailed statutory requirements." The statutory appraisal rights commonly require shareholders wishing to assert the rights to comply with exacting advance notice requirements. Del. § 262 and MBCA chapter 13 are illustrative.

While there are detailed statutory provisions governing how a shareholder must assert her right to be paid the "fair value" of her shares by her corporation, there are virtually no statutory provisions governing how a court determines what that "fair value" is. Reported cases use a number of different judicially developed standards for determining the "fair value" of the dissenting shares.

b. Sale of Assets

Sale of assets is another possible end game for a corporation. Consider the different legal consequences if Bubba's Burritos sells all of its assets to McDonald's instead of merging into McDonald's.[2]

(1) Effect of Sale of Assets on the Creditors of the Selling Corporation

There are significant differences in the effect on the creditors of Bubba's Burritos, Inc. between a merger of Bubba's Burritos into McDonald's and sale of assets to McDonald's. Recall that if Bubba's Burritos, Inc. merges into McDonald's, the merger provisions of the relevant state corporate law makes the creditors of Bubba's Burritos, Inc. creditors of McDonald's.

---

2. There are also significant differences in the tax consequences. We will leave that for your tax teacher to explain when you take the course in taxation. It is outside the scope of this book.

There are no comparable statutory provisions making a buyer of the assets of a corporation liable to that corporation's creditors. And, the general common law rule is that the buyer of a corporation's assets is not liable for the selling corporation's debts. Accordingly, if Bubba's Burritos sold its assets to McDonald's, creditors of Bubba's Burritos could not collect from McDonald's. Rather, Bubba's Burritos creditors would "generally" be limited to collecting their claims from Bubba's Burritos. [We use the "weasel word" "generally" because there is a statutory basis for environmental claimants recovering from the acquiring corporation and there is a more limited judicial basis for products claimants recovering from the acquiring corporation. We leave the consideration of such successor liability concepts to your environmental and torts courses.]

And, there will still be a Bubba's Burritos, Inc. to collect from. By selling all of its assets, Bubba's Burritos, Inc. may be going out of the burrito business but it does not go out of legal existence. A corporation's sale of assets does not automatically terminate the legal existence of the corporate entity.

Often, however, sale of all of a corporation's assets is followed by that corporation's dissolution—which does terminate its legal existence. We have already considered dissolution. Remember that any corporation that is considering dissolution and distribution to shareholders should remember to pay off its creditors in full before making a distribution to shareholders. A corporation's failure to do so can make its shareholders personally liable to these creditors.

Reread the last sentence of the prior paragraph. We are not saying that the shareholders of a dissolving corporation are always personally liable to its creditors. We are merely saying that if a dissolving corporation makes distributions to shareholders even though there is not enough left to distribute to creditors to pay their claims in full then. . . .

(2) Effect of Sale of Assets on Shareholders

If Bubba's Burritos merges into McDonald's, then the shareholders of Bubba's Burritos receive McDonald's stock or cash from McDonald's (if it is a cash merger). Similarly, if Bubba's Burritos sells all of its assets to McDonald's then Bubba's Burritos, Inc., will receive McDonald's stock or cash from McDonald's which can be distributed to its shareholders. The economic consequences to Bubba's Burritos' shareholders and McDonald's shareholders of a sale of assets are substantially the same as the economic consequences of a merger.

The legal rights of Bubba's Burritos and McDonald's shareholders in a sale of assets are, however, different from the legal rights of the shareholders in a merger. While state corporation statutes require a corporation to obtain the approval of its shareholders in order to sell all or substantially all of its assets, Delaware and some other states do not provide appraisal rights for the shareholders of the selling corporation. More significantly, under most state corporate statutes, the shareholders of the buying corporation have neither appraisal rights nor the right to vote on their corporation's buying the assets.

c. Sale of Stock

McDonalds could buy a controlling block of Bubba's Burritos stock from Bubba's Burritos itself (if there is sufficient authorized but unissued shares) or from some or all of Bubba's Burritos shareholders. As consideration for the purchase of such shares McDonald's could either issue the selling shareholders of Bubba's Burritos shares or McDonald's stock or it could pay cash for the shares acquired.

In this type of a transaction Bubba's Burritos would then become a subsidiary of McDonalds (either a wholly owned or majority owned subsidiary) depending on the percentage of shares acquired. Bubba's Burritos, Inc., as an entity would not be affected by the transaction. Only its ownership would change.

To state what needs to be obvious, all three types of transactions—mergers, sales of assets and sales of stock—despite differences in the effects under both corporate and tax law, have the same result. McDonald's acquires control of Bubba's Burritos.

Operating considerations may play a part in determining which type of deal to do. For example, since Bubba's Burritos sells a different product than McDonald's (Mexican food rather than hamburgers) it might make operating sense to keep the entity alive and operate Bubba's Burritos as a McDonald's subsidiary.

It is worth passing mention that some people refer to the three types of friendly acquisitions, discussed above, as

A, B and *C* reorganizations (*A*—mergers; *B*—sales of stock; and *C*—sales of assets). This is merely a reference to subsections of § 368 of the IRC, which governs the tax consequences of mergers and acquisitions. This information will likely only become relevant to you, if your professor happens to be a tax expert who is a junior member of the faculty in terms of seniority, and is teaching business associations because someone was needed to teach the course. Many such tax lawyers have difficulty communicating without reciting sections of the IRC.

d. De facto Merger

Similarly, if your professor is a real old guy he may cover the de facto merger doctrine since it was covered in his class in corporations 40 years ago. If so, he will likely teach *Farris v. Glen Alden Corp.* There *S*, a small company, acquired all of the assets of *MB* a much bigger company by issuing new *S* stock to *MB*; *MB* then distributed the *S* stock to its shareholders. Because *MB* was much bigger than *S*, the former shareholders of *MB* now held much more *S* stock than the original shareholders of *S*. Even though the deal was structured as a sale, the court held that the dissenting shareholders had the same appraisal rights as in a merger. The de facto merger rule of *Farris* is, at best, a minority rule.

3. HOSTILE TAKEOVERS

A shareholder's selling her shares is the end of the game for that shareholder but not the corporation. If that selling shareholder is selling a majority of the outstanding shares or a controlling block of the outstanding shares, the sale can be the end of the game not only for the selling shareholder but also for the management of the corporation.

The term "hostile takeover" is used to describe an attempt to gain control of a corporation over the objection of that corporation's management. In other words, if Alpha Corporation wants to acquire Beta Corporation and Alpha's management does not believe that Beta's management will be amenable to negotiating a friendly acquisition, Alpha may bypass Beta's management and make an offer directly to Beta's shareholders.

The acquiring company or individual is politely described as the "bidder." More colorfully, the acquiring company may be described as the "raider" or the "shark." The company whose stock is targeted for acquisition is called the "target company."

Sometimes the acquiring company can acquire control of the target company by buying a controlling block of outstanding shares from a control person. See for example *Perlman v. Feldmann* previously discussed in § VII.B.4.b., *supra.* But in the typical hostile takeover, the bidder is not able to acquire a sufficient number of shares of the target company to gain control of it from a single shareholder or even a single family or allied group. And, the bidder does not want to pay for any shares of the target company unless it is able to buy a sufficient number of shares to gain control of the target company.

If the target company is a public company, the usual process for acquiring sufficient shares is a "tender offer."

In a tender offer, the bidder makes a public offer of cash or securities of the bidder (or a package of cash and securities) to the target stockholders who tender their stock. The tender offer will typically be conditioned on a sufficient number of the target's shares being tendered to ensure that the bidder gains control of the target company.

While taking over control of a company by acquiring a majority of that target company's outstanding stock, does not require any action by the management of the target company's board of directors, it usually triggers defensive action by the management of the target company to prevent the takeover. Lawyers for companies that have been or are likely to be targets of hostile takeovers have been creative in developing (and naming) responses to takeover threats: "poison pills," "golden parachutes," "shark repellent bylaws," "white knights" and "pac-man defenses." All of these are colorful names for specific actions taken by management of the target company designed to prevent or repel a takeover. They are referred to as "defensive measures."

A defensive measure is simply a maneuver or transaction undertaken for the purpose of making it more difficult for a bidder to acquire control of the target company. When management uses defensive measures to prevent or repel a takeover, the action is often challenged on grounds that the officers and directors of the target company breached their fiduciary duties through the use of such measures to defend against a hostile takeover.

The courts, particularly the Delaware courts, have created a body of case law which deals with the standard to apply in reviewing challenges to these defenses. These Delaware judicial opinions are based on the specific facts of the particular cases, which tend to be extremely complex.

In broad overview, these cases present conflict of interest problems similar to the conflict of interest problem which we have already discussed in other contexts. Officers and directors of a target company who oppose a takeover of their company have an obvious conflict of interest: there is a very high likelihood that they will lose their jobs if the takeover is successful. This is not, however, as clear cut a conflict of interest as when a director is doing business with the corporation or usurping a corporate opportunity. See § VII.A.3., *supra.* Management of the target company may be opposing the takeover for reasons which they honestly and reasonably believe are in the best interests of the target company.

This raises the difficult question: How far can management go in their defensive measures without violating their fiduciary duties? The question is difficult, because the answer depends on the motives or subjective state of mind of officers and directors. Often there are multiple overlapping motives. And all of this is complicated by the extremely complex nature of the facts usually encountered in these lawyer intensive take over battles.

That having been said, while there are many factually sensitive variations and nuances, the foundation for the rules applied in cases involving the scope of defensive measures rests on tests developed by the Delaware Supreme Court in two famous cases decided in 1985:

Unocal Corp. v. Mesa Petroleum Co. (the "Unocal case") in which Mesa Petroleum Co., which was controlled by T. Boone Pickens, attempted to acquire control of Unocal; and

Revlon, Inc. v. MacAndrews & Forbes Holdings, Inc. (the "Revlon case") in which Ronald Perelman, through his holding company, MacAndrews & Forbes, acquired control of Revlon.

These two cases established two basic doctrines which have been applied in numerous subsequent cases involving litigation arising out of takeover attempts. Today these cases are part of the jargon of corporate lawyers, who often refer to companies as being in the "Revlon Mode" or as invoking their "Unocal Defenses."

The *Unocal* case speaks to the question of what defensive measures are proper.

The *Revlon* case speaks to the question of when management of the target company has to give up the fight—*i.e.*, when they can no longer engage in defensive measures.

In the *Revlon* case, the management of Revlon, the target company, did not want Mr. Perelman to acquire control of Revlon. It was clear that if Mr. Perelman acquired control of Revlon he would terminate the senior managers of Revlon. Looking for a "white knight," Revlon gave Forsman Little & Co. an option to acquire two of Revlon's most desirable divisions (*i.e.*, "crown jewels" of Revlon) for over $100 million less than the appraised value of the two divisions. Presumably management felt that if Revlon no longer owned these "crown jewels," Mr. Perelman would no longer want to acquire control of Revlon.

The Delaware Supreme Court invalidated the Forsman Little option and held that once a takeover becomes inevitable, the board must discontinue defensive measures and assume the role of an auctioneer. Their fiduciary duties required management to maximize shareholder values—*i.e.*, get the best offer possible for the target company or its assets.

Obviously questions have arisen in subsequent cases as to: (1) what is the best offer and (2) when must a company discontinue defensive action (in the jargon of the industry—when does the company get into a "Revlon Mode").

The factual variations are infinite and beyond the scope of this book. But two basic points should be remembered: (1) the highest price, though usually the most single important factor, does not necessarily equate to the best offer and (2) a company gets in the Revlon Mode when it becomes clear from the facts that the company will no longer remain independent in its present form.

The main consequences of the *Revlon* case are: (1) if the target company is in the "Revlon Mode," management has to give up the fight but (2) the converse is also true—until the company gets into the Revlon Mode it can use defensive measures——its management can fight to make it more difficult for the bidder to acquire their company.

The *Unocal* case sets the limits on the kind of defensive measures the target company's management can take prior to getting into the "Revlon Mode." In the jargon of the industry, lawyers say that "until it gets in the Revlon Mode" a target company can invoke its "Unocal Defenses"—meaning assert defenses that meet the test laid down in the Unocal case.

The *Unocal* case sets forth a broad based test by which the courts determine whether or not the board of the target company went too far in their defensive actions. The test fashioned by the Delaware Supreme Court in the Unocal case puts the burden on management of the target company to prove that:

(1) they acted in good faith,
(2) based on reasonable investigation they felt there was a threat to their company and
(3) the defensive measures they took bear a reasonable relationship to the threat that they perceived.

In general, this test requires management to show that it took defensive measures for the purpose of protecting the company's interests, rather than for the purpose of protecting management's jobs or negotiating better severance packages.

There are no court-imposed fiduciary duty limits to takeover efforts by the bidder company's board. The bidder does not owe a fiduciary duty to the target's shareholders.

While there are no cases imposing fiduciary duty limitations on the takeover efforts of bidders, there are federal and state statutory limits. In 1968, Congress regulated tender offers by enacting the Williams Act, which amended §§ 13 and 14 of the 34 Act. The Williams Act applies only to companies registered under § 12 of the 34 Act (the same subset of companies subject to the proxy rules discussed in § VI.B.4.b., *supra).* The Williams Act focuses on disclosure by the bidder or perspective bidder but also contains substantive rules relating to a bidder's high-pressure tactics and fraud. And, some states have enacted statutes that make hostile turnovers more difficult, regardless of whether there has been complete compliance with the Williams Act standards.

4. BANKRUPTCY

For a growing number of corporations and other business structures, the end game is being played in bankruptcy courts. Chapter 11 and then sometimes Chapter 7.

That is another law school course. And, another nutshell.

INDEX

391

TIPPERS AND TIPPEES, 316-22

—U—

ULTRA VIRES, 54-55

USURPING CORPORATE OPPORTUNITY
See Corporate Opportunity

—V—

VOTING AGREEMENTS
See Shareholder Agreements

VOTING TRUSTS, 174-76

—W—

WATERED STOCK, 105-08

WINDING UP, 358-60